Lean and Digitize

Lean and Digitize

An Integrated Approach to
Process Improvement

BERNARDO NICOLETTI

Routledge
Taylor & Francis Group

LONDON AND NEW YORK

First published 2012 by Gower Publishing

2 Park Square, Milton Park, Abingdon, Oxon OX14 4RN
711 Third Avenue, New York, NY 10017, USA

Routledge is an imprint of the Taylor & Francis Group, an informa business

First issued in paperback 2016

Originally published by Franco Angeli Publishers. Original title *'Le Metologie del Lean e Digitize'*(2010). This English edition is produced with their permission.

British Library Cataloguing in Publication Data
Nicoletti, Bernardo.
  Lean and digitize : an integrated approach to process
  improvement.
  1. Lean manufacturing. 2. Six sigma (Quality control
  standard) 3. Process control. 4. Technological innovations.
  I. Title
  658.5'14-dc23

ISBN 978-1-4094-4194-6 (hbk)
ISBN 978-1-138-26176-1 (pbk)

Library of Congress Cataloging-in-Publication Data
Nicoletti, Bernardo.
  Lean and digitize : an integrated approach to process improvement / by
  Bernardo Nicoletti.
    p. cm.
  Includes bibliographical references and index.
  ISBN 978-1-4094-4194-6 (hardback)
  1. Process control. 2. Lean manufacturing. 3. Six sigma (Quality
  control standard) 4. Technological innovations. I. Title.
  TS156.8.N52 2012
  658.5--dc23

2012011050

Contents

List of Figures

List of Tables

Abbreviations and Definitions[1]

ABC Analysis See **Pareto's Principle**.

Accord A decision-taking strategy based on persuasion and agreement between all of the parties involved, who strive to keep the decision taken.

Affinity diagram A powerful method of organizing and categorizing ideas collected during a brainstorming session at the beginning of a project.

Andon The Japanese word for lantern. It refers to the management techniques of acknowledging typical errors and downtime in the devices engaged in **autonomation**. In general, it consists in a signboard and a sound alarm system (siren) which can be activated automatically or by pressing a button located near the workstations.

Anova Analysis of variance. A statistical method used to analyse variations.

Autonomation The second pillar of the Toyota production system. Essentially it means intelligent automation: transfer labour and even intellectual work to machines.

B2B Business-to-business. Providing solutions from one organization to other organizations.

B2C Business-to-consumer. Providing solutions an organization to consumers.

BAM Business activity monitoring: monitoring the organization's activities.

Belt Belts are the members in the teams for Lean and Digitize projects. They know the methodology and act as enablers of its application.

Benchmarking Comparing processes and/or measures to others implemented by competitors or by best-of-the-breed organizations.

BI See **Business intelligence**.

Black belt A term used to denote a level of competence. The Black belt can help or manage a team that is applying the Lean and Digitize and other process improvement initiatives. A typical Black belt should have passed a series of training courses and

---

1   These definitions are synthetic so they will not necessarily be precise. Please consult the text for a more complete presentation of most of these ideas. Only some terms have been explained in this glossary, based on the need for the reader to find a quick reference. For a more thorough description of these terms, see Nicoletti, B. 2010. *Gli strumenti del Lean and Digitize*. Milano: FrancoAngeli

managed at least one relevant project. Some organizations have an official certification process beofre team members can become a Black belt.

BOA Business-oriented architecture. A set of computer systems modules to support **business process management** (BPM). **SOA** computer architecture combined with **BPM** (business process management).

BPA Business process analysis. The analysis of business processes.

BPM Business process management. Management of processes in order to improve them substantially.

BPMN Business process modelling notation. Documentation of process modelling.

BPMS Business process management systems. Application which help support **BPM**.

BPO Business process outsourcing, also known as business process optimization. Process optimization obtained through outsourcing.

BPP Business process platform. A platform for processes.

BPR Business process re-engineering. Process re-engineering for drastic improvement.

BRE Business rule engine. Component of a **BPMS** for managing the rules of an organization process.

Business intelligence In short, the art of extracting useful information from large databases and present information so that they are comprehensive in terms of business.

CASE Computer-aided software engineering. Software to support engineering.

Cause–effect diagram Also known as Ishikawa, Cedac or Fish diagrams, they show the relations between a problem, the characteristics of quality (effects) and the factors (causes) that produce them. Effective in analysing concrete problems, but not so effective in the case of cultural or organizational problems. One of the seven classical tools for quality control.

Cedac Cause–effect diagram with additional cards. See **Cause–effect diagram**.

Cell A cell is a way of organizing the resources in a manufacturing environment to improve quality, speed and cost within the process. They are small continuous manufacturing line for a part or all the production process. Cells improve the process flow and eliminate wastes and are usually U-shaped.

Champion The person sponsoring a project in the organization, with the necessary authority and power. Usually a member of the senior management, they are an important factor for the success of the project.

CMMI-Dev A capability maturity model integration for devolution. Standard for the development and integration of software products.

COBIT Control objectives for information and related technology. Methodology for ICT governance.

Common causes Inputs of the system which impact on the quality of the outputs. They may depend on materials, people, or design. They are constant and predictable. In order to be able to eliminate them, the system must be modified.

Compliance Respect for the internal and external rules of the organization.

Continuous flow In this situation, a certain number of sequential processes are balanced, allowing the material or the information to flow continuously from one station to the following station immediately. It is an efficient way to manufacture products or services serially when the characteristics of the product and the market allow using it.

Control chart A graphical representation of values that show a process's behaviour. It allows the user to discern which causes of variation are acceptable and which are not. It is also used to forecast the future behaviour of a process and is one of the seven traditional tools of quality management.

Control limit A limit in a control chart, applied to define an interval of acceptable process behaviour.

CPM Corporate performance management. An information system for the management of the key metrics of the organization.

CPM Critical path method. Programming and control tool for projects through network techniques.

CRM Customer relationship management. Information system for managing the relationships with the customers. It is a tool to manage the whole customer cycle, from the acquisition of new customers to the intensification of relationships with the most important ones, to loyalty building with those customers who have more relations with the organization. It allows reducing the costs of the transactions between the customer and the organization and integrates the management processes of the customers.

CTQ Critical to quality. The variables critical to quality. Element of a process that directly affects the quality perceived by the customer. Those attributes of a product which the customer considers to be the most important.

Customer Also Client or Citizen (the latter in the case of a government organization). The person who pays for the product, service or activity. The customer is not necessarily the user of the product, the process or the activity and can be external or internal with regard to the organization. In the latter case, unless there is an in-house 'transfer pricing' system, the internal customer does not pay for the product, service or activity, but only uses it. Customers must be regarded as a reason for the process to exist, rather than simply as the recipient of the outputs of the process.

CWQC Company-wide quality control. A methodology introduced to improve the quality in the entire organization, not just in one of its sectors.

Cycle of improvement See **PDCA**.

Cycle time This term is applicable to different situations. Cycle time gives an idea of the time it takes for a product/service from start up to the delivery of the output. In case of a manufacturing company, the cycle time for production is the time from the arrival of the raw materials to the release of the final product. From the point of view of the end customer, the cycle time is the total amount of time that a customer has to wait to get a product/service once they have ordered it.

Data collection The process of generating information that can be used to make decisions. In the case of manual data collection, check sheets are used to collect the information and proceed to their first classification.

Database Computer files, usually single-function.

DDDD Define, discover, develop and demonstrate. A methodology used to structure innovation.

Design of experiments A discipline of planning and analysing the experiences in which multiple and possible interconnected measurements can be operated.

DFSS Design for Six Sigma. Another denomination for **DMADV**.

DMADV Define, measure, analyse, develop and verify. Six Sigma method for drastic process improvement.

DPMO Defects per million opportunities. Opportunity is a chance of non-compliance or a defect, the latter being a process result in which some specifications are not met.

ECM Enterprise content management. Management of all contents (data, unstructured documents, e-mail, voice, video, etc.)

EERP Extended enterprise resource planning. It is an ERP evolution, adding tools to control connected third parties (such as companies controlled, resellers, customers, suppliers, etc.).

EFQM European foundation quality model. A model for managing quality, based on the indications of a certain number of European organizations' CEOs.

E-procurement A tool to manage the procurement cycle with the integration of providers **B2B** (business-to-business). It integrates the acquisition process, minimizes transaction costs to the customer by simplifying the flows, and for the vendor, thanks to the access to an open market.

ERP Enterprise resource planning. The extension of **MRP II** to the remaining functions in the organization, such as engineering, finance and personnel administration and management. Consists of a software package with a single data model that facilitates the horizontal and vertical integration of all interorganizational processes, improves process efficiency and monitors processes through special **KPI**s (key performance indicators) according to quality, service levels and timeliness. Components of an ERP include accounting, industrial accounting, payrolls, sourcing, warehouse management, production, project control, sales, distribution and facility maintenance.

Facilitator The person who helps the team achieve their full potential, through the identification and the elimination of obstacles. They lead the team to accomplish their mission.

Fish diagram See **Cause–effect diagram**.

Flow chart A diagram or a process map. It uses symbols (for activities, decision joints and other events) in a horizontal or vertical sequence to show what happens in a process or in the design of a new process.

Flow The progressive execution of operations from the beginning of the process through to the delivery of the result. According to one of the principles of Lean Thinking, the flow must proceed forwards, that is to say towards the customer (internal or external), and occur uninterruptedly and without waste. All activities that create value should flow without interruption from beginning to end, so as not to allow waiting time, downtime or waste during a given phase, or between phases.

FMEA Failure mode and effects analysis. A tool for analysing the modes of failure and their effects.

FMEAC Failure mode, effects and criticality analysis. A **FMEA** which also takes into account the criticalities arising from the FMEA analysis.

Gantt A diagram which helps organize the different activities included in a project into manageable groups of tasks. In a Gantt diagram, activities are shown as horizontal bars in a timeline. It can be used to refine the programme, to form different strategies and to make the plan more efficient. It was introduced by a Swedish engineer named Gantt in 1900.

GE General Electric Corporation. An American company known for having popularized the use of Six Sigma methodologies.

Gemba System parts that add value to the inputs, in the interest of customers.

GERT Graphical evaluation and review technique. A variation of the **PERT** that allows us to consider situations of uncertainty.

Green belt A facilitator or a member of a project team. As a participant, a Green belt helps the team to apply improvement methods effectively, so that they can improve the way work is done.

H2H Human-to-human relations.

H2S Human-to-system relations.

Heijunka A production levelling box used near the pacemaker and the remaining production cells. *Heijunka* allows a levelling up of production, balancing the workload of the cells and minimizing fluctuation in delivery.

Histogram A graphical display for showing a variable's distribution: one of the seven classical tools for quality control.

ICT Information and telecommunication systems.

IDE Integrated development environment.

Improvement teams See **Project teams**.

In-process kanban Used for signalling the production of a product or a small amount (up to one pitch). It is used where the flow is continuous.

Input A resource introduced in the system or used during the operation, which contributes in obtaining a result or output.

Internet of things The use of the Internet to get objects, machines and other inanimate things interconnected.

Interprocess kanban Withdrawal/collection kanban. It is used for signalling the need to withdraw objects between the supermarket and the upstream process in the plant.

IoT See **Internet of things**.

IPMA International project management academy. A project management certification entity.

ISE Integrated service environment.

Ishikawa diagram See **Cause–effect diagram**.

ISO 9000 A family of standards for continuous quality improvement managed by the International Standard Organization (ISO).

ITIL Information technology infrastructure library. Methodology for the management of ICT services.

Java EE Java platform, enterprise edition. Computer programming language freely available.

Kaizen A Japanese term meaning continuous improvement. It indicates the improvement seminars in a Lean action.

Kanban The tool which facilitates information and materials flow in a process' environment. The concept is relatively simple. A productive unit must be activated to produce the amounts required by the next downward department, according to a card (such is the meaning of the term in Japanese).

Kano model An elegant way to represent the opinions of different customers: expressed, implied or desired.

KPI Key performance indicator. Indicators of key performances (e.g. of a process).

Lead time See **Throughput time**.

Lean and Digitize Committee See **Steering committee**.

Lean and Digitize To simultaneously make a process lean and automated. It is the methodology introduced in this book, based on re-engineering the process to make it lean and at the same time to automate wherever it is necessary.

Lean manufacturing See **Lean production**.

Lean production The application of improvements and standardizations as well as many other concepts and tools to improve quality, costs and time of production. Many lessons learned with lean production can be applied also to leaning operations in services.

LRC Linear responsibility chart. See **Matrix activity/responsibility**.

Matrix activity/responsibility The matrix used in project management to assign different types of responsibility to the team members.

Matrix diagram A means of connecting two or more sets of characteristics to help, for instance, prioritize efforts to improve processes. It is one of the key **QFD** tools.

Milestone The end of a stage that marks the completion of a work package or phase.

Mission The mission is the way to proceed towards the Vision.

MRP Material requirements planning. A computer application which provides times and quantities relative to procurement and production automatically. The outputs of these packages are obtained by analysing the input data (cycle times, different base, inventory state, reorganization policy, etc.), obtained from one or more databases, and processing them with specific algorithms.

MRP II Manufacturing resources planning – the successor of MRP. MRP II adds the scheduler: a module to compute productive capacity and level the work load.

Muda Waste in Japanese. The objective of the Lean Principle is to eliminate muda in the processes.

Norms Optional indications for standardization.

OandM Operations and maintenance. The production function.

Open UP Open unified process. It is a software process inspired in the rational unified process (**RUP**). It was launched with open source licence within the Eclipse process framework. It describes the best practices for software development according to RUP and involves iterative development, usage of use cases and scenarios as leading entities for the development, risk management and a development approach focused on architecture.

Organization In this book, this term indicates a company, a public institution, either central or local, or a non-profit organization.

Output The result produced by a system or process. The final output is a product or a service.

Pareto principle This principle states that 20 per cent of the few 'vital' elements justify the 80 per cent of the consequences regarding the many 'trivial' elements. It was popularized by Joseph Juran and introduced by Vilfredo Pareto, an Italian economist, in the nineteenth century.

PCK Process capability key – a process capacity measure with a short-term aprioristic value. It indicates the processing capacity to comply with the specification limits in the future. The specification limits are obtained by analysing the **CTQ'**s and assigning the acceptable variances and tolerances.

PDCA Plan-do-check-act. Improvement cycle introduced by William Edwards Deming. It is based on the sequence of actions: plan, do, check and act.

PERT Programme evaluation and review technique. Programming and control tool for projects based on reticular techniques.

PMbok Guide to the project management body of knowledge. Document describing the project management methodology of the PMI – the **Project Management Institute**.

PMI Project Management Institute. One of the most accredited project certification entities.

PMO Project management office. The organization created to provide support to a leader of a project of large dimensions.

Poka-yoke Means 'mistake proof' and describes the selection of projects with regard to devices, equipment and spare parts which allow self-inspection even before the production process is running.

PPK Process performance key. A process capacity measure which indicates if the process is centred, if it has complied with the specifications, coming within lower and upper limits as established in the project management office.

Prince 2 Project in a controlled environment. Project management methodology.

Process control The action of obtaining and keeping a process stable. In fact, stability is not a spontaneous status for any process.

Process improvement A continuous effort to learn from the causes and effects in a process, aiming at reducing the complexity, the variation and the cycle time. It is obtained by improving and eliminating the wrong causes and then by redesigning the process in order to reduce the root causes of the most common variations.

Process management A methodology used to optimize the organization as a system, determine which processes need to be improved and/or controlled, define priorities and encourage leadership to initiate and sustain process improvement efforts. It manages the information obtained because of these processes.

Process owner The person responsible for the whole process, they are in charge of communicating the process objectives, optimizing performances in the context of the whole system and leading the efforts to improve. It is a position not present in many organizations. When it is, s/he must closely coordinate with the responsibles of the functions involved in the process.

Process A set of interconnected activities that transforms a set of inputs in one or more results. Sometimes a process is identified with a system. In fact, it would be more correct to consider it as a system component.

Processes of change Taking feedback from customers and the context to develop policies and conduct relevant changes in the **Gemba**.

Processes of support These allow the operation of the **Gemba**.

Programme Set of projects with similar objectives, for example, for the improvement of systems installed in different branches of the same group.

Programme and control A neologism used in this book to indicate the process of programming and control. The new term emphasizes the inseparable relation of programming and control: It makes no sense to programme without controlling and it cannot be controlled if it has not been programmed.

Project charter Describes the problem, defines the objectives to achieve and plans the main project activities.

Project teams Groups of people coming from the same sector or, ideally, from different sectors, who work on process improvement during a period of time.

Provider A person or organization that provides goods or services for use in the environment of the specific process.

QFD See **Quality function deployment**.

Quality assurance The set of planned systematic actions appropriate to ensure that a product or a service complies with the predefined quality requirements.

Quality control The operative tools and activities used to satisfy quality requirements.

Quality function deployment A set of disciplines based on a deep understanding of the customers' needs and desires. It is used to accelerate the development of relevant projects and of new products and services. Based on many hierarchies, it gathers and analyses strategic information.

Quality This concept is not easily defined because there are many variations, sometimes determined by an adjective or specification accompanying the name. In general, quality is customer satisfaction achieved in such a way that it is profitable for the organization.

RUP Rational unified process. Process for software development managed by IBM/Rational. RUP does not determine a single specific process but an adjustable framework which can lead to different processes in different contexts (for instance in different organizations or in the context of projects with different characteristics).

S2S System-to-system. Computer-to-computer interface.

SaaS Software as a service. Using the software as a service offered by a third party on one's own computers.

Sigma (σ) The eighteenth letter of the Greek alphabet. In statistical theory, it is related to variance.

Signal kanban Kanban for signalling the production of a relatively big lot. It is used by supermarkets to guide the process upstream and to allow them perform fine tuning which is usually very time-consuming.

SIPOC Supplier input process output customer. A document summarizing an overview of the process, customers and providers, regarding the measures, the actual performance and the justifications about the possible causes of variations.

Six Sigma A philosophy and a performance objective. As a method, it is a structured approach to the continuous improvement of processes. The objective is a measure of process performance defined in terms of defects, with 3.4 defective parts per million opportunities.

SMED Single minute exchange of die. Tool used in the Toyota Production System to indicate setting time reduction.

SOA Service-oriented architecture. ICT architecture based on the use of 'services', components of information systems reusable in different applications and platforms.

SPC Statistical process control. A methodology to study a process and reduce variations over time. The resulting data are then analysed to identify the root causes of the variations. People with knowledge of the process work to identify and reduce the recurrence of the unpredictable causes, and to understand and reduce the predictable causes.

Special causes These are not features of the system. They are unpredictable and cause anomalies during the process. Special causes can be unexpected breakage of machines, non-compliant materials, etc. They are specific and must be considered in order to intervene to eliminate the causes of variations.

Sponsor This term has the meaning of Champion. It is used to define the role of one member of the senior management, in charge of supervising and supporting a programme or a project.

Stable process A process that is predictable because it is subject to controllable variations. Also the property of being within a statistical control limit.

Stakeholder A part or person interested in the project.

Steering committee Also known as Lean and Digitize committee in this book, it includes the representatives of senior management, the project leader and the facilitators. Its main responsibilities are the management of the efforts of process improvement, the assessment of needs, the supervision of support and education and training, the communication of the progress to the stakeholders and the guidance of the efforts to improve the process.

Supermarket (also manufacturing supermarket). A factory analogous to a retail supermarket for consumers. The workers, similar to the customers in a supermarket, take components from the 'shelves' as they need them. The provider of the components can take notice and refurbish the article.

Supplier kanban Withdrawal/collection kanban. Used for the movement of materials outside the site/the organization according to the management of the procurement. It indicates the cycle of kanban, in other words the type of product to be supplied, the quantity and frequency of shipment.

System According to William Edwards Deming: 'A network of interacting components which cooperates for achieving the goals of the system.' It could also represent the organizations as they are a set of resources used to provide on a flow of materials and information.

Takt time The sales rate of products assigned to a cell.

Technical rules Compulsory indications for technical standardization.

Telematics Synergy of telecommunications and informatics. In this book, it is synonymous with ICT.

Throughput time Time taken for a part or a service transaction to move along an interconnected set of processes or a value flow, from beginning to end. This time includes also the time of non-processing and waiting time.

TPM Total productive maintenance. Variation of the Toyota production system methodology applied to maintenance.

TPS Toyota production system. Introduced by Toyota, this later evolved into Lean Thinking.

TQC Total quality control.

TRIZ *(TeoriyaRresheniya izobretatelskikh Zadatch)*. A problem-solving, analysis and forecasting tool derived from the study of patterns of inventions in the global patent literature.

Uni EN 28402 ISO quality standards terminology.

Uni EN 9000 ISO standards regarding company management of quality and quality assurance. Criteria for selection and use.

Uni EN 9001 ISO quality standards terminology. Criteria for the assurance of quality regarding design, development, implementation, installation and assistance.

Uni EN 9002 ISO quality standards terminology. Criteria for the assurance of quality regarding design, development, implementation, installation and assistance.

Uni EN 9003 ISO quality standards terminology. Criteria for the assurance of quality in the final controls and tests.

Uni EN 9004 ISO standards on the criteria related to company management for quality and the company quality systems.

Unstable process A process that is subject to variations originating in predictable and unpredictable causes.

UPC Universal product code. Standard used to name products in a unique way.

Value analysis An organizational technique that allows the organization to obtain alternative solutions at the lowest cost.

Value engineering Value analysis applied to design.

Value flow The set of activities required to design, order, produce and deliver (or supply in the case of services) a given product. These activities cover all the product/service throughput time in the organization up to the end customer. The objective of the value flow analysis is to categorize the activities.

Value stream mapping Identifying and graphical representation of all the activities performed during the Value flow relative to a product/service or a family of products/ services. The activities can be classified in: value adding for the customer; not value adding and unnecessary (easily eliminated); not value adding but not immediately dispensable.

Value Value is defined by the end customer. Conceptually, it is the relationship between benefits and cost/damage of a product or service. It is expressed in terms of a product/ service that can meet the customers' demands at a given price and at a given moment. It is also possible to refer to value as perceived by customer, meaning all the product/service characteristics that the customer considers as necessary and valuable. Any activity that consumes resources (including time) and does not brings value to the customer or to the organization is waste (**muda** in Japanese)

Variance In statistics, the squared media error. It is a parameter of dispersion.

Variations Quantitative changes in the value amongst cases or over time caused by predictable and unpredictable causes.

Vision Expression of what would represent a success for the organization. The objective is to produce a mental image to aim at – generate creative tensions between the current reality and the vision in the organization. In order to be valuable it must be shared by the whole organization. This requires much effort and much patience. The mission is the way to proceed towards the vision.

VoC Voice of the customer. The voice of the customer, or voice of the citizen, in the case of public organizations.

VoP Voice of the process. A description of the requirements of a process.

Useful Websites

ec.europa.eu: website of the European Union
www.aberdeen.com
www.aigi.net
www.aigi.net/index.htm
www.asq.org, The American Society for Quality
http//it.encarta.msn.com, Enciclopedia Encarta Online 2009
www.qualitiamo.com
www.itri.loyola.edu/ep/cost.htm
www.in.net/deming/html
www.isixsigma.com
www.sixsigma.com
www.aicq.it, Associazione Italiana Cultura Qualità
www.iso.ch, International Organization for Standardization
www.geminieuropa.com
www.uni-bocconi.it
www.iqualityprocess.com/
www.iso-9000.co.uk/
www.lean.org
www.peterkeen.com
www.processexcellencenetwork.com
www.qmtmag.com/default.cfm?CFID=179769andCFTOKEN=36682636
www.quality.nist.gov
www.sinedi.com/
www.sixsigmaiq.com/video.cfm?externalid=24
www.smartenterprisemag.com/
www.towersassociates.com/articles.html

Acknowledgements

This volume has gone through a long process. It summarizes my working experience, readings and thoughts, during a long period.

Similarly to a Lean and Digitize project, many people contributed to this book. I wish to thank all of them. The contribution of each of them has been essential.

Particular thanks go to:

- Dr Thomas Bortolotti, who worked with me on a thesis on the subject of this book, and helped me systematize my years of experience and thoughts on the method. Some sections of this book originated from this thesis;
- All of the people I have interviewed. They have contributed to the development of this method with their knowledge and experience. Special thanks to one of my most beloved bosses, Leonard Kim, who encouraged me to apply and conceptualize the method, during my job at GE Money, as a Global CTO, and as Group CIO at GE Oil and Gas;
- All colleagues, Belts and participants of the Lean and Digitize projects in the organizations in which I worked and learnt so much.

A big thank you to my family. They have suffered out of the long hours I spent in front of my personal computer, in addition to my daily ordinary working duties, in order to synthesize experiences and summarize them in this book.

Preface

And one should bear in mind that there is nothing more difficult to execute, nor more dubious of success, nor more dangerous to administer than to introduce a new order to things; for he who introduces it has all those who profit from the old order as his enemies; and he has only lukewarm allies in all those who might profit from the new. This lukewarmness partly stems from fear of their adversaries, who have the law on their side, and partly from the scepticism of men, who do not truly believe in new things unless they have personal experience with them. The result, however, is that whenever the enemies of change make an attack, they do so with all the zeal of partisans, while the others defend themselves so feebly as to endanger both themselves and their cause. Niccolò Machiavelli (Burd L.A. (2009))

We are living in times of a deep economic crisis characterized by scarcity of raw materials, energy and credit and an increase in volatility and globalization. All of which leads to considerably increased competition with regard to the quality and price of products and services. This challenge is due, on the one hand, to the increase of knowledge, demands and the power of customers[1] and, on the other hand, to the number and aggression of competitors.

Every organization must seek to satisfy customers' requirements in terms of quality and price of products and services. At the same time, it must improve the cost structure of production and service supply; in other words improve business processes.

The Six Sigma and Lean Thinking methods are effective for supporting and making process improvement projects. However, they leave a number of important issues unresolved:

- Is there a coherent model that covers both the aspects of Lean and Six Sigma methodologies and those of digitization?
- In what way can Information and Communication Technologies (ICT) support such improvement projects rather than hinder them?

Lean and Six Sigma methods work on the analysis and subsequent optimization of physical and organizational flows. They leave aside the study of the automation flow and of the interactions between information systems and telecommunication networks with physical and organizational activities. The risk, consequently, is for any desired improvement to remain trapped within the constraints imposed by such systems.

An empirical rule states that 50 per cent of the processes are independent from automation, while the remaining 50 per cent of the processes are closely based on

---

1   When we refer to customers in this book, we mean also citizens in the case of public organizations.

automation and highly dependent on information systems and networks. These percentages are changing, and automation is acquiring an increasing relevance.

It is important to integrate automation methods and management rules with improvement and optimization projects of Lean Six Sigma. This is the only way to optimize typical processes for improving competitive advantage, and is especially true in those service companies that traditionally have not assigned significant priority to the improvement of processes, but which now depend increasingly on digitization.

Sustainable business improvement requires a holistic, methodological approach, designed to improve and optimize processes from all points of view. Such an approach should:

- be complete and operational;
- be structured (Six Sigma);
- be guided by customers' demands (Lean and Six Sigma);
- not be stuck in a specific sector;
- make use of digitization wherever this makes sense;
- enhance the benefits brought about by processes and projects of management automation and the rational use of information systems and telecommunications.

Process digitization should go together with the improvement of the organizational and physical flows. Collectively they enable you to eliminate any source of waste from the logical flow caused by physical, organizational and digitization activities and their interfaces. It is only once you have streamlined or redesigned the new process that it is possible to introduce or re-introduce automation in an effective, efficient and economical way. At that stage you can speed up and automate activities, adding value that will be recognized by the customer. You can also avoid waste in the information and communication system and in the automation flows. This waste causes the production or supply processes to slow down or stop altogether.

Different methodologies are generally accepted in Lean Thinking and Six Sigma. There are several systematic approaches to ICT and to automation. These may be from the project management point of view, e.g. the Digitize Project Management Method (DPMM), in General Electric Corporation (GE) or the Project Life Cycle (PLC), of the European Union. The approaches can be also from an operation point of view, e.g. the Information Technology Infrastructure Library (ITIL). There are no integrated approaches blending Lean and Six Sigma with digitization.

This book intends to introduce a method for the improvement, optimization and automation of processes. We call this 'Lean and Digitize' and it provides a coherent and integrated method which:

- Can manage and optimize simultaneously organizational, physical and automation flows;
- Uses the information system and telecommunication networks as levers for process improvement and for project management; and
- Can help solve non-alignment problems between the organization and the ICT initiatives.

In order to achieve this objective, this book aims to:

- Define and introduce the 'Lean and Digitize' method;
- Analyse the development of automation and of information and telecommunications systems;
- Review the development of technologies related to quality and process improvement management, particularly Six Sigma and Lean Thinking;
- Analyse several real cases of organizational approaches and of the management of process improvement initiatives;
- Compare organizational realities and the best (and worst) practices with the proposed method. In this way, it allows its validation at the operational and organization level, based not only on real cases, but, above all, on the author's personal experience in a number of best-in-class organizations.

Lean and Digitize helps to solve the following problems:

- Incomplete alignment of ICT and process improvement initiatives;
- Initiatives redundancy;
- Excessive time lost in the analysis and implementation phases;
- The difficulties in the measuring and verifying control improvements.

By engaging information and communication systems in your initiatives together with process improvement and optimization, you can secure excellent results. The method is quantitative: based on facts. This allows a quick and accurate measurement process whether in an analysis or control phase, which helps facilitate and accelerating all project activities.

From an organizational point of view, the Lean and Digitize method:

- Includes information and communication systems in improvement initiatives, making it possible to improve and optimize physical, organizational and automation flows concurrently;
- Provides ongoing improvements to projects delivering new or updated information and communication systems by integrating them with those projects associated with process improvement and optimization;
- Automates only those processes that have already been improved and optimized.

The Structure of the Book

- The introduction deals with the development of Lean Thinking and the approaches for streamlining organizations. It also explains how, over time, the Lean Six Sigma method was introduced in synergy with Six Sigma;
- Chapter 1 describes the relevance of ICT to process improvement:
- Chapter 2 introduces the method and tools of Lean and Digitize;
- Chapter 3 analyses the approach to Lean and Digitize;
- Chapter 4 describes how to organize a Lean and Digitize project;

- Chapter 5 is about people. It focuses on culture, roles and responsibilities associated with the application of the Lean and Digitize method;
- Chapter 6 covers communication and its impact on those both outside and inside the organization;
- Chapter 7 deals with the use of ICT to support the Lean and Digitize projects;
- Chapters 8 and 9 present the main aspects of the application of the method in manufacturing and service organizations respectively;
- The last chapter shows possible future developments of the method in the light of the kind of scenarios you might expect in the near future.

I recommend you read all chapters of this book consecutively. Alternatively, you may start with Chapter 2 for an overview of the method and to understand briefly the development of a Lean and Digitize project, and then read the chapters related to those specific topics of interest.

My aim is to be beneficial and useful to the reader and carry out a missionary action in the use of this method. In this way, I hope that as many organizations as possible can benefit from it. This is my only purpose.

Enjoy reading and learn a lot.

Bernardo Nicoletti

List of References

Burd, L.A. (2009), *Il Principe*, Ithaca; Cornell University Library

1 Introduction to Lean Thinking and Lean Six Sigma

Customers' demands for ever-lower prices, higher quality, more options and faster and safer deliveries are increasingly conditioning organizations. Rapid modifications in the socio-economic environment and in the market have brought a number of changes in organizations, and all of these elements have increased the complexity and cost of process management.

Increased costs, competitive pricing and the growing purchasing power of consumers have tended to drive down profits. In order to survive and grow, a fundamental revolution must take place inside the business and at the level of the organizational culture.

Lean Thinking is a philosophy, a method and a set of tools and techniques. Lean Thinking allows you to bring your processes closer to the customer, to eliminate any activities that do not add value to your products, and to produce faster with lower costs and higher quality.

This chapter provides an overview of the Lean Thinking concepts and basic tools/ techniques, such as the pillars of the Toyota Production System (just-in-time and autonomation), followed by a discussion of the five principles of this method – Value, Stream Value, Flow, Pull and Perfection.

The second part of this chapter is a presentation of Lean Six Sigma: a synthesis between Lean Thinking and Six Sigma. These methods along with digitization form the basis of the Lean and Digitize approach, presented in the next chapter.

Lean Thinking

Any organization based simply on a traditional production and management model is unlikely to survive the current competitive pressure. The economic crisis, the fall of geopolitical barriers with the subsequent entry of competitors such as China and India, and the excessive increase of supply over demand are some ingredients of the heated battle within many markets.

Organizations typically used to make pricing policy based on the cost incurred according to this formula:

Production/supply cost plus budgeted profit equals selling price of a product/service to the customer (Cost + Profit = Price)

The dynamic nature of the market has shifted purchasing power towards the customer. It is now the customer and the activities of your competitors who determine the price and the quality of the products and services that the customers wish to buy. Therefore, the new logical scheme is as follows:

Subtract production/delivery costs from the selling price as determined by the market. The result will equal the profit that the organization can get (Price – Cost = Profit)

It is no longer acceptable to raise prices to mitigate poor efficiency and lack of effectiveness. This then puts three elements at the heart of your organization's competitiveness:

* quality improvement
* reduced cycle times
* costs reduction.

To achieve these, the organization needs to eliminate all sorts of waste: indeed, everything that does not add value for the customer.

The causes of waste in organizations are mainly:

* deficient organization and management of production spaces and times
* bad maintenance
* lack of methods and attention to details
* inadequate equipment
* low-quality materials and components
* excessive inventories
* non-necessary transport
* misunderstanding the requirements of the customers.

According to some estimations, 80 per cent of the activities in a process do not add value. 15 per cent is waste and just 5 per cent add value. An activity that adds value is one that transforms the product physically, is performed correctly first time and satisfies the customer's requirements. An activity with no added value consumes time and resources but does not add value to the product itself.[1]

The customer dictates what adds value and quality in the product or service. Everything else is waste, unless required for other reasons (for instance, compliance). When we refer to the customer, we mean not only the user of the product or service, but also the department that receives the output of internal activity: the internal customer.

It follows that you need to determine what the requirements of external and internal customers are in order to define which activities do not add value and make the product/service less attractive.

---

1   Available at: http://www.Leanmanufacturing.it

Development of Lean Thinking

During the last century, quality management had a single approach in the management world. Taylor influenced Ford. It was the beginning of mass production. Shewhart introduced statistics as a quality control tool in the business world. Organizations all over the world followed these approaches in a uniform way. Since 1945, the paths of quality management in Asia and the West have divided.

QUALITY IN JAPAN (1945–1980)

During the 1940s, the general quality of Japanese products was poor in the context of the severe economic crisis following the defeat in the Second World War. The Japanese embraced post-war reconstruction as an opportunity to address the root of the problem. And to do this, they turned to the American gurus of quality: Deming, Juran and Feigenbaum.

THE GURUS OF QUALITY

These quality gurus succeeded in translating some innovative theories into Japanese culture: theories which, ironically, struggled to gain acceptance and adoption in the Western world, which was still closely bound to mass production and the ideas of Henry Ford.

Edwards Deming (1900–1993) arrived in Japan in 1947, to assist in the preparation of 1951 census. He worked with statistics teachers, advised some Japanese organizations and introduced the concept of statistical quality control. He was in contact with the JUSE (Japanese Union of Scientists and Engineers), sponsoring entity for the development and diffusion of a quality control culture in Japan. Deming's aim was to give senior management responsibility, and he claimed that 94 per cent of the problems stemmed from its lack. His ideas focused on the following principles:

- continuous improvement of products and services
- professionalism at every level of the organization
- defect prevention, rather than defect detection
- quality assurance of supplies
- use of statistical methods
- training in quality
- supervision as support, rather than as a passive control
- creating a motivating atmosphere
- breaking down barriers between functions
- management as a promoter of quality.

The Deming Prize was established in 1951 to recognize contributions to research and application of statistics.

The Japanese authorities invited also Joseph Juran (1904–2008) to give two seminars at the main Japanese organizations. His approach was different from Deming's in that it focused on the management and organizational aspects of quality. Juran's quality trilogy – planning, control, improvement – connects quality to customer satisfaction and emphasizes the concept of quality improvement, which is achieved through a sequence of projects, directed by a strong management. His *Quality Control Handbook* (1957) remains a standard reference for quality improvement (Defeo and Juran, 2010).

Armand Feigenbaum (1922–) published the book *Total Quality Control* in 1951 and brought forward total quality as a system for continuous improvement. The main argument of his book was that it is necessary to engage the entrepreneurial structure completely in order to produce and provide products and services at the lowest price and at the highest level of customer satisfaction (Feigenbaum 1991).

These three gurus provided Japanese organizations with some clear and basic principles for quality improvement:

- The importance of quality management as a competitive factor;
- The importance of strategy applied by senior management to promote improvement actions; and
- The statistical method as an educational factor to sustain the qualitative evolution of the organization.

Company-wide Quality Control

The concept of Total Quality spread in Japan as Company-wide Quality Control (CWQC). Following the teachings of the American gurus, quality became a mantra for many Japanese organizations. The application of the P-D-C-A model (also called the Deming Cycle) was particularly successful:

- Plan: planning goals and conditions;
- Do: perform the activities;
- Check: measure improvement in processes and in activities;
- Act: work to improve.

The main aim of this cycle is to enable quality and make it visible to the customer. Profit is a natural consequence, not a primary goal. It is necessary to control quality continuously and extend it to every aspect of the organization's systems. Quality should involve all the professional positions, from the general management of an organization to the lowest level of personnel. There is a direct connection between quality, strategy and profit.

Total quality needs to be at the heart of the organizational culture. To do this you need to train employees in the seven tools of quality and their application:

- data sheets
- stratification
- histograms
- Pareto analysis
- cause–effect diagram or CEDAC
- correlation diagrams
- control charts.

You also need to eliminate barriers between functions, which are anathema to the concept of the 'internal customer'. The satisfaction of all internal customers, up and down the value chain, is the key to satisfying the external customer.

Romano Bonfiglioli (2004: 29–30) describes the main points of CWQC:

Why does the company exist? The answer is not that of the West 'to make profit,' but rather: organizations exist because clients exist. Therefore, this is the starting point (point 1): the client is the main objective of the company. Following this idea, if the client is not satisfied they will choose another product, so the main aim of the company is more precisely defined as follows: client's satisfaction becomes the organization's main objective (point 2) ... 'Client's satisfaction can be obtained through quality' (point 3) ... profit is no longer the main objective of the company, but a secondary objective which stems from the choice for quality made by the company which is well expressed by the motto 'Take care of quality, profit will take care of itself.'

He continues:

If quality is the main objective of the organization, then (point 4): all people and all sectors of the organization will be interested in quality – not just in production, as it was believed in the past: the real 'killers' of quality can be those who have never even touched the product! Therefore (point 5): each one must be responsible for the quality of their own work. ... The concept of continuous improvement (kaizen) (point 6): if total quality is the main objective of the company, the organization should not just control quality but strive to improve it continuously ... However, if the customer is far away, I have not met them, how should I obtain their satisfaction? Again, here is an innovative answer: the department immediately below is your client ... The development of the model proceeds with the implementation of statistical methods (seven tools, PDCA, etc.) (Point 7) in order to obtain quality improvement ... If I should strive to obtain total quality and continuous improvement ... then it is necessary to make massive training, that is, (point 8) to provide training for the entire personnel in terms of quality and the use of statistical tools ... Training must begin at the top (point 9).

According to Ishikawa (1991), a key figure of this evolutionary phase, CWQC involves the following:

*   Management must be the leaders;
*   Applying the Deming Cycle (PDCA) to the entire organization in order to prevent possible defects;
*   Approach quality. As a dynamic objective;
*   Pursue continuous improvement;
*   Consider the client to be a king: their satisfaction should be the final objective of every activity of the organization;
*   Train the whole staff, raise the cultural level and change ways of thinking;
*   Encourage autonomy and motivation in people involved in the organization processes;
*   Make quality circles;
*   Control variability by means of the seven quality tools;
*   Spread control down the production chain, beyond the organization.

Value Analysis

As these revolutions were taking hold in Japan, the Western world began to talk about the 'value' of the product. Value analysis is an organizational technique used to obtain alternative solutions to the way the product was built at minimum cost, based on three basic points:

• Recognition and assessment of value through the identification of functions;
• Assessment of functions/costs;
• Development of alternatives.

Value engineering applies this concept to the design of products and services.

Value analysis goes back to the post-Second World War period. It remains a relevant technique (Weiller 1987), especially as part of a process of continuous improvement.

L.D. Miles studied and developed value analysis in 1942–43. At that time, he was in charge of the purchasing department at General Electric Corporation (GE). His main focus was searching for new low-cost and easy to find materials, which could replace other much more rare and expensive materials; particularly in the context of wartime shortages. Consequently, he only initially applied value analysis to the purchasing function.

In 1947, Miles extended the use of value analysis to the planning department within GE. His first practical application was in an automatic temperature control system. Encouraged by the results they obtained, GE applied the same method to other components and products, gradually improving the technique.

Value analysis started to spread to other companies by 1950. The first experiences in Europe date back to 1956, while a number of leading Italian companies, such as Pirelli and Fiat, introduced it into their production in 1965.

Value analysis can be applied in all sectors of an organization, from general purchases to production cost, planning for investments cost, components of the product, scheduling to the working method, the purchase of raw materials to the purchase of semi-processed products. Value analysis enables you to review and control, indirectly, the productivity and results of each part of the organization.

Value analysis provides a platform for corrective actions to bridge any gaps between functions within the organization. It enables analysts to:

• Conduct precise cost analysis;
• Solve problems caused by specialization, conducting studies outside the normal operational framework;
• Encourage creative and imaginative actions;
• Improve the connection amongst the services; and
• Develop knowledge.

It is important to apply the method rigorously and address the human factors associated with its introduction. Once you have piloted the concept you can apply the method to new products in the design phase or to other sectors, such as organizational structure cost and industrial investments. Some organizations have achieved cost savings of between 10–20 per cent without undermining the quality of products. Value analysis requires a serious investment in time and money but the annual savings should cover their cost several times over.

The Toyota Production System

The founder of Toyota, Sakichi Toyoda, his son Kiichiro Toyoda and the engineer Taiichi Ohno introduced the Toyota Production System (TPS) during the 1950s, using the company-wide quality control (CWQC) approach. Toyota adapted CWQC to fit their specific environment: the production of vehicles. The Toyota Production System was the origin of many of the tools now present in Lean Thinking, including two of the most important: just-in-time and jidoka.

The Japanese economy was in bad shape after the Second World War and faced strong competition from international products. One of the consequences was that the car market in Japan had a limited and inelastic demand. In that context, mass production really did not make sense. The volume and mix required did not allow a serial production process similar to that of the 'Model T' produced by Ford.

In addition, Japan was geographically distant and detached from the most interesting markets: the United States and Europe. Nor did the Japanese have a network of technical support available in these markets. This made product quality the fundamental hurdle to exporting their products to these markets. The new developing markets such as Africa and Latin America had similar needs, essentially due to the lack of maintenance organizations.

In order to be competitive and survive, Toyota organized and structured their production system to enable themselves to use the infrastructure, personnel and materials in the most effective way, cutting the costs. The key concept at the heart of the Toyota production philosophy is the total elimination of the three M's: *muda* (waste), *mura* (unevenness) and *muri* (overburden), which represent activities that do not provide added value for the customer. Therefore, TPS aims to eliminate:

- Overproduction: waste of material, time, personnel, goods, space, money;
- Defective products: waste of material, time and money. They decrease customer satisfaction;
- Unnecessary transportation: unnecessary movement of raw materials, work in progress and finished products;
- Manual movements: useless workers' actions during the production of a specific product;
- Delay/hold on: waiting time wasted by operators due to delay, damage or movement of materials;
- WIP (work in process): materials and components used to hide the problems of production balance;
- Manufacturing: time devoted to unnecessary processes.

In order to eliminate these wastes, it is important to balance production (*heijunka*) and apply a set of tools belonging to just-in-time (JIT) and autonomation (*jidoka*). These are the pillars of the Toyota Production System:

- Just-in-time allows running the productive flow without the need of stocks, at the right time and in the right volume and mix. Materials are 'pulled' according to the customer's demand;
- Autonomation makes the machine 'intelligent', automatically treating each anomaly, digitizing the routine and therefore facilitating human work.

The first applications of TPS were in the production of Toyota car engines. It then spread to the assembly line and the supply chain.

Kaizen

The TPS is a development of the Japanese theory called kaizen or continuous improvement. Kaizen means to solve a problem with a different point of view (*kai* = change, changing your way of seeing things). It requires everyone to produce ideas for improvement, and to share them. In this way, they can be immediately useful (*zen* = good, to the best). The main objective is to involve people to improve processes and products. In this way, you can reduce the. natural resistance to change.

The kaizen plan represents short, medium and long-term planning (30, 60 and 90 days) for those activities associated with the implementation and monitoring of the progress of a Lean project.

Kaizen planning consists in:

- Deciding the sequence of improvement activities defined during the meetings of the improvement team;
- Assigning of tasks and responsibilities of each single activity (design, construction, test, and launching of the production of the new component/application/interface/ etc.);
- Planning of timing, resources and budget assignment.

The organization defines the terms and approaches of improvement actions on the basis of how difficult it would be to implement the solutions: the greater the complexity of the intervention, the greater the need to schedule more time in the kaizen plan. This, in turn, requires detailed monitoring of the progress of the intervention.

One of the tools used in the kaizen is Five-S. Its main aim is eliminating waste and helping implement improvements. Table 1.1 shows the key components of this tool (Miklovic 2008).

Table 1.1   The Five-S kaizen tool

Japanese word	English translation	Explanation
Seiri	Sort	Examine the workstation in order to eliminate materials or tools that are not used. Clean up.
Seiton	Set, straighten, store	Organize the remaining articles. A place for everything and everything in its place.
Seiso	Shine, sanitize, scrub, sweep	Establish a cleaning routine that includes an initial cleaning, as well as a continuous cleaning, and a daily clearing up activities.
Seketsu	Standardize	Guarantees that the best practices become part of the daily work on the work station. Establish the processes.
Shitsuke	Sustain, self-discipline	Review the first four S's on a continuous basis in order to guarantee that there are no backward steps, but only continuous improvement.

A KAIZEN MINI-WORKSHOP UNDERTAKEN IN A GRAPHICS COMPANY. WWW.RIVISTEDIGITALI.COM/ITALIA

The Kaizen Institute developed a mini-workshop in a company called Ciemme in Cinisello Balsamo, Italy. The company is involved in the customization and distribution of mailing envelopes and company prints one million units per day.

Similarly to many other companies in the sector, Ciemme follows a number of production rituals, with some methodologies repeated over and over again. It is a working environment that does not encourage either workers or managers to reflect on possible improvements.

In Ciemme, the kaizen workshop was on the 'gemba', the operations floor. The workshop focused on the reconfiguration of a printing machine. This is a delicate operation because it requires machine downtime and a halt in production. Typically it uses 15 per cent of the overall production time. Carlo Ratto, from the Kaizen Institute, introduced the new method to the managers and workers. The machine operators were impressed. They had not considered the possibility of reducing the downtime, because during the reconfiguration of the machine, they were constantly active and did not consciously waste time.

The team video recorded each operation required to reconfigure the machine:

- washing the nozzles for the next printing
- cleaning the machine
- preparation of colour
- replacing ink, washers, plates and so on.

Back in the classroom, watching and analysing the video, the operators were able to see all the unnecessary actions they performed:

- Each operator walked considerable distances to collect tools which could have been available in a basket near their normal position;
- They repeated a number of actions;
- Several operations would be more effective if performed in reverse order; and
- Other activities required much less time.

The machine operators, initially sceptical, started to see their own operations through fresh eyes. They began to realize how to improve their daily routine. The operators themselves were the source of the best ideas to improve the effectiveness for the machine reconfiguration.

Their response is interesting: following a natural resistance – 'what are these guys doing here?' – they began to feel involved. They emerged from the session with a much better knowledge of the process.

Overall Ciemme provided very positive feedback, both in terms of results and in terms of process improvement. They understood that kaizen motivated people.

Kaizen always needs a starting point, in this case, the printing machine. Subsequently, a number of people in the organization were able to apply what they had learned to extend their experience independently to other machines and later to the entire organization. You can use kaizen to redesign the core processes: sales, product definition, operations and so on. From an initial starting point it is possible to adopt kaizen throughout the company. At that point, that process of managed improvement gives way to one of continuous improvement in which everyone participates.

Fordism vs. Toyota Production System

Table 1.2 summarizes the main differences between the traditional production model initially adopted by Ford and the Toyota Production System.

Table 1.2   Fordism and the Toyota Production System compared

Fordism	Toyota Production System
Push: product is pushed into the market	Pull: product is pulled by the customer
High volume	Low volume
Low mix	High mix
Inspection	Prevention
Discrete improvement	Continuous improvement
Fragmentation of activities	Integration of activities
Individual knowledge	Shared knowledge
Not qualified worker	Polyvalent worker
Management controls	Management leads
Vertical integration	Network enterprise
Compulsory automation	Flexible automation

Difficulties in the Introduction of the TPS Principles around the World

During the 1970s and '80s, Japanese products had great success in Western markets. Western manufacturers pondered the reason behind such success and started to study the TPS and the principles of CWQC.

They studied in detail the different techniques of just-in-time, quality circles and so on and initiated some early attempts to introduce these tools in their own organizations. The results were disappointing, largely due to:

*   Cultural problems;
*   The confusion generated by a wrong assessment of the production system; and
*   Poor understanding of some tacit elements at the base of the method.

Stephen Spear and H. Kent Bowen believe that the reason why US companies rarely obtained the results that Toyota obtained was that they were not able to use the tools correctly. According to Spear and Bowen (1999), there are four rules you need to follow in order to benefit from the essential knowledge of the Toyota Production System (Berry and Parasuraman 2004, Bertels 2003: 7–8):

*   Each activity must be specified in terms of scope, time and results;
*   Each client–provider connection must be direct. There must be a correct and univocal way to send requests and receive answers;
*   The path of each product and each service must be simple and direct;
*   The organization should get each improvement by means of a scientific method, under the supervision of a facilitator, at the lowest possible level of the organization … The TPS and Japanese concepts about quality in general link processes, people and behaviour with the culture of continuous improvement.

In order to obtain worthwhile results from any changes on the basis of the TPS, your organization needs to be willing to change and must understand the new method in full.

From TPS to Lean Thinking

The Americans created the terms Lean Production, Lean Manufacturing, Lean Enterprise and Lean Thinking. They described and abstracted the TPS to make it understandable and thus applicable in any context. John Krafcik, researcher at the Sloan School of Management, MIT of Cambridge, Massachusetts, introduced the term 'Lean' for the first time in 1988, in a study carried out by MIT on 90 automobile production sites in 17 different countries.

There are subtle differences between these terms:

*   Lean production: in 1990, James Womack, Daniel Jones and Daniel Roos used this expression to describe the TPS in their book *The Machine that Changed the World* (1990). The book is about the role of the automotive industry in the world economy, as studied during the project called International Motor Vehicle Program (IMVP);

- Womack and Jones introduced the term 'Lean Thinking' in their 1996 book. They generalized the lessons learnt during the IMVP project, introduced the principles of Lean and made them applicable to any sector.

In 1997, Womack founded the Lean Enterprise Institute with the objective of increasing the number of organizations using Lean Thinking.

Thanks to the contribution of a number of research institutes and a variety of published papers, Lean Thinking has nowadays become part of the patrimony of the corporate culture of the West. Organizations increasingly apply the method to all sectors of manufacturing and are extending Lean Thinking to the entire supply chain. The end game is the 'Lean Enterprise', and in recent years, service organizations too have started to use it.

During a workshop on 'Lean Six Sigma,' Leonardo La Pietra, General Manager of the European Institute of Oncology (EIO), focussed on the use of Lean Thinking and cultural change in services www.ieo.it. He pointed out that in order to become a centre of excellence such as the EIO it was not enough simply to possess great technical-scientific knowledge. You also need to have a wider vision, one that takes into consideration the patient's perspective. That involves devoting care to some aspects that at first sight might seem to be irrelevant, such as the organization and total quality of the service. Womack and Jones 1996

The Lean Thinking Method

Lean Thinking is a philosophy, which is focused on the systematic elimination of waste, (*muda* in Japanese). The concept aims generally at the elimination of the 3Ms: in Japanese *muda*, waste, *muri*, something unreasonable, impossible, without any logic, and mura, unmanaged and sudden variation. Organizations apply Lean Thinking with a series of tools consisting in the just-in-time (JIT) and autonomation (*jidoka*) approaches. It is a well-defined method based on the following principles:

- value: define the value
- value stream: identify the value of the flow
- flow: make the identified flow run
- pull: make the flow pulled
- perfection: seek perfection.

The application of Lean Thinking methods and tools should involve everyone in the organization, once suitably trained. The Lean concepts are simple in theory but difficult to apply to the day-to-day flow of work. They require a change to employee's cultural approach; the adoption of a continuous improvement culture, known by the Japanese term *kaizen*.

Eventually, all people in the company will acquire the principles. Difficulties arise when these principles must be applied to ordinary reality, when people have to change their mentality and their working habits, when the whole organization must change their working habits, when providers must change their working habits, and so on. Bonfiglioli 2004: 85

Change needs to come from the top. Senior managers need to introduce a sense of urgency and provide an engaging vision for everyone, through a plan of incentive and communication. Employees need to change their way of thinking to accept the challenge associated with continuous improvement.

Lean Thinking is a model that should simplify the whole organization and its way of working. However, it requires considerable effort in order to overcome the resistance to change. The primary objective is customer satisfaction, achieved by eliminating all waste; those activities that do not add value. The organization's profitability is also an important objective but only as a by-product. The lean organization tends to perfection, is not overly worried about competitors since the objective of Lean is perfection.

AN EXPERIENCE OF LEAN PRODUCTION (ALFIERI 2009)

Flavio Berto, from the Berto textile industry (200 employees with €24 million profit) provides the following example:

We have applied the principles of Lean production for two years now, not without difficulty in its implementation, because it is difficult to make the entire chain responsible ... [But there have been results] ... We have reduced the time of machine reconfiguration by 50 per cent without having to increase the investment; we have simplified the internal statistics system. In addition, we have multiplied the range by increasing productivity by 30 per cent: from 20 jean products per year to 120 per season.

Lean in the Evolutionary Pyramid

The CWQC and TPS belong to Asian culture. They originated in the 1950s through to the 1980s. From the 1990s onwards, the West joined the party with Lean Thinking: a generalization of the TPS principles and tools (Womak,Jones, Roos 1996).

Figure 1.1 shows a graphic representation of the evolution of process and quality.

The final missing element is represented by the summit of the pyramid: Lean Six Sigma, a synergy of Lean and Six Sigma.

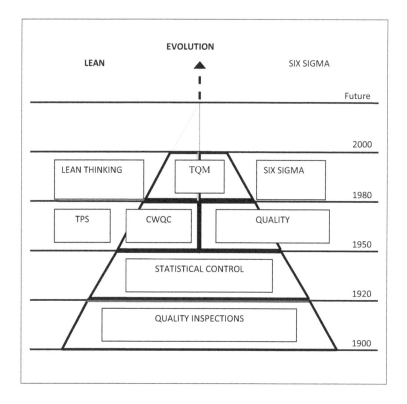

Figure 1.1 The quality management evolutionary pyramid

Lean Six Sigma

Lean Six Sigma represents the current phase in quality improvement methodology. It reduces process defects using Six Sigma and improves the cycle time thanks to Lean Thinking tools.

When applied individually, both methods have limitations:

- Six Sigma eliminates the defects but does not directly tackle the problem of improving cycle time. Six Sigma focuses on the reduction of variability and the subsequent improvement of the process. It follows the Define, Measure, Analyse, Improve, Control (DMAIC) approach and uses statistical instruments; whereas
- Lean Thinking focuses on flow optimization but does not guarantee a reduction in defects. The five principles of Lean Thinking guide the Lean approach. They focus on the elimination of redundancy and continuously improving the process flow, and above all, reducing the cycle time.

Table 1.3 shows the main differences between Lean and Six Sigma, and the effects produced by implementing them.

Table 1.3   Characteristics of Lean and Six Sigma

	Lean	Six Sigma
Aim	Cycle time improvement/defect elimination	Process improvement/variability elimination
Applicability	Mainly manufacturing	All the processes
Project selection	Guided by value stream map	Several approaches
Project duration	From one week to three months	From two to six months
Infrastructure	Ad hoc	Resources used
Training	Learning by doing/no formal training	Learning by doing/formal training and extended to all the organization
The primary effect	Cycle time reduction	Reduction of variability in the processes
The secondary effect	Uniform resulting process	Cycle time reduction

The Benefits of Lean Six Sigma

Lean Six Sigma:

- Minimizes costs;
- Streamlines, accelerates and makes processes flexible;
- Makes it possible to meet the customer's requirements efficiently;
- Increases the qualitative level of the product and the service.

> *The aim of Lean Six Sigma is to improve a system by reducing defects and activities of no value for the customer. They represent costs, expenses and money for an organization and therefore a reduction in the price-cost profit margin ... By applying Lean Six Sigma, it is possible to revolutionize the presentation of efficiency in each company area, both at the strictly productive level and everything related to transactional processes. Aggogeri and Gentili 2006: 16–17*

The Lean Six Sigma method makes it possible to address improvement projects with real rigour, based as it is on two distinct methods and two heterogeneous and complementary set of tools.

Reducing both cycle times and defects (which in turn makes it possible to reduce time for control and re-evaluation) is paramount in a context in which time will be an increasingly essential factor for competitiveness. Peter F. Drucker (1966), considered one of the modern gurus of organization management, said 'Time is the scarcest resource and unless it is managed, nothing else can be managed.'

TIME AND COST REDUCTION WITH PROJECTS LEAN SIX SIGMA WWW.PETERKEEN.COM

A study of business process management (BPM) initiatives, based on Lean Six Sigma, analysed the effect of BPM on reducing cycle time and showed that BPM has been a successful approach. Companies in the study successfully reduced their cycle time from 30 per cent to 70 per cent. Examples of successful application of these principles include:

- Ford Motor Company: management of the approval of warranty services (time reduction by 69 per cent with a US$1.5 million reduction per year);
- International Truck and Engine: special quotations for personalized vehicles (reduction of 40 per cent)
- Lockheed Martin: resolution of production problems (savings of 50 per cent with savings of US$1 million per year);
- Lubrizoil: development of new products for special chemical product (dramatic impact; the exact figure of benefits has not been published);
- General Motors: ICT solution development (80 per cent time reduction, with 69 per cent staff cost reduction);
- RR Donnelly and Sons: personalized production and collaboration with suppliers (general increase in productivity by 15 per cent);
- The Laser Centre: opening of a new centre (40 per cent reduction);
- Telecom Inc. (fictitious name): (25 per cent reduction, 25 per cent savings over salaries, 90 per cent reduction of problems with invoices).

The synergy generated by applying the Lean Six Sigma method enables clear results in terms of:

- increases in productivity
- reduction in costs
- improvement of product/process quality and customer satisfaction.

The combined and synergistic effect of high quality and speed of the cycle necessarily brings many benefits. Less production time implies a prompt response to clients' diverse requirements and it therefore allows the possibility for higher profits. High quality implies more satisfaction for the customer and at the same time, a significant reduction of costs of support. Aggogeri and Gentili 2006: 18–19

Figure 1.2 represents an example of the results obtained with Lean Six Sigma. It illustrates a typical logistics process involving a level of variability of the process, which is equal to three sigma over a certain cycle time. The Lean contribution equals the sum of both primary and secondary effects:

- The primary effect, directly linked to the application of the Lean method, corresponds to the improvement in the cycle time. In the example, the cycle time is reduced by about 60 per cent;

- The secondary effect, which is directly linked to the primary one, corresponds to the decrease in process variability. The variability of the whole process depends on the variability of the single phases with it. The primary effect eliminates some of these phases, removing the contributions of connected variability, and therefore decreasing the total variability. In the example, the variability improves by about 0.7 sigma.
  The Six Sigma contribution also equals the sum of both primary and secondary effects:
- The primary effect, which is directly linked to the application of the Six Sigma method, corresponds to the decrease of process variability. In the example, the variability improves by about 2.3 sigma.
- The secondary effect, which is directly linked to the primary one, corresponds to the improvement of the cycle time. The total process cycle time depends on the duration of the individual phases involved in the process itself. The primary effect eliminates the re-processing and disposal phases of non-conforming products, thus decreasing the total cycle time. In the example, the reduction in the cycle time is about 15 per cent.

The Lean Six Sigma synergy equals the sum of the contributions of Lean and Six Sigma combined; that is, the sum of the primary and secondary effects of both contributions. In the example, cycle time improvement corresponds to a 75 per cent reduction (60 per cent + 15 per cent) and variability improvement corresponds to 3 sigma (0.7 sigma + 2.3 sigma).

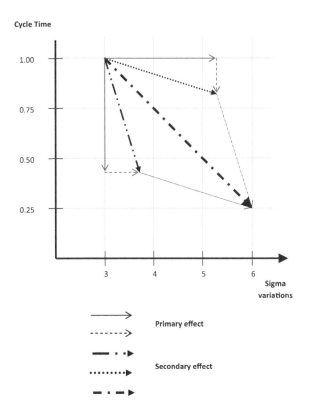

Figure 1.2   An example of the synergy generated through Lean Six Sigma

---

THE BENEFITS OF LEAN SIX SIGMA

At a seminar on 'Lean Six Sigma Strategies,' Gianpiero Cancelli – Corporate Quality and Process Manager – presented the example of the integration of World Class Manufacturing and Lean Six Sigma at the Radici Group. The system they use derives from WCOM (World Class Operations Management), closely linked in concept to TPM, Toyota production maintenance. The aim of these systems is to maintain high and controlled levels of productivity. With an investment of approximately €300,000 this represented a benefit to the value of €1.5 million. www.eccellere.com

---

Characteristics of Lean Six Sigma

The integrated approach of Lean Six Sigma starts with process mapping. The value stream map enables you to visualize the 'as-is' (the current value flow) and to trace the 'to-be' (the state you are aiming to achieve). Using the mapping, you can draw a project plan (or kaizen plan) indicating the intervention strategy for bridging the gap between the as-is and the to-be and achieving the planned objectives. The kaizen plan includes a list of improvement projects, based on the application of Lean and/or Six Sigma tools.

Lean projects generally focus on critical operational problems such as actions to reduce set-up times, cell creation or workload levelling. Without the benefit of advanced analysis tools they tend to last only a short time.

Six Sigma projects can involve any type of processes; they are suitable for complex problems, use advanced problem-solving tools and tend to last longer than Lean projects.

Lean Six Sigma takes advantage of the positive features of both approaches. It defines and accelerates the improvement process. It creates the flow and eliminates variability from processes.

Figure 1.3 shows an example of an approach to integrate Lean and Six Sigma, including a project plan to schedule the interventions from process maps and change plans. The tools you use could be either Lean or Six Sigma. The main scope of the application of Lean tools is to:

- accelerate the operations flow
- reduce setting-up time
- level the workload
- improve supplier relationships; and
- apply the total productive maintenance on the basis of the five principles of Lean thinking.

The aim of the Six Sigma interventions is to reduce variability through the DMAIC or Define, Measure, Analyse, Develop, Verify (DMADV) approach, according to your specified objectives.

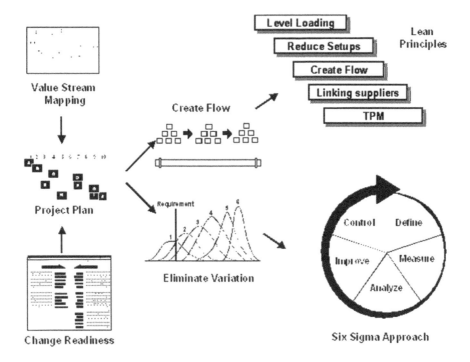

Figure 1.3   Example of integration of Lean and Six Sigma

LEAN SIX SIGMA AT GE MONEY.CNN.COM

GE Money offers a private-label credit card in support of large stores or websites. Originally, it was taking 63 days to examine and accept/reject the request by each new retailer. After some Lean Workouts and with the participation of the best people available, it was possible to reduce the 63 days to just one day. This enabled the CEO of that business to launch a marketing campaign using the catchphrase 'Enrol today. Transact Tomorrow', with a consequent doubling of sales. And this is just one example from amongst 30 projects carried forwards at GE in one year.

The Complete Evolutionary Pyramid

This chapter ends with the graphical representation of the evolutionary stages in quality from 1900 to the present in Figure 1.4. It was a long journey, over more than a century, which ended with the introduction of Lean Six Sigma.

Figure 1.4 shows the evolution of Lean Six Sigma. This method represents the union of two paths developed in parallel.

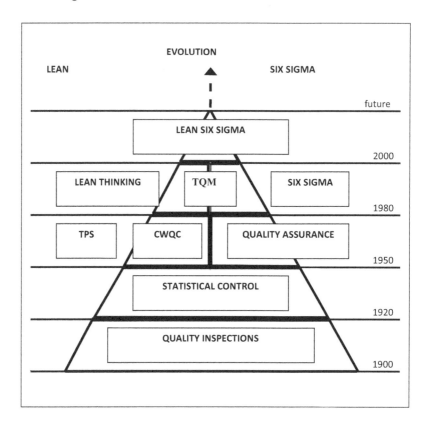

Figure 1.4 Graphical summary of the history of quality management: the evolutionary pyramid

List of References

Aggogeri, F. and Gentili, E. 2006. *Lean Six Sigma: la nuova frontiera per la qualità. La sinergia tra six sigma e lean production per un innovativo metodo di gestione e miglioramento dei processi industriali.* Milano: FrancoAngeli.

Alfieri, M. 2009. Il laboratorio Nord-Est sa parlare giapponese. *Il Sole 24 Ore*, 9 October, 2.

Berry, L. and Parasuraman, A. 2004. *Marketing services. Competing thourgh Quality.* New York: The Free Press.

Bertels, T. 2003. *Rath and Strong's Six Sigma Leadership Handbook.* Hoboken: John Wiley & Sons.

Bonfiglioli, R. 2004. *Pensare Snello. Lean-Thinking alla maniera italiana. Costruiamo l'impresa competitiva (più produttività – minori sprechi). 5 nuovi casi italiani di successo.* Milano: FrancoAngeli.

Defeo, J. and Juran, J.M. 2010. *Juran's Quality Control Handbook*, 6th edn. New York: McGraw-Hill.

Drucker, P.F. 1966. *The Effective Executive.* New York: Harper Business Essentials.

Feigenbaum, A.V. 1991. *Total Quality Control*, 3rd edn. New York: McGraw-Hill.

Ishikawa, K. 1991. *What Is Total Quality Control?: The Japanese Way (Business Management).* Upper Saddle River: Prentice Hall Trade.

Miklovic, D. Nov. 2008. *Q&A: Moving Lean from the Plant to the IT Organization, Part 1.* Gartner Report.

Spear, S. and H.K. Bowen. 1999. Decoding the DNA of the Toyota production system. *Harvard Business Review* (September–October): 97–106.

Weiller, G. 1987. *L'analisi del valore. Guida teorico-pratica all'applicazione dell'analisi del valore per la riduzione sistematica dei costi*. Milano: FrancoAngeli.

Womack, J.P., Jones, D.T. and Roos, D. 1990. *The Machine That Changed The World*. New York: Rawson Associates.

Womack, J.P. and Jones, D.T. 1996. *Lean Thinking: Banish Waste and Create Wealth in your Corporation*. New York: Simon and Schuster.

Websites

http://www.eccellere.com/public/rubriche/gestionestrategica/Lean_Six_Sigma_Strategies-85.asp

http://www.ieo.it/formazione%20esterna/qweek.shtml

http://money.cnn.com/magazines/fortune/fortune_archive/2008/07/21/105711270/index.htm

http://www.peterkeen.com/recent/articles/z_pk_it.htm

http://www.rivistedigitali.com/Italia_grafica/2009/4/054/scaricaPdf

The Theory of Lean and Digitize

2 Information Communication and Technology and Process Improvement

Introduction

The traditional methods Lean Thinking and Six Sigma were excellent when they were introduced. At the same time information communication and technology (ICT) has developed at an incredible speed. ICT can support process improvement in a big way but such analysis has not been taken into proper consideration until now. Before writing on how Lean and Six Sigma can revolutionize organizations, it is worth analysing in more detail the relationship between ICT and process improvement. This chapter focuses on this aspect.

ICT as a Lever for Process Innovation

Existing ways of working have strongly influenced the early applications of computers in organizations. The situation slightly improved with the coupling of computers and telecommunication networks – ICT. Organizations gradually started to use the new technology to modify processes and the fields and ways to apply computers widened. So did the possibilities for the organization to benefit from automation.

However, even with ICT the improvements obtained were often incremental rather than drastic. There are several reasons for this limitation in innovation and the corresponding benefits:

* ICT business analysts are usually systems analysts. They have little authority from their managers to introduce, or even suggest, fundamental changes in processes;
* Management sometimes devotes little time to understanding how to change functions in order to make the best of new technology. This problem often occurs in organizations, especially public offices, in which process changes might be subject to new laws or regulations;
* The use of formal and consolidated methods to apply ICT for changing processes or procedures is not widespread.

Everybody says they are in favour of interfunctional systems. They often give rise to difficult issues about organization policies and differences in relation to the information requirements of the different functions. Some initiatives of application during the 1980s and '90s prove that the use of ICT allows the introduction of substantial changes in interfunctional processes. Many strategic systems originating in that period were very successful because they introduced substantial changes in business processes (Fontana et al. 1996). Computer reservations systems (CRS), for instance, have simplified dramatically all processes used by travel operators, such as booking and ticket issuing, hotel and excursions reservations. With CRS, the interorganizational relations between travel and leisure operators and agents have changed profoundly. This kind of system has always been strictly interfunctional, as it includes marketing, sales and operational aspects. From the analysis of this case, one particular element stands out: those who have succeeded in the use of ICT implemented systems which changed processes in the organizations

On the other hand, process improvement methods often did not consider the role of ICT. Practitioners considered it dangerous because it introduced rigidity in the processes. It is only recently that some organization researchers have started discussing the role of ICT in process improvements (see Figure 2.1) (Porter 2008).

This chapter presents an integrated method for process improvement in organizations. It analyses how, by means of organizational methods or by means of digitization, process improvement and optimization can integrate. We introduce a method called Lean and Digitize, based on the following principle: make processes lean and high quality while at the same time digitize them.

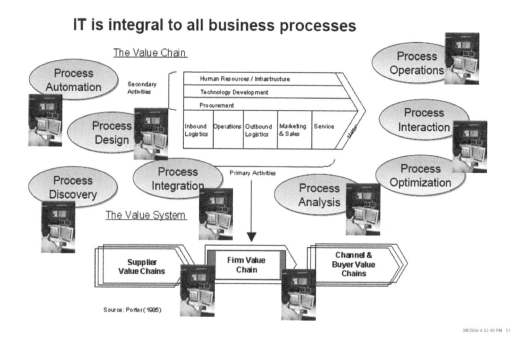

Figure 2.1   The close connections between ICTs and business processes

Information and Communication Technology and the Crisis in Productivity

Data on productivity indicate that organizations are often not successful in employing ICT for relevant changes, even though the functionality of technology has improved continuously. The following are some examples of improvements:

- Telephone networks were for transmitting voice. Nowadays, they can transmit data, voice, image and video, sales orders, money transfers, project design of products, documents, telephone meetings, video conferences and so on;
- Computers initially automated accounting. Nowadays, they support decision-making, archives and make available large amounts of documents and graphic images. They simulate processes and control the behaviour of spacecraft and artificial hearts, etc.

In spite of its widespread use in many organizations, ICT has not fulfilled its promise of substantially influencing business transformation. There are indeed some examples in which the new technology has increased productivity and reduced costs considerably. However, there is no evidence to prove that these new technologies in all cases increase productivity (one of the most relevant aspects of organizational management) or that they necessarily increase profitability (Brynjolfsson 1993) There are several examples of investments in ICT on a large scale, with limited or even no process changes. ICT is often used solely for text processing and spreadsheets by individuals and organizations. These implementations do not assure process innovation. Many technology applications have dealt with the automation of routine work: only in relatively few cases have they tackled process innovation.

In a famous book, Nick Carr from the Harvard Business School wondered *Does IT Matter?* (Carr 2004) because of the poor results in its application.

Organizations developing new applications should do it in an innovative way. The general trend is to automate the existing practice, with the consequence that most of the ICT applications support specific vertical functions of the organization. They often only automatize manual activities:

- Marketing systems only resolve marketing operations problems;
- Sales systems tackle only sales problems; and
- Manufacturing systems consider only what relates to manufacturing.

This approach makes difficult to support process improvements in the organization, because these systems tend to confine the data inside each individual function. For instance, in certain situations, they do not allow the new product information to be readily available for production, or make the sales data readily available for the manufacturing function. They do not allow for the fact that customers for a certain product could be customers for another different product of the same organization.

The ICT–Process–Productivity Relationship

Process improvement and innovation are important prerequisites to obtain a greater value from investment in ICT. Unfortunately, people working in ICT and those in charge of the different functions do not focus rigorously on changing processes as a basic step in transforming organizations. On the other side, only in this way ICT initiatives or investments in organizational changes can bring good results from an economic point of view (Figure 2.2).

In other words, people working with systems applications who strive to bring benefits by using ICT, and people in charge of organizations who struggle to maximize the value of this technology, have to start thinking about process improvement, using Lean Six Sigma as an essential factor to make technological innovation. Only in this way can they bring substantial returns in economic terms. This chapter introduces a new method called Lean and Digitize. Using this approach means adopting a radical change in perspective. Investments in ICT by themselves cannot assure a return in economic terms. Only an improvement in the processes along with the correct digitization can bring real and substantial benefits. The main role of ICT (along with other factors) is to make possible the design and the operation of a new improved process (see Table 2.1).

Managers who expect to have significant returns from investments in ICT must digitize a substantially changed process. It is necessary to modify working habits. If the role of ICT is simply to automate an existing process the benefits, both tangible and intangible, will be few.

Besides process improvements and ICT, other levers will affect the change. Few organizations think of using ICT combined with another key lever for change, namely new approaches for people management. Chapter 6, Organization for lean and digitize, will touch on this aspect.

Figure 2.2   ICTs–process–productivity relationships (Davenport 1993)

Table 2.1   A matrix to maximize the impact of ICT (Davenport 1993)

	ICT initiatives	Process changes	Economic result
Individual	Laptop system	Sales contact	Sales
Teamwork	Product database	Product moves	Product management
Business unit	Product management system	Channel relationships	Competitive position

THE RELATIONSHIP BETWEEN PROCESS AND INFORMATION SYSTEMS

The ultimate aim of a process innovation project is to implement a new process in the organization. This would allow the organization to reach several objectives of drastic better performance. The term 'drastic' implies an improvement in the range of 40–50 per cent or more. Process innovation should have objectives directed to three aspects that are strongly interconnected. The strategic objectives lead to specific objectives related to process, which, in turn, refer to the objectives related to the information system. Summing up, the objectives of the information systems are only a part of the challenges of process innovation.

It is important to apply approaches oriented to the information system as systems engineering, bearing all these objectives clearly in mind. The tools and techniques useful for process improvement are different in their application from those useful only for attaining the objectives of system development. Some ways to impose this mindset are the following:

- Give priority to strategic processes and vision aspects during the project;
- Progress towards a definition of a process improvement vision before engaging in any design or development of an ICT system.

ICT can be helpful in many ways and in many phases of the process improvement. There are also some dangers if one fails to take these opportunities. Some points are fundamental:

- Success in process improvement often depends on the speed of its implementation. Not using ICT tools could affect the speed of design and execution;
- The success of a new process is less likely when the initial development is of poor quality. It is important to use tools in advance to analyse and manage the project properly. This would improve quality;
- Supporting the process with ICT procedures allows the organization to increase the probability that the process is executed as it was designed and with less variability (and thus with a better value of Sigma);
- Failing to recognize and take advantage of ICT to facilitate the implementation of process innovation can be an indicator that management is insufficiently aware of how process innovation relates to key processes. In other words, this situation can be an indicator of a possible failure in changes related to the new process.

The list of activities related to process innovation must include the technologies (as shown in Figure 2.3) which can be useful for developing the innovation.

Computer-Aided Software Engineering (CASE)
Code generation
Applications for electronic conferences
Conventional programming
Current Applications
Tools for collection and analysis of data
Software for decision analysis
Computerized graphic applications
Executive Information Systems (EIS)
Fifth generation Languages
Communications technology
Team Decision-Support Systems (GDSS)
Hypermedia
Idea generation tools
Information engineering
Object-oriented programming
Prototyping tools for the PC
Process modelling tools
Data bank and programmable electronic spreads
Project management tools
Prototyping
Techniques for quick system development
Simulation
Graphic animation
Databases for strategic applications (generic or CASE-based)
Products of system re-engineering
Databases based on new technologies
High-level languages

Figure 2.3   The ICT levers for process innovation development (Davenport 1993)

The teams of process innovation must ensure that their approach towards ICT developments allows an appropriate management of the other key aspects of process innovation, namely:

- analysis
- design
- business and process development
- implementation
- human resources management
- communication.

PROCESS INNOVATION

Digitization can be an important lever for process innovation. ICT is also powerful when there is a change in an existing process, rather than a completely new process (supporting action: see Figure 2.4). ICT does not only allow better design, it also helps to turn the process into a sustainable working behaviour. Used in this way, it can bring continuous benefits to the organization. On the other hand, ICT is a tool to implement a successful process innovation only if accompanied by Lean and Six Sigma methods and techniques.

The main five stages of process innovation, listed in Figure 2.4, involve the following key activities according to Davenport. Some of them are implicit and others explicit. Here ICT can be particularly helpful to (Davenport 1993):

- Identify and select the processes to be redesigned;
- Define the business strategy and the process view;
- Understand the structure and the flow of the current processes;
- Measure the performance of the current process;
- Identify the levers for improving the process;
- Design the new process;
- Build a prototype of the new process;
- Make the process and the related systems operational;
- Communicate the positive results of the project;
- Ask for commitment with the solution in every phase.

There are two kinds of knowledge required in order to design a new process:

- Knowledge of the actual state, of the possible developments of the key technologies and of the levers for change; and
- Knowledge on how these levers for change have been (or could be) applied to the target process.

There is documentation of either kind. It is possible to use expert systems and consulting services in order to get the information contained in this document, based on parameters that relate to the specific situation of the organization analysed.

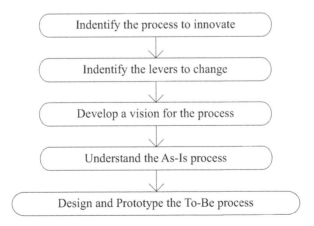

Figure 2.4   A high-level approach to process innovation (Davenport 1993)

PROCESSES AND INFORMATION

The information helps in a number of supporting roles in making processes more effective, efficient and economical. The availability of more information in a process could lead to radical performance improvement in order to, for example:

- Introduce new products and services;
- Integrate activities across and inside processes;
- Measure and control the process performance;
- Adapt the processes to particular customers; and
- Facilitate long-term planning and process optimization.

Only on certain occasions, ICT gave special importance to the information in the processes they tackled. One reason to separate them is that ICT does not manage most of the information relative to organizations and processes (more than 85 per cent, according to some estimations). Sometimes this information could be too unstructured for a computer to recognize and process. It always represents a useful input or an output element in the process. Eventually, if these entities were detached, information would play a secondary role in the analysis. Information is the most important element in ICT and it plays a fundamental role in process design and innovation.

Despite speaking about the age of information, not all organizations consider information management as a valuable issue worth improvement. Therefore, managers seldom describe or measure progress in information management. Large amounts of information enter and leave the organization without anybody really realizing their impact, value or cost. Information management is a natural objective in guiding the process. Some authors claim that in the future this will be the key for getting competitive benefits: they say that information management and its role in business processes is a prerequisite to attaining the success of the organization.

Information is the glue that holds organizational structures and can be used to better integrate activities inside or through multiple different processes. The information used in a process is useful for other processes. For instance, the information collected by door-to-door sales representatives, call centres and calls received by customer care is an important source of data, with possible analysis at different levels. It should be collected centrally and analysed. This information, whether it is the customer's voice or a large database containing information about customers, represents the foundations for business intelligence to improve marketing and sales. The source of information needed to integrate existing processes can be inside the organization or purchased from external suppliers. Useful sources are commercial information organizations, labour unions or professional associations.

From the customer's point of view, a key role of information is to enable the fitting of products to their requirements. ICT and the professional press call this approach mass customization. Nowadays the amount of customer data available in databases (both internal and public but accessible) is rising. There are also powerful means to analyse them through a process called data mining. It is possible to use all these data in order to improve the process of selling to the customer (Davenport et al. 2010).

The degree to which a process can provide different products has become an important indicator of its quality. Successful organizations have taken advantage of customer databases. They can easily use customer data to:

- classify
- store
- analyse
- retrieve; and
- maintain.

These organizations have determined and used the information in order to offer products and services customized for specific customers or market segments. By recognizing the value of product and process differentiation, they have stressed the importance of their activities related to information and have invested in them.

Information-oriented Processes

The result of a process can consist of physical and tangible products or services. The latter could also be an information product. There are two types of processes oriented to information:

- Processes designed to help decision management and activities
- Processes with operational objectives.

The operational processes oriented to information can be destructured or transactional. Figure 2.5 summarizes the different kinds of information-oriented processes dealt with in this section.

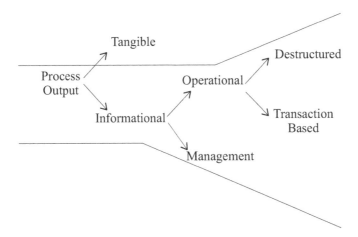

Figure 2.5   Information-oriented process types (Davenport 1993)

The Management Processes

In general, the situation of information-oriented processes is not so rosy. People responsible for the organization need external information about customers, competition and the market. However, most information processes are still including only internal information.

One of the reasons why ICT has not much affected managers is that the information needed (such as reports, information and simulations) is often not processed with ICT systems, due to their external and unstructured nature. Most ICT systems supporting the management do not abide by the law of variety required. In other words, people in charge of the organization do not obtain the information from as many different sources as would be required due to their complex decisional needs. Almost all of the decision information systems used in organizations rely at most on one or two external information sources. Often they deal with product pricing services or press releases, not because of lack of available information but because of errors in the evaluation of the information needs of those in charge.

Furthermore, many decision information systems tend to use information in a way that is more oriented to functional departments rather than to processes. As long as there are no available systems capable of supporting the whole process, one can only get information about process performance manually by:

- sampling
- paper reports purchased outside the organization
- manual distribution of process documentation; and
- other similar ways.

Only when organizations turn to process management do they start developing methods to analyse the validity of real-time processes. For this purpose, it is normally useful to focus on a limited number of metrics with indicators, financial or not, about process performance or about the organization as a whole.

Operational Processes

Some operational processes process and generate information. Unless they are highly transactional and repetitive, as for instance in banking and insurance processes, they are seldom recognized and treated as such. In general, it is not clearly understood where performances start or end, or how to measure them.

Even if they generate information, information processes based on transactions are often similar to manufacturing processes. The result is a progressive measurement and improvement of this kind of process over time. However, it is possible to change these information processes radically, based on transactions, by eliminating irrelevant phases or functions or computer applications.

Not all information-oriented operational processes are particularly structured. In professional services organizations and in the management of information delivered to customers, such as marketing research, there are some examples of less structured information processes.

When organizations start valuing information, even if it is unstructured, they understand the need of creating more formal information processes for middle and senior management. There are some emerging strategies regarding this kind of processes. The following four are amongst the most important.

- Since information processes are unstructured, the simple fact of moving towards structuring them is an innovation. The key is creating basic information management processes and then enlarging them;
- Information management processes should contain the entire value chain of information. Unless the information is not treated as part of the process, the relationship between the information provided and the decisions or actions taken will not be understood or improved;
- ICT tends to be fundamental in many processes because it allows the distribution of information within the organization. This emphasis is not necessarily true. Ironically, just because information needs and flows are unstructured, ICT should not be so much relevant as a lever for the process. Venturing into the maze of an organization's information set often requires the active assistance of experts, at least with the technologies available in the organization and in the market. Until technology does not solve this problem, it is necessary to focus on more people-based aspects rather than on those based on information processes. This is true at least in the initial phases of design and improvement;
- In times of crisis, management cut down the resources for ICT. As a result, many talents are lost. Moving towards analysing processes, it could be useful to institutionalize unstructured information processes (thus measuring their economic value). In this way, it would be possible to provide information to prevent loss of talents by making efforts to retain them.

Process Information Management

In an environment in which the amount and availability of information is growing exponentially, it is necessary to implement radical changes in the practice of information management. In most cases, even when ICT has been widely used for automation, managers neglect the issue of information management via ICT. The causes of this situation are complex. Some believe that information technologies and systems, because of their nature, are routine work for technicians. Another reason is that ICT tends to be sold by the sales representatives, consultants, journalists and by employees of the sector, as the solution for every need for information management and productivity.

Information systems managers tend to focus on specific organizational needs to break through functional barriers. They often work on their projects with operators who do not have authority in respect of the rest of the organization. If organizations understood the importance of information for their management, it would be more efficient and more effective to assign the control and responsibility of information to people with a higher position in the organization. Some organizations are now also assigning the responsibility for information and process improvement management to the people in charge of information systems.

In one of these large organizations, the general manager was concerned about information having a limited circulation within the organization. He introduced the new role of 'information owner'. He assigned this role to different managers, according to the nature of the information. These people are responsible for:

- Defining what kind of information should be used within the different specific processes throughout the organization; and
- Standardizing the processes in the use of information.

This initiative succeeded because qualifications required to perform information management processes are sufficiently different from those held by most managers in the organization. The organizations interested in doing this type of approach must form 'hybrid' teams to lead the initiatives. They must have experience not only in the business but also in information-processing technology.

Another key aspect of the process-oriented information is its structure, or architecture. Systems engineering involves the construction and maintenance of detailed models and reports for the use of information throughout the whole organization. It rigorously splits applications from data. The so-called 'service-oriented approach' – SOA – does the job even better. It prevents filing redundant information and ensures requirements are met. However, it may not be the correct paradigm to follow in order to construct information-oriented processes.

Although data are the basis of a system-engineering model, maybe higher-level information units would be more appropriate. They would potentially be much better prepared for the design of process-oriented information structures. Instead of detailed description of the data entering and leaving a phase, it would be simpler to elaborate the documents required or provided by the process activity.

Retrieving the information in order to view it as a document implies simplicity, less details and a deeper capacity to elaborate less structured data. In this way, it is possible to dematerialize or make them dematerializable. Systems engineering allows developing robust and basic well-managed files. Much work done today to provide input data to processes seems to come from other sources: the so-called hybrid (automatic and manual) information systems, less structured but more effective. Besides these hybrid information systems, the structures of process communication often make use of the concept of data warehousing and data mining. To take these concepts into account, it is necessary to store the information useful for processes for frequent access, whether it be documents, database extracts, or files.

List of References

Brynjolfsson, E. 1993. *The Productivity Paradox of Information Technology*. Communications of the ACM, December.

Carr, N. 2004. *Does IT Matter?* Cambridge: Harvard Business School Press.

Davenport, T.H. 1993. *Process Innovation: Reengineering Work Through Information Technology*. Cambridge: Harvard Business School Press.

Davenport, T.H., Harris, J.G. and Morison, R. 2010. *Analytics at Work: Smarter Decisions, Better Results*. Cambridge: Harvard Business School Publishing Corporation.

Fontana, F., Lacchini, M. and Nicoletti, B. 1996. *Casi di organizzazione e management*. Torino: Giappichelli G. Editore.

Porter, M.E. 2008. *On Competition*. Cambridge: Harvard Business Review Book.

3 *The Lean and Digitize Method*

Introduction

This chapter presents the Lean and Digitize method, which was developed based on best practices and experiences. We will consider all the steps necessary to apply the method and include a detailed comparison with other methods. We also analyse the application of the method and the criteria to move from one macro phase to another.

The Lean and Digitize Method

Thus far in this book we have emphasized the importance of blending process improvement and ICT technology. Based on research and experience, one can profitably use the Lean and Digitize method, which can be summarized as follows: it can be divided into 6 macro phases and 20+1 micro phases. The twenty-first phase is optional.

At the end of each macro phase, the project needs to be checked by the Lean and Digitize Committee, called Tollgate.

MACRO PHASE 0: PRELIMINARY

1. Context: identify the requests of customers, shareholders and employees; the challenge of competitors and the extent the firm has to comply with legislation and regulations;
2. Culture: detect the culture of the organization, of the community and of the nation in which the organization is located;
3. Vision: tackle the problems of effectiveness, efficiency, economy, quality of processes or, if necessary, of the entire organization;
4. Strategy: define the processes to be improved and the plans.

MACRO PHASE 1: DEFINE AND MEASURE

5. Kick-off: launch the project during a special meeting and notify all of the stakeholders;
6. Governance: define how to manage the project and form the team;
7. Voice of the customer: listen to the voice of the customers associated with the processes. In the case of public administration, it is the voice of the citizen. In both cases, the acronym VoC is used;
8. Metrics: translate the VoC into Critical-to-Quality factors – we will use the acronym CTQ;
9. As-is: map the existing process.

MACRO PHASE 2: ANALYSE AND PROCESS DESIGN

10. Lean: define how to improve the project with the support of the team in workshops and meetings (in General Electric this is referred to as AWO! – Action work out);
11. Kaizen plan: define the improvement intervention plan.

MACRO PHASE 3: ARCHITECTURE DESIGN

12. Architecture design: define the rules, policies and process structure.

MACRO PHASE 4: BUILD, TEST AND DEPLOY

13. Build and test: implement and test the chosen solutions (including the digitization of the relevant management aspects);
14. Change management: manage the changes;
15. Deploy: implement the chosen solution;
16. Documentation: issue the documents related to the new process.

MACRO PHASE 5: VERIFY

17. Verify: control the improvements,
18. Internal and external benefits: assess the benefits:
    - External: take notice of customers/citizens, shareholders and employees satisfaction;
    - Internal: assess the profitability, market share and internal improvements related to the new process;
19. Lessons learned: learn from the initiative;
20. Celebration: acknowledge the team's work.

OPTIONAL MACRO PHASE 6: REPLICATE

21. Roll-out: replicate the solution to the different departments or organizations in the same group.

The macro phase replicate or roll-out is optional. It consists of extending the implemented solution to other similar environments (other functions, departments or organizations in the same team).

Figure 3.1 is a summary of the method. For the purpose of continuous improvement, once the project is completed, one must use Define, Measure, Analyse, Improve, Control DMAIC. DMAIC typically leads to the need for a technological change.

In the following paragraphs we describe each macro phase with a general introduction, the best practices and a detailed analysis of each phase. Each phase is described with its main points, results and accelerators (factors that speed up and improve the execution of the project).

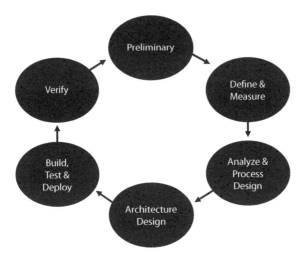

Figure 3.1   The Lean and Digitize method

A CONCLUSION OF EACH MACRO PHASE

- A list of the completeness acceptance criteria for a given phase (indicated as exit criteria); in other words, the actions which must be completed in order to proceed to the following macro phase;
- The featuring actions are summarized, compared and validated with the fundamental points of the literature collected for the analysis of the Six Sigma method: Aggogeri, Gentili (2006); Barney, Mccarty (2002); Bertels (2003); Tartari (2008); for the Lean Thinking method : Bonfiglioli (2004); Harris, Rother (2001); Smalley (2004), for the Lean and Digitize method: Bortolotti, (2007–2008) and Bortolotti et al. (2010).

At the end of each macro phase, we summarize the relational model with the sequence and the links amongst phases. They are located in their competence area:

- Market: customers, competitors, regulations;
- Organization: structure, people and knowledge.

For each phase related to the improvement process, the relational model includes the main elements associated with the organizational, physical or digitization flows.

The Preliminary Macro Phase: Context, Culture, Vision and Strategy

The Lean and Digitize method starts with the preliminary phase, in other words with the activities to begin the improvement and change project.

Focusing on change implies mainly:

1. Understanding the context in which the organization is operating, the demands of customers, colleagues and shareholders, the legislation and regulations that apply, the status of the competitors;
2. Understanding the culture;
3. Defining an overall impression;
4. Having an operational strategy.

THE 'PRELIMINARY' MACRO PHASE

Context

An organization must establish objectives in order to excel in its market and aim to satisfy its three main stakeholders:

- customers;
- shareholders; and
- employees.

In general, there can be other stakeholders, such as the community where the organization is based. For the sake of simplicity, we will not consider those aspects connected with their satisfaction. However, it would not be difficult extend the objectives in order to include other categories.

Process improvement and digitization has three objectives:

1. Provide products and/or services with customer-defined quality and capable of adding value for them: in order to continually meet the customers' needs, it is necessary to aim at process excellence and measure customers' acceptance of the products and services provided by the organization;
2. Generate returns for shareholders: in order to satisfy them, it is necessary first to satisfy the customers. In this way, you can generate profit margins. It is also important to control the process costs structure and assure that the company brand is not damaged;
3. Be an excellent working place for the employees: it is important not to neglect the human factor within the working place. This is fundamental to the proper functioning of the processes. Entrusting people with more relevant and valuable activities can be an excellent strategic benefit for the entire organization.

If the organization fails to its satisfy customers (or citizens), those groups can search for a competitor who can meet their needs. Losing loyal customers causes loss of revenue, reduced profits, lower dividends and lower profitability for shareholders. The latter could divest their assets from the organization and invest with the competitors. Clearly it is important to benchmark by analysing the competitors' offerings and how they operate.

In order to excel, however, it is not enough to meet the customers, shareholders and employee's needs. It is also necessary to comply with the applicable laws and regulations. Organizations (especially services) are highly regulated. Not considering this during the improvement and design phases could cause high costs for non-compliance.

Culture

Culture is an important aspect when defining a vision and choosing a strategy. Context refers especially to the external environment of the organization. Several factors influence culture:

- the context;
- the community in which the organization is located;
- the management;
- the organization's history.

As in the case of context, organizational culture is not easy to modify. A new CEO or President can undertake this mission but it will take time. At the level of the individual departments, some slight interventions can be undertaken in order to modify the culture, e.g. with appropriate training or incentives. Without senior management support, it is difficult to obtain any result.

Therefore, it is necessary to take into account the context and the organization culture. This is necessary not only at the time of defining the vision and the strategy, but throughout the whole Lean and Digitize project.

Vision

Vision is:

- A guideline describing what the organization is aiming at;
- An overall picture of the future state the organization intends to reach; and
- A way to encourage and move people towards change.

The vision should drive improvement interventions and align business strategies to the context in which the organization operates. It must integrate the long-term strategic aims with the operational process objectives from start to end, beyond the limits of each individual function.

By means of the vision, the organization can define objectives in terms of:

- competitive benefits;
- strategic differentiation;
- reduction of operational costs;
- orientation to a market niche;
- acquisition of customers;
- increase of productivity, effectiveness, quality and agility.

The Malaysian bank CIMB offers a list of best practices in terms of the definition of vision.

CIMB TEAM CONTEXT

CIMB Team customers want:

- Access to banking services at any time and in any place (online and mobile access);
- A personalized offer (above all relative to financial advice);
- Fast, reliable and efficient services (no waiting lines, comfortable environment, etc.); and
- A particular solution for each financial issue.

The Vision of CIMB Team:

'Southeast Asia's most valued universal bank'

'We want to be the bank which represents the most obvious option for customers, the favourite organization for employees and the most profitable opportunity for shareholders all over Southeast Asia.'

Strategy

To ensure the success of the improvement project, it is necessary to translate the vision objectives into operational strategic objectives. Too often, planning of improvement projects is isolated in respect to the other departments, which can lead to isolated and marginal results. It will not lead to process optimization from start to end.

To maximize project results an overall vision of what the organization intend to achieve is necessary. For this reason, it is important to connect vision with operations, so that one can identify the processes which need improvements.

Operational strategy alignment to vision means indirectly aligning the operational strategy to context, to customers and competitors. In this way, operational improvement will be global (related to vision) or adding value to the end customer (related to context) and taking into account the organizational culture.

The result of the strategy-related phase must be a high-level plan (objectives, resources and timing) of the interventions on processes connected with the improvement projects.

In order to track projects and facilitate the analysis of the final connections and the lateral synergies, it is advisable to manage the project portfolio with a database of extraordinary initiatives (this would be an 'accelerator' for the project).

The development of a business strategy and of a process vision is based on:

- Clear understanding of the organization's strengths and weaknesses, and particular attention to the structure and the opportunities in the market;
- Awareness of innovation activities of competitors and other organizations active in the same market.

ICT can play a role before or during the process innovation development. Before innovation, the existing information system is the main source of information related to functions and current performances.

Once a formal innovation process has started, it is possible to define the vision by means of brainstorming sessions amongst the team members and other stakeholders. Information technologies can offer valid support to the execution of these activities, allowing, for example, fast simulations.

Processes to be Redesigned

In the 'business processes identification' phase those processes that are to be improved must be selected. One can then continue with the other phases. In order to identify and select the target processes, it is necessary to collect and analyse information regarding two aspects:

* The performances and structure of the processes under consideration;
* The extent to which the organization is prepared to support the redesign of those processes.

The first step in this phase is the collection of documentation and the study of the organizational processes.

First, the team needs to collect the organization's requirements for the process. The staff working on that process can make the best contributions to this analysis. In order to perform this activity, it is necessary to:

* Count on experienced people; and
* Carefully and precisely, understand the customers/market in which the organization operates.

From the point of view of the selection of the target process, it is particularly useful to have a database of processes or activities.

DATABASE OF UNICREDIT PROCESSES AND SUB-PROCESSES (BORTOLOTTI 2007–2008) (MAJORANA 2008)

Unicredit processing and administration (UPA) launched an initiative for process mapping in the year 2000. A consulting firm helped to involve and train the internal resources.

At first, UPA determined the process and its competence in them. Then, it defined the following items:

* All levels in the process hierarchy;
* The sub-processes; and
* The support activities, lateral to the various sub-processes.

Next, for every process and sub-process, UPA plotted the external interfaces. In other words, they identified the input and output players of the processes and the organization's responsibilities.

The variables used to identify each sub-process were:

- inputs and outputs;
- volumes
- applications used
- deadlines to meet
- relations with other sub-processes
- offices involved with existing FTEs (full-time equivalent employees)
- risks and associated controls
- volumes, itemized per each customer, in order to allow charging back the costs to each one of them.

Timing has not been measured In fact, the initial objective was only to understand the way in which activities were developed, who developed them and for which purpose. In this way, it was possible to get a ballpark cost benefit analysis for the project.

Activity databases

During the analysis phase, Unicredit's senior management often needed to know which activities could eventually be:

- Outsourced offshore or given to an external organization, due to their low added value;
- Modified in order to reduce materiality.

It was not easy to answer these questions, because each process had to be analysed in detail.

By interpreting the requirements of past information, and trying to forecast the possible future needs, 830 activities, part of 80 processes, were analysed, observing and measuring the following:

- Legal commitments to applicable regulations, national or international, if necessary;
- Legal restraints to internal regulations;
- Active contracts (if outsourced);
- Levels of service established and included in the contracts with customers;
- Jurisdiction (in case there are regional conventions or territorial constraints);
- External relations;
- Type of activity (input data into the system, input data which need to be analysed, control, audit, research, assistance and consulting, removing anomalies);
- Input and output types, storage;
- Expertise required: specialization, functional or relational;
- Periodicity of the activity;
- Operational modes: individual or team management;
- Security levels required;
- Duration of the learning process: classified into classroom training and training on the job;
- The possible anomalies: missing data, erroneous data, procedure problems, others.

UPA studied some of these entries in detail. Knowing the kind of activity (input data into the system, input data, which need to be analysed, audited and researched, assistance and consulting) is very useful in revealing which activities could be potentially automated or outsourced. Usually, the focus is on simple activities, such as entering data into the system.

They can be easily digitized or outsourced because they do not require important expertise and knowledge. In order to quantify the time spent by the resources in activities not completely operative, all of the activities classified as assisting or consulting were observed to determine whether they were necessary for the process or not.

The information relative to the type or input/output and storage can be useful in the projects of de-materialization. They are useful to understand to what extent the activity is still conventional (need paper-based documents) or digitized. Once de-materialized, it is relatively easy to digitize the activity which, in turn, can be the object of a digitized workflow.

Project Selection and Priority Criteria

Projects are the main means for the improvement of quality and productivity. Juran (Defeo and Juran 2010) attached great importance to quality improvement projects. The selection, management and successful completion of the Lean and Digitize projects must be part of any effort to improve processes. Selecting an appropriate project is an essential factor in obtaining the short- and long-term acceptance of a Lean and Digitize programme from the managers and employees in any organization. The project selection process within a Lean and Digitize programme must listen to four important voices:

- the voice of the customer;
- the voice of the organization;
- the voice of the process; and
- the voice of the other stakeholders.

In order to select a specific process, it is often necessary to prioritize some potential processes to attack. Good Lean and Digitize projects have the following characteristics:

- The project must be clearly connected with the strategic objectives of the business;
- The aspects to be improved are acknowledged to be very important for the business, in terms of costs, quality and customer's satisfaction;
- The quality of the data in the source system should be good;
- The new process needs to be flexible;
- It should require less than six months for its development. If the scope of the project is too ambitious, the costs associated with the project development could be large. This could create frustration amongst key players due to the long time to progress, the need to provide human resources for a long period of time, a delay in achieving a financial impact on the front line, etc.

The project must:

- Have clear, measurable, attainable objectives;
- Be completed on time;
- Count on measures to quantify the success of the project, to apply before the project start and after its completion;

- Count on the support and the approval of senior management.
- The project selection and priority criteria are:
- The project's alignment with the strategic objectives of the organization;
- The impact of the project on customer's satisfaction;
- The impact of the project on the organization's profit (in financial terms);
- The impact of the project on the cost of poor quality and cycle timeline;
- The risks associated with the project;
- The cost of project management;
- The level of expertise required by the project etc.

Nowadays, the information and communication technology required to support this selection process is readily available. This technology includes graphic diagrams of process flows or the possibility of creating and processing different views of the organization. However, the capacity of the project team in identifying and evaluating the selection criteria limits these functions. The base for these criteria is often very subjective assumptions.

Unicredit use key performance indicators (KPIs), both at a strategic level and at the level of the bank, to build a matrix or prioritization (see Figure 3.2).

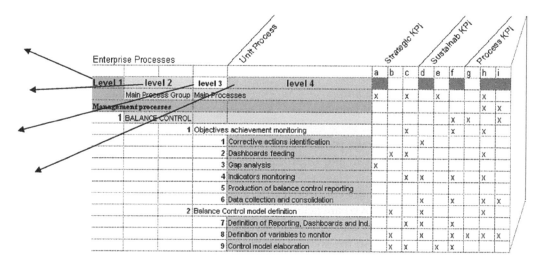

Figure 3.2   Project prioritization at Unicredit (Majorana 2008)

The Acceptance Criteria for Tollgate 0 – the Preliminary Macro Phase

Before moving into the following phases, it is important to answer the following questions correctly:

1. Did the team clearly understand whom the affected customers, shareholders and employees are and what they want? Ignoring the demands of the customers, shareholders and employees is one of the most common causes of energy and

resource waste in initiatives. They may be useless or even harmful to the profitability of the organization. Before initiating any improvement project, it is necessary to analyse the customers the organization aims at, and to involve the employees and the shareholders (at least the most relevant ones);

2. Did the team clearly understand the competition and what it is doing? Ignoring who the competitors are, what they offer to the market and what their results are can originate an erroneous vision of the objectives in terms of competitive benefits and of the strategic differentiation which could be obtained through a Lean and Digitize project;

3. Does the team know the applicable regulations? Regulations represent an essential constraint in organizational processes. Ignoring them implies a cost increase due to penalties and the need for a subsequent realignment;

4. Does the team know the economic, financial and operational performances of the organization? Ignoring these means ignoring what the organization is doing and, as a consequence, not having the possibility of correctly addressing the actions beng take to improve matters;

5. Did the team translate the vision into strategic objectives? Lacking a connection between vision and strategy causes the absence of a long-term global guideline. The team needs to manage the improvement actions through an integrated vision with a full inclusion in the organization's context. In this way, it is possible to obtain better results;

6. Does the team have a high-level plan of the interventions to improve the process? Lacking a high-level plan in this macro phase could mean underestimating or overestimating the objectives, time and resources of the different projects. It could also delay the improvement actions.

Answering the above questions correctly ensures the completion of the preliminary analysis of the organization. It is essential to assure that the team has:

- Identified customers, competitors and regulations;
- Described market demands, challenges and constraints;
- Identified the main financial and operational measures;
- Established the objectives to achieve for those indexes;
- Analysed the processes; and
- Planned the improvement actions in order to achieve the objectives stated in the vision and the strategy.

THE RELATIONAL MODEL AND ACTIONS – THE PRELIMINARY MACRO PHASE

Figure 3.3 helps us understand the connections between the initial phases of the Lean and Digitize method.

Context is located in the Market column because it represents the forces outside out of the organization. It conditions the vision, by pointing out the demands of the customers, the challenges of the competitors and the constraints of regulations. The vision of the organization must define the objectives of effectiveness, efficiency, economy and quality, in order to solve the problems found when analysing the organizational context.

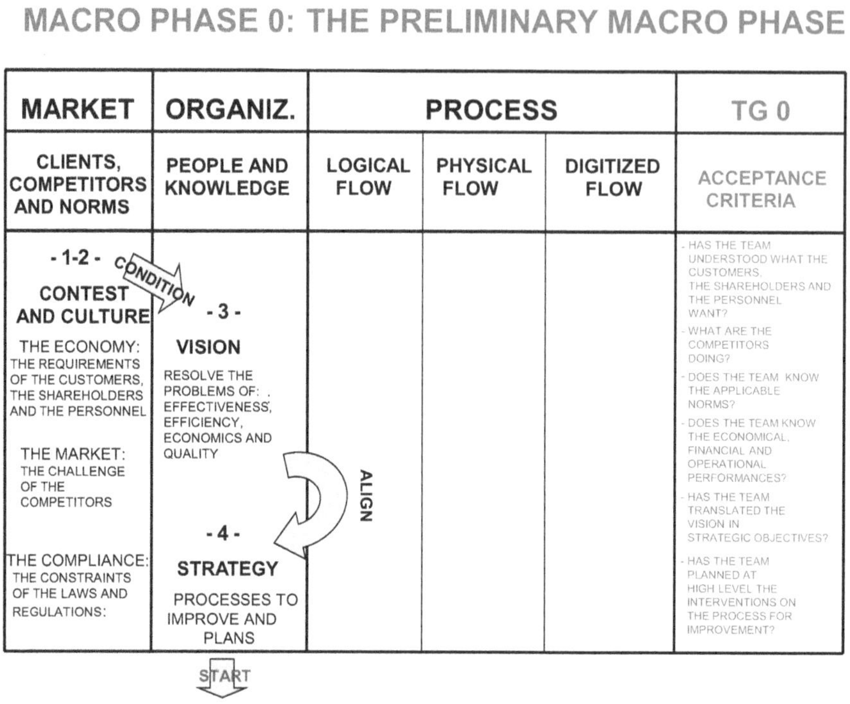

MACRO PHASE 0: THE PRELIMINARY MACRO PHASE

MARKET	ORGANIZ.	PROCESS			TG 0
CLIENTS, COMPETITORS AND NORMS	PEOPLE AND KNOWLEDGE	LOGICAL FLOW	PHYSICAL FLOW	DIGITIZED FLOW	ACCEPTANCE CRITERIA
- 1-2 - CONDITION CONTEST AND CULTURE - 3 - VISION THE ECONOMY: THE REQUIREMENTS OF THE CUSTOMERS, THE SHAREHOLDERS AND THE PERSONNEL RESOLVE THE PROBLEMS OF: . EFFECTIVENESS, EFFICIENCY, ECONOMICS AND QUALITY THE MARKET: THE CHALLENGE OF THE COMPETITORS - 4 - THE COMPLIANCE: THE CONSTRAINTS OF THE LAWS AND REGULATIONS: STRATEGY PROCESSES TO IMPROVE AND PLANS		ALIGN			- HAS THE TEAM UNDERSTOOD WHAT THE CUSTOMERS, THE SHAREHOLDERS AND THE PERSONNEL WANT? - WHAT ARE THE COMPETITORS DOING? - DOES THE TEAM KNOW THE APPLICABLE NORMS? - DOES THE TEAM KNOW THE ECONOMICAL, FINANCIAL AND OPERATIONAL PERFORMANCES? - HAS THE TEAM TRANSLATED THE VISION IN STRATEGIC OBJECTIVES? - HAS THE TEAM PLANNED AT HIGH LEVEL THE INTERVENTIONS ON THE PROCESS FOR IMPROVEMENT?

START

Figure 3.3   The relational model of the preliminary macro phase

In order to achieve the objectives established, the team must align the operational strategy with the vision. It is then possible for the Team to connect the operational process improvement projects to the objectives of the organization and to the demands/challenges/constraints of the market. The team needs to translate the operational strategy into plans for the process improvement and optimization projects. Later the team should state them in a project database.

This project database allows the organization to manage process adjustments. Processes change because there are modifications in the environment and organization, or because volumes increase, or because there are changes in the regulations. Therefore it is necessary to survey all the events that are exceptions to the normal activity:

* extraordinary activities
* process re-engineering projects
* lean and Six Sigma projects;

THE PRELIMINARY PHASE MACRO ACTIONS

* Market 1 database (if present).
* Analysis or shareholders and employees;
* Analysis of regulations;
* Determination of the vision;
* Alignment of the strategy to the vision;

- Planning of the project portfolio;
- Update of the project database (if present).

THE NEW ELEMENTS OF LEAN AND DIGITIZE – THE PRELIMINARY MACRO PHASE

The new elements, contributed by the Lean and Digitize method for the preliminary macro phase, consist of the analysis of the demand of the organization and the management of project planning through a specific database:

- Analysis of the organization demands: employees have the same relevance as customers and shareholders. Staff satisfaction is very important because employees are the main players in conducting the re-engineered processes. Satisfied people keep benefits coming from the improvement and optimization project for a long time, because they are encouraged and motivated in their own work. These considerations are valid in general, but in particular they apply to services, in which staff contribution is essential;
- Project database: managing project planning through a specific database provides benefits when the organization schedules a new project and inserts it into the database. It is possible to connect the process under analysis with other flows and documentation coming out from previous projects. Every new process improvement and optimization project could benefit from the innovations of previous or parallel projects, not yet completed or scheduled for the near future. This is an important element, especially in large organizations.

The Define and Measure Macro Phase: Governance, Voice of the Customer, Metrics, As-is

Once the preliminary phase has been completed, the project starts with the define and measure macro phase. In this phase, the team working on the project needs to guide, govern and develop process improvements:

- Listen to the voice of the customer (VoC);
- Quantify it in CtQ metrics;
- Design the activities and the process services; and
- Measure CtQ metrics.

At the beginning of this macro phase, it is necessary to select the members of the team.

THE TEST OF BEST PRACTICES – THE DEFINE AND MEASURE MACRO PHASE

Table 3.1 shows the main elements of the Lean and Six Sigma methods and the most commonly used tools regarding the governance and team, VoC, metrics and as-is phases.

**Table 3.1   The main elements of Lean and Six Sigma methods and their tools –
define and measure**

	Six Sigma	Lean	Lean Six Sigma tools	Lean tools
Governance	DEFINES: 1. To select the members of the team; 2. To issue the project charter; 3. To analyse the interesting parts; 4. To define the customer; 5. To analyse VoC; 6. To identify the CTQ	VALUE: 1. Definition of the value; 2. The customer defines the value; 3. Everything that does not add value is waste (*muda*); 4. Improvement is obtained through change;	DEFINES: • Project charter; • Quality function deployment; • SIPOC diagram; • Risk analysis; • Project plan MEASURE: Data collection plan;	VALUE: • The seven wastes VALUE STREAM: • Value stream mapping
Voice of the Customer	7. To individualize the processes; 8. To map the process; 9. To update the Project Charter, the project plan and to organize a plan for communication. MEASURE: 1. To identify the variables to be measured; 2. To issue a data collection plan; 3. To identify and select the Y's (the results) and the X's (the inputs) to be measured; 4. To identify the definition of a defect in operation mode;	5. It is necessary to hinder inactivity. VALUE STREAM: 1. Mapping of every process regarding the product families; 2. Mapping of the materials and information flow; 3. Analysis of the current state map.	Stratification; Data collection sheet; Measurement System Analysis MSA–Gage R&R	
As-is	5. To analyse the measuring system; 6. To compute the processing capacity; 7. To measure the process presentation; 8. To stabilize excessive data collection.			

GOVERNANCE

Senior management should support projects and assign a team to each one of them. The Lean and Digitize Committee assumes the responsibility and guidance of the project while the team has the task of participating actively in the operational phases of the improvement activities.

Members of senior management, with process responsibilities, the champion and the process owner should be part of the Lean and Digitize Committee. Besides the responsibility of the result of the project, the members of the committee also perform the task of mentoring the team.

The team should be composed of persons from all the areas of the organization involved in the process. This must be as diverse as possible, in terms of both knowledge and attitude. The members of the team must know the process, be innovative and know how to manage a project.

The first act of the team consists of writing the project charter. This formal document describes:

- objectives
- activities
- timeline
- members of the team and their respective roles
- competencies; and
- project responsibilities (in scope and out of scope).

The elements able to accelerate this phase are:

- Training and certification courses for the participants of the team;
- The presence of people with good experience in the process and in project management.

PROJECT KICK-OFF

The launch of the project is an important moment in its life. A member of senior management should join the event. If the project includes many areas, the CEO and the general manager should participate at the launch meeting. Apart from a meeting with all the stakeholders, the communication of the launch of the project should go to the entire organization using all of the communication tools available.

THE VOICE OF THE CUSTOMER AND THE METRICS

The team must listen to the voice of the customer (VoC) concerning the processes involved in the improvement initiative. Listening to the voice of the customer allows focus on what is important for the success of the organization.

The preliminary macro phase analyses customers. It is necessary to detail what their requirements are in the area of each process. Quality functional deployment is a good tool to find the metrics to measure, improve and monitor.

The most important metrics are the following:

- cycle time
- throughput time
- cost
- quality
- inventory.

The plan for data collection depends on listening to the VoC and defining the characteristics that are CTQ. The data collection plan defines the sampling plan. During the observations, it is necessary to define:

- the operational conditions
- the data collection
- the modes, the frequency and the number of data surveys.

Before mapping the data, it is advisable to analyse the measurement system by applying the MSA–Gage R&R tool.

THE AS-IS PROCESS

Once the team has identified the metrics it should then map the as-is process (or current state) based on the data collection plan. The mapping must include the organization, the physical and the digitized flow, in order to obtain the full flow design of each activity and process operation.

The team members during this phase need to observe:

- The sequence of operation and physical activity procedures and the layout. They will then be able to understand how the organizational and physical flows work;
- The applications, systems and digitization sequences, to understand how the digitized flow works.

The team should describe and integrate both flows in such a way as to map of the as-is process logical flow. Once this is done, the team should measure the CTQ's and identify the critical points and the regulations connected to the various activities or sub-processes. They represent the as-is process constraints.

In practice, actual conditions may not allow direct measurement of the CTQ's (for instance the process cycle times). This is the case when:

- Processes are too variable: this situation is typical for instance in service supply processes based on people. In this case, it is necessary to resort to alternative methods of measurement, such as planning a series of interviews with operators about the time required by each activity;
- Processes with long throughput time. In this case, it is necessary to measure the CTQs using historical data, if available in the organization's databases.

The results of the process as-is phase are:

1. Graphic mapping of the process current state (SIPOC or the current state of value

stream mapping) which represents all the activities of the logical flow, from the observed sequence of organization, physical and digitized activities. They must include all the CTQ measures, the critical locations and the applicable regulations;
2. The high-level project plan of the improvement project;
3. The communication plan linked to the project charter timeline and to the project plan.

The database of the activities and the processes represent the accelerating factor of this phase. Having a database containing all data related to organization activities and processes allows to reduce the time dedicated to mapping the as-is process. The team should take data updated and representative of the organization's reality, rather than the standards described inside the operational handbooks.

THE ACCEPTANCE CRITERIA FOR TOLLGATE 1 – THE DEFINE AND MEASURE MACRO PHASE

In order to move to the following phase, the TEAM should get positive answers to the following questions:

1. Did the team allocate correctly the resources? Mis-allocating the Lean and Digitize Committee's resources may cause the project to fail, due to different reasons:
   - Leadership within the Steering Committee: only senior management can guide the effective implementation of the project improvements. The absence of adequate support from senior management or leadership may make it impossible to effectively modify the process;
   - Deep knowledge of the process: not knowing how the process works may cause evaluation errors both in the as-is and to-be mapping phases.
   - Heterogeneity: if the team members come from a similar role, the improvements are conditioned by their limited knowledge of other roles;
   - Innovation and propensity to change: if there are no members in the team who are creative, innovative and ready to change the solutions end up being obvious, simplistic and trivial;
2. Did the Lean and Digitize Committee approve the project charter? The project charter is a tool that allows constantly visualization of the advance of the work, in time and manner. It also officially assigns the roles and the tasks to the members of the committee and the team. Not writing the project charter (or writing it in a bad way, or the lack of approval by the Lean and Digitize Committee) may be the cause of time and priorities mismanagement;
3. Did the team collect the internal and external customer's VoC correctly? The VoC the key element that shows which activities are (or are not) adding value. Not knowing the VoC may lead to assessment errors and make it impossible to eliminate the sources of waste;
4. Did the team identify measure and analyse the CTQs? The CTQ parameters represent the objective metrics that allows overcoming the subjectivity of the VoC in the process. Not knowing how to correctly translate the VoC into CTQ has the same effect as not knowing the VoC. It causes evaluation errors and makes it impossible to eliminate all the sources of waste;

5. Have the team correctly mapped all ofthe organization's, physical and digitization flows? The as-is mapping process must represent all possible activities and all the waste identified in the process. An incorrect detection of all the activities, either organizational, physical or of automation, may produce an inaccurate design of the logical flow and, as a consequence, inaccurate consideration related to the improvement phases;

6. Did the team identify the critical points? The immediate identification of the critical points, which slow down or stop the value flow, helps the following waste elimination phases;

7. Did the team identify all applicable laws and regulations? They must respect these constraints to avoid penalties and the resulting impact on the cost structure. Lack of awareness of the laws and regulations may result in the failure of the project. That lack would make an efficient implementation of an appropriate solution difficult;

8. Did the team plan communication activities at a high level? Once the as-is process mapping phase has finished, the team needs to plan all the remaining activities of the project and communication modes with the stakeholders. Reporting the project progress is important to achieve consensus: it also provides an opportunity for dialogue between the team and other process operators. Lack of regular communication of results and other objectives may increase the stress and fear related to expected changes.

Accurate answers to these questions assure the completion of the definition and measurement of the problems related to the process improvement and optimization objectives.

*   The steering committee and the team must include the most suitable people;
*   The project charter must be planned and approved at a high level in order to support the management of schedules and resources of the project;
*   The team needs to listen to the VoC and translate it into measurable CTQs;
*   The as-is project logical flow must include all organizational, physical and digitization flow activities.
*   The team needs to identify all legal constraints and the main criticalities; and
*   Needs to plan communication actions.

THE RELATIONAL MODEL AND ACTIONS – THE DEFINE AND MEASURE MACRO PHASE

Figure 3.4 helps understand the relations between the define and measure macro phase of the Lean and Digitize method and the preliminary macro phase.

According to previously set plans, projects begin with the constitution of the steering committee and the team, formed by the organization staff and eventually by supporting consultants.

The team listens to the customer's voice coming from the market, from outside the organization, that is to say the demands of customers and the staff, the challenges of competitors and the restraints of compliance. The Team needs to quantify these voices by identifying the CTQs related to processes.

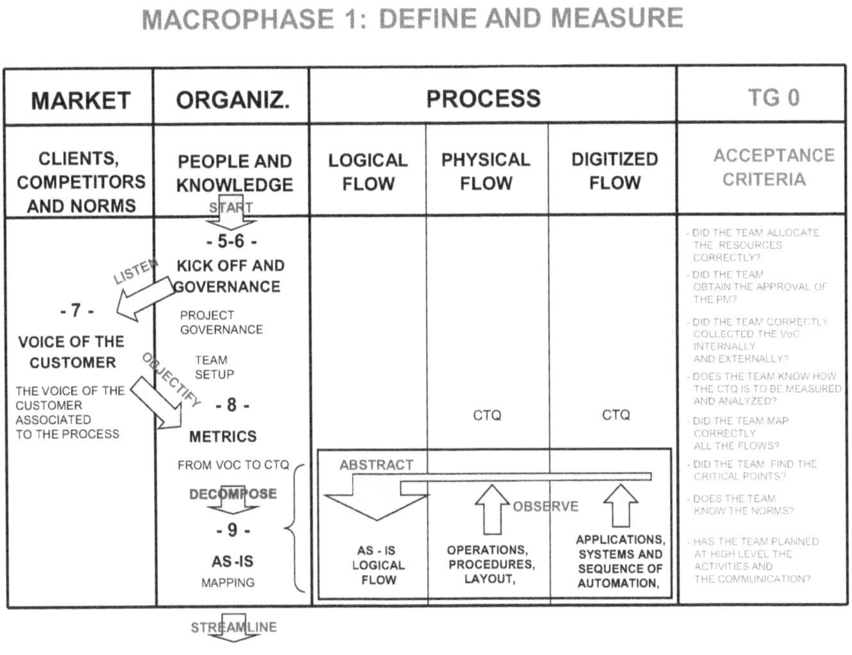

MACROPHASE 1: DEFINE AND MEASURE

MARKET	ORGANIZ.	PROCESS			TG 0
CLIENTS, COMPETITORS AND NORMS	PEOPLE AND KNOWLEDGE	LOGICAL FLOW	PHYSICAL FLOW	DIGITIZED FLOW	ACCEPTANCE CRITERIA

Figure 3.4   The relational model of the define and measure macro phase

Then the team observes directly, or by means of the analysis of the data in specific databases (in case the organization have these):

- The physical and organizational flow of the as-is process (how operations are performed, how procedures are related, the plant layout and the location of the workstations); and
- The as-is process digitization flows (which applications are involved in the process, on which systems these applications are used, in which operational mode, and which is the automation sequence flow).

The team in charge of designing the as-is needs to summarize the flows observed and represent them. The sequence of organizational, physical and digitized activities and the interfaces between them form the logical flow.

The activities in the define and measure phase are:

1. Setting up of the Lean and Digitize Committee and the team;
2. Writing the project charter;
3. Collecting the voice of the customer;
4. 'Translating' the voice of the customer in measurable parameters critical to quality;
5. Writing the plan of data collection;
6. Analysing the measurement system by means of the MSA method–Gage R&R;
7. Executing the data collection plan;
8. Designing the as-is process;
9. Detecting the critical points;

10. Evaluating the compliance;
11. Writing the high level project plan;
12. Communication planning;
13. Pass Tollgate 1 to get the approval of the committee.

LITERATURE - THE DEFINE AND MEASURE MACRO PHASE

The define phase goes through the following steps:

1. Setting up the team: participants must have heterogeneous and complementary knowledge and must know how to work in a team.
   ✓ Model: setting up the Lean and Digitize Committee and the team;
2. Issuing the project charter; describing the problem, defining the objectives to be achieved and planning the project main activities;
   ✓ Model: writing the project charter;
3. Analysing the interested parties; analysis of the stakeholders;
4. Defining the customer: selection of internal and external customers;
5. Analysing the VoC: collect opinions and expectations from the customers;
   ✓ Model: collecting the VoC;
6. Identifying the CTQs; translation of the VoC into the critical features of quality;
   ✓ Model: objectification of the VoC in CTQ parameters;
7. Identifying the processes; identifying the relations between the CTQs and the production and/or supplying processes;
8. To map the process;
   ✓ Model: design of the as-is of the process;
9. To update the project charter, the project plan and to plan for communication.
   ✓ Model: writing the high-level project plan.

The tools most commonly used during the define phase are:

- Project charter: used to schedule the work and define the roles;
  ✓ Model: writing the project charter;
- Quality function deployment: links the VoC to the CTQs;
  ✓ Model: collecting the VoC and quantifying the VoC in CTQ parameters;
- SIPOC diagram: maps the process flow, the inputs (X's), the outputs (Y's), providers and customers;
  ✓ Model: design of the as-is process;
- Risk analysis: useful to evaluate the opportunities and risks related to the project;
- Project plans, used with the project charter to schedule the work.

The measure phase goes through the following steps:

1. Identifying the measurement variables, product/service and process analysis, identifying the quality features which most affect the satisfaction of customers;
   ✓ Model: translation of the VoC in parameters CTQ;
2. Issuing a data collection plan: quantification of the number of the variables and the time needed to detect;

✓ Model: writing the plan of data collection;

3. Identifying and selecting the Y's (the results) and the X's (the inputs) to be measured;
4. Identifying the definition of defects, in the operational model; define the lower and upper specification limits for all the variables which must be measured;
5. Analysing the measuring system: choosing a reliable measurement as an analysis tool (deviations and uncertainties); validation of the measurement system;
   ✓ Model: analysis of the measurement system by means of the MSA method–Gage R&R;
6. Computing the processing capacity: computing the main capacity indexes, e.g. Potential Capability Index (PPK) and Process Capability Index (CPK);***
7. Measuring the process performances: measuring the variables identified under item three;
   ✓ Model: execution of the data collection plan;
8. Establishing the analysis to perform after data collection. Planning the data stratification and choosing the methods for the analysis.

The most common tools and (methods) used during the measure phase are:

- Data collection plan: method for the collection of data;
  ✓ Model: writing the plan of data collection;
- Stratification: modes of data clustering;
- Data collection sheet: tool for entering data;
- MSA–Gage R&R: method for analysing the measuring system.
  ✓ Model: analysis of the measuring system by means of the MSA method–Gage R&R;

The key points of the first principle – define the value – are:

- The improvement process starts when the value is defined;
- The customer defines the value, quality, price and timeline;
- Everything that does not add value is waste (muda);
- Improvement is obtained through change;
- It is necessary to counteract inertia;
- Tools: the seven wastes.
  ✓ Model: CTQs represent the value defined by the customer (VoC). What deviates from the CTQ targets represents waste, and needs to go.

The key points of the second principle – identify the value stream – are:

- Mapping of every process regarding the product families;
- Mapping of the flow of materials and information: current state map;
- Tools: value stream mapping.
  ✓ Model: the value stream mapping workshop map the as-is. Materials and information flows (mainly through the mapping of the digitization flow).

The New Elements of Lean and Digitize – the Define and Measure Macro Phase

The new elements introduced by Lean and Digitize in the define and measure macro phase are the simultaneous mapping of the digitization, the organizational and the physical flows, and the practical advice regarding the formation of the team and the possible use of specific database for the as-is mapping.

1. Mapping the digitization flows: the activities typically included in the Lean and Six Sigma improvement projects are part of the organizational and physical flows. Some teams neglect the information systems or do not consider them thoroughly. Therefore, a digitization flow definition and measurement represent a new element. By mapping the logical flow regarding the physical activities and digitization sequence, automation is integrated into the classic Lean Six Sigma improvement projects and implemented at a management level;
2. Database of activities and processes: using databases especially designed to define and update activities and processes accelerates and facilitates mapping operations, particularly in the case of processes with long throughput time, or in the case of processes which are difficult to observe in operation;
3. Team: including project management experts of the organization in the team assures the best and fastest results.

The Analyse and Process Design Macro Phase: Lean and Kaizen Plan

Once the team has defined and measured the as-is process, the Lean and Digitize project continues through working seminars. The team works in these seminars with the objective of:

*   detecting waste in the process;
*   designing the to-be process, freed from any waste; and
*   planning execution of the improvement actions.

THE TEST OF BEST PRACTICES - THE ANALYSE AND PROCESS DESIGN MACRO PHASE

Table 3.2 shows the main elements of Lean and Six Sigma methods and the most used tools regarding the Lean and kaizen plan phases.

**Table 3.2   The main elements of Lean and Six Sigma methods and their tools –
analyse and process design**

	Six Sigma	Lean	Lean Six Sigma tools	Lean tools
Lean **Kaizen plan**	ANALYSE: 1. Validating the data collection 2. Analysing the data 3. Analysing in depth 4. Updating the project charter and the project plan IMPROVE: 1. Identify potential solutions 2. Assessing the risks 3. Assigning priorities to solutions 4. Choosing the solution	VALUE STREAM: 1. Identification of added value activities 2. Identification and elimination of waste flow: 3. The flow runs if the following aspects are tackled: wasting time, discrepancies, unproductivity, batches, codes, inventories (warehouse) 4. Reschedule of the process in order to make the productive flow run 5. Redesign concerning the layout and the infrastructure	ANALYSE: Five whys: Histogram Box plot Correlation diagrams • Test f/t ANOVA • FMECA (Failure Mode, Effects and Criticality Analysis) A IMPROVE: Brainstorming *TRIZ (TeoriyaRresheniya izobretatelskikh Zadatch)* (a problem-solving, analysis and forecasting tool derived from the study of patterns of invention in the global patent literature) • Value engineering • Design of experiments; Taguchi's robust design	VALUE STREAM: value stream mapping Flow: • Cells

Lean

Once the define and measure phase is over, the team gathers in a working seminar (in General Electric this is called a workout). The seminar will last from two to five days, according to the complexity of the project. The tasks of the seminar are:

- Detect the wastes appearing in the logical flow of activities (organizational, physical and/or digitized);
- Redesign the sequence of the process activities so that the process is flowing, continuous and free from any source of waste and variability.

The working seminar differs from the classical seminars in that team members focus on action speed. The team should implement and measure the performance of the new ideas as soon as possible. Later they should go through an iterative cycle of tests, observations and improvements, using a technique called Trystorm. From this viewpoint, the contribution of the team members with an information systems background is very important.

The Map of As-is

By means of the as-is map, it is possible to define the aspects that should be improved. There can be:

* bottlenecks
* excessive queuing and inventories
* poor standardization
* useless operations
* unneeded transport and moves
* necessary activities which add little value
* excessive and poorly controlled automation
* lack of digitization.

Analysis of As-is and Detection of all Sources of Waste

The working seminar starts with the validation of the data collected and the description of the logical sequence of the activities observed during the define and measure phase. The team then works to identify the corrective actions.

Using all the information collected, the team brainstorm looking for solutions, benchmark references in the market and define critical KPIs. The latter become the target of the new re-engineered process.

The aim of this phase is to critically evaluate the as-is process observed in operation and to analyse the inefficiencies, bottlenecks and criticalities defining possible solutions.

The phases of the analysis of collected data and identification of the corrective actions are:

1. Analyse the collected data: read critically the effective as-is process (analysing the causes of dissimilarity with the process documented) and list its critically;
2. Assess profitability: compare management costs with the possible benefits, considering the impact of anomalies detected and wastes;
3. Compare with internal and external KPIs: identify and analyse critically through organization-wide and/or partial KPIs;
4. Identify benefits and corrective actions: itemize the actual corrective actions for each detected criticalities/inefficiency and explain the benefits obtained by eliminating them. Classify criticalities according to their severity. Define the corrective actions that require minimum organizational interventions and result in immediate benefits

as quick wins (e.g. collect documentation in the place in which it is produced).

The facilitators of analysis of collected data and identification of the corrective actions are:

- Identifying the drivers (e.g. cost recovery, elimination of inefficiencies, decentralization of the process) constitutes a facilitator for the entire team. The team will then perform their own analysis by applying common guidelines and thus obtaining homogeneous results;
- Apply the KPIs as a useful working tool to identify the scenarios for improving efficiency and reducing costs.

Once the team has validated the as-is process, the data and activities for detecting the sources of waste are analysed (organizational, physical or digitized activities which do not add any or low value to the customer).

The typical wastes in this phase of the project are:

- Overproduction; useless reports, batch processes which result in the accumulation of spread sheets, excessive production, production before it is necessary, etc.;
- Inventory: work in progress, material used due to lack of workload balance, transactions not yet processed, etc.;
- Unnecessary activities: time devoted to unnecessary activities which do not add value, such as the use of unnecessary applications, entering the same data in more than one point in the process, searching for missing or erroneous data, etc.;
- Physical movements: operators' unnecessary movements during production, such as climbing stairs, manual data entry, inappropriate use of photocopies and files, movements between distant machines, etc.;
- Transportation: useless motion of raw materials, work in progress and finished products due to a disorganized layout (departments, warehouses, offices, etc.);
- Waiting: employees waiting for materials, or because of failures or settings, waiting times due to computers blocked in batch processes, failures in photocopiers and printers, time spent waiting for data entering into the system, or for applications not momentarily available, etc.;
- Rework (defects): defective finished or half-elaborated products, inaccurate information or data, defects in design and software code; etc.

The To-be Design

The team must find ways to eliminate the waste found in the as-is process (unless there is some applicable regulation restraints) in redesigning the process to-be. The result of this phase is a brief but detailed list of critical issues, with shown corrective actions for each single issue and expected benefits from them.

Process design should take place only after the team has:

- Created the overall vision of the new process;
- Established the measurement criteria;

- Defined an evolution as from the existing process; and
- Identified the key opportunities of changing the new process with the support of ICT.

At this point, the attention focuses on creating models and analysing the new process, by redesigning it and using ICT. Whenever possible, it will be useful to make a prototype. The process of identifying the levers of change must consider at the same time:

- what is feasible
- the obstacles due to the current technology
- the organization required by the new process
- the possible changes in the physical layout.

The team must analyse the levers for change in order to determine the degree of freedom that the organization has, when developing new technologies and organizational ways, as from their present state. This approach is important for a correct benefits–costs analysis and a correct intervention planning.

ICT as a Process Innovation Tool

One of the ICTs available for process analysis is information engineering. The aim of information engineering is to describe, in terms of information (data-oriented), an already conceptualized process. Then a system can be rapidly and rigorously built supporting the design of a new process. This is certainly a valid objective. It still includes some risks that should be avoided as far as possible, for example changing too many steps of the current process.

ICT and other levers can play an even more important role in process innovation (see Figure 3.5).

Figure 3.5 shows how ICT can facilitate process innovation. It can also support operational changes. The team should design the new processes only when they understand how to use technology in innovative ways. If the team believes that they can develop process improvement without ICT or other levers, they are ignoring excellent tools for process innovation.

One technology can have either positive or negative characteristics. A given tool can make a process simpler or more complex. ICT, for instance, offers a number of solutions but may at the same time impose several constraints on the design of the new process:

- The opportunities offered by ICT relate to new ways in which organizations can use technology in order to innovate processes;
- The constraints are those aspects of the existing or prospective technology facilities which limit the possibility of innovation and which cannot, for some reasons, be modified in a short period of time;
- The main constraint introduced by ICT is a certain rigidity of process. ICT makes it difficult to introduce subsequent changes as well as to replace the system and, therefore, to change the process itself. In this sense, SOA-based systems should offer more flexibility (see the Chapter 8, Information systems, which details the support that ICT can provide to Lean and Digitize projects).

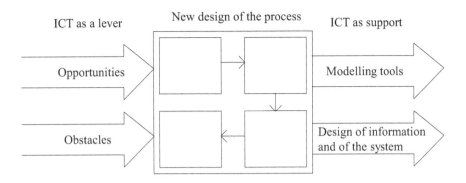

Figure 3.5   The role of ICTs in process innovation (Davenport 1993)

THE OPPORTUNITIES OF ICT FOR PROCESS INNOVATION

The opportunities of supporting process innovation with ICTs fall into nine different categories according to Davenport (see Figure 3.6) (Davenport 1993). They require general objectives of the organization related to cost reduction, cutting down cycle times, and so on. The categories show the specific means by which ICT can achieve these objectives.

These aspects belong to two big families:

* Processes implicit in the organization's assets; and
* Processes integrated in the assets of ICT.

The following paragraphs explain these processes. We also include some other aspects which are possible thanks to new ICT technologies, already developed or under development.

Impact	Explanation
* Digitization	Elimination of the human work in a process
* Information	Capture of process information in order to understand
* Sequencing	Change in the process sequence or parallel processing
* Tracking	Monitoring of the process and object status
* Analysis	Improvement in the analysis of the information And decisions
* Geography	Remote coordination of processes
* Integration	Coordination among tasks and processes
* Knowledge	Collection and distribution of intellectual activities
* Disintermediation	Elimination of the intermediaries in a process

Figure 3.6   The impact of ICTs on process innovation (Davenport 1993)

Processes implicit in the organization's assets are:

- Digitization. The most commonly acknowledged benefit of ICT is the power to reduce the need for human labour and to create more structured processes. The first applications of ICT mostly used this opportunity. Examples of these are robotics, numerical controls and the like. Services organizations' processes use document flows extensively. ICT can support the storage and processing of documents and images, the so-called electronic content management (ECM). ECM also supports workflows, in order to define the routes that the sequences of activities should follow through a certain process. In processes based on phone work, such as telemarketing, the fulfilment of orders, customers service, call management systems – a call centre or automated response system, such as an interactive voice response unit (IVR) – can provide effective support;
- Information. Shoshana Zuboff (Zuboff and Maxmin 2004) proved that managers can use information not only to reduce the need for human labour in the process, but also to improve the use of organization's information. ICT within a process can help in obtaining information about the process functions. The analysis of this data, even if done manually, can provide considerable benefits. It will eventually be possible to automate this analysis. The work to be done in this area is still considerable, but the applications of this approach, also known as data mining, are interesting and promising;
- Sequencing. ICT allows changing the sequence of processes or transforming a process from sequential to parallel, in such a way as to reduce the cycle times in the process. For instance, this opportunity is at the core of new processes called concurrent engineering (CE). The latest developments in CE also integrate procurement and production – the so-called product life cycle (PLC) management systems. According to this, different areas engaged in the design (and eventually external providers or production units) design in cooperation a new product component or the entire product, together with its manufacturing process;
- Tracking. In order to conduct some process optimization projects successfully a high degree of control and tracing is required. This is true particularly in organizations working in the transportation and logistics areas. Federal Express, a huge US logistic organization, for instance, controls each package up to 10 times as it goes through their system which enables them to locate a lost package and provide the customer with information about the delivery status. This organization uses GPS searching systems to track the exact location of each unit of their fleet. The use of sensors, such as Radio Frequency Identification Devices (RFID), opens new and interesting prospective in this sector;
- Analysis. In the processes that involve information and decision analysis, ICT allows the use of complex analytical tools which can process huge quantities of data to support the decisional process. Such is the case at American Express, with an expert system used to authorize credit card purchases. This system, called the Authorizer's Assistant (Dzierzanowski et al. 1989), allows the collection of a significant amount of information. It also helps in taking better decisions in less time than any employee in charge of authorizations in the organization could do. In other situations, neuronal systems allow the identification of unusual behaviour in the use of credit cards. They can even block the cards before any fraud can thrive or even occur;

- Geography. A key benefit of ICT, related to the association between telecommunication and information technology, is to solve problems created by the distance amongst people or teams who have to work together, coordinated or in sequence. Globalization pushes for development of processes in cooperation, efficiently and uninterruptedly, in different geographic areas. ICT can support this trend much more efficiently and with minimum costs thanks to the Web.

Processes implicit in the ICT assets are:

- Integration. Organizations find difficult to make drastic improvements in their process performance. This is because there are often fragmented tasks throughout many areas or even different organizations. New approaches are possible. For instance, one individual or work team completes or at least manages all the releasing aspects of a product or service, thanks to the accessibility of information through the computer;
- Knowledge. Many business reports mention the knowledge and experience of the staff as one of the most relevant assets of the organization. Unfortunately, sometimes organizations do not manage these resources well. Moreover, people do not treat the activities that require high levels of knowledge as processes. Some organizations are attempting to acquire and distribute knowledge in a more open and consistent way, by means of process knowledge data banks and the so-called expert systems(Read 2009);
- Disintermediation. There is an increasing awareness that people are not always efficient in communicating information, even when it comes to relatively structured transactions, such as stock exchange transactions or ordering spare parts. For instance, many brokers are automating more and more of their transactions processing. In markets with a high number of operators or a relevant number of choices, ICT technology can help in exchanging information between buyers and sellers (or even their computer applications), during the commercial transactions.

Besides the aspects mentioned by Davenport, today the focus is on other aspects of ICT:

- Collaboration (Nicoletti 2009). Thanks to the association between computers and the Web, ICT allows people who are distant geographically to collaborate actively, in addition to communicating, as previously mentioned. This aspect is particularly important in improving processes, especially those involving players outside the organization, such as distributors or suppliers;
- The treatment of wider type of contents (data, images, video, voice, etc.) (Nicoletti 2008: 38–43). Many processes rely on unstructured data. ICT is more and more able to process this contents;
- Distributed processing performs complex processing as part of distributed processes (referred to as cloud computing);
- Composition. Create and orchestrate new processes based on elementary reusable services, such as service-oriented architecture (SOA).

A process optimization team, which is testing the ways in which ICT can affect the process, should identify which of the above opportunities are relevant for them. Then, they should find examples of other organizations, not necessarily in the same sector, with the experience of such ICT technologies. The team can visit organizations that are using ICT in similar situations, in order to study the different aspects of the optimal process design. It is like a kind of benchmarking, or intelligence on process innovation.

Identifying the Process Innovation Tools

In order to get all the potential of ICT for the transformation of the organization, it is necessary to consider ICT as a lever for process innovation. The team can identify other opportunities/obstacles are identified in the preliminary phase of the implementation of a process innovation initiative, through activities such as those listed in Figure 3.7.

> * Identify the technological potential and the human opportunities for the change in the process
> * Identify the potential factors which could be a technological or human obstacle
> * Search for the opportunities in terms of application to the specific processes
> * Find the typologies of obstacles which could be accepted

Figure 3.7   Key activities to identify the levers for change (Davenport 1993)

SETTING OUT NEW PROCESSES AND RELEVANT SYSTEMS

Project management tools can be useful in Lean and Digitize initiatives in two ways:

* They can help identify, structure and estimate project, development and re-engineering activities;
* They can facilitate a quick analysis of the management of improvement projects and classify developments.
  There are information tools that facilitate project management. Some of them are:
* Applications of the method called system-development life cycle (SDLC), to manage the project life cycle;
* Information engineering tools on computer-aided software engineering (CASE), to support continuity between design and development;
* Design systems and object-oriented programming (OO), which allow the applications to be split into manageable objects.

The To-be Validation Process

In the to-be phase, the idea is to give a concrete form to all the proposals, arguments and creative ideas from the previous phase. The aim is to design the new procedure in detail in order to understand if the flow is feasible or fluid.

Different scenarios are possible, and more challenging every time. One should start from an initial scenario that resolves the simplest problem, which anticipates the quick win interventions (e.g. doing a new screen rather than filling out a data sheet by hand or working on the current documentation on the computer and only printing at the end of the day, rather than printing each processed file). Then pass on to a more complex proposal but with better performance, until one achieves the final scenario.

During this phase, it is necessary to quantify the following data relative to the to-be process:

- financial details
- resources
- management
- general expenses
- timescales.

The aim of the to-be design phase is to identify the future process that better responds to the organization demands.

The follow-on state design phases are as follows:

- Designing the future state process (to-be): representing the process flow in full respect of the regulations;
- Proving the benefits and the risks: listing the expected benefits and the potential risks connected with the future design implementation;
- Identifying the actions for going from the current to the future state: listing the organizational and infrastructural interventions to carry out in order to achieve the to-be scenario. For example:
  - Sizing resources;
  - Allocation of activities and resources;
  - Identification of the most suitable training channel (course, seminar, training on the job, etc.);
  - Externalization of activities related to third-party contracts;
  - Modified/new application procedures;
  - Infrastructural intervention;
  - Distribution of workstations and other input/output devices.
- Writing a detailed cost–benefit analysis; quantifying the expenses and the benefits for the as-is and to-be scenarios in order to facilitate the comparison and prepare the elements to support the decisions on the organization, physical layout or digitization. The costs to consider should be:
  - Personnel (organization expenses, transfers, liquidations, etc.);
  - Systems (hardware, software, network, maintenance, etc.);
  - Support for change (training, selection, etc.);
  - Cost of infrastructure (rent, extra services, etc.);
  - Acquisitions/divestitures (supplies, consultancy, etc.);
- Defining the governance: showing the organization's KPIs are useful to monitor the new process and the improvements obtained. Determining who is responsible for the monitoring and the identification of corrective measures possibly necessary to improve the KPIs;

- Validating as part of the steering committee: validating the future state design in order to carry out the implementation.
  The complete future state design should include:

- Driver's identification: as per in the previous phase;
- Process KPI identification, being based on the sectors experts' opinions.

The Lean results are the following:

- The to-be process mapping: activity sequence to form the future process workflow;
- Identifications of associated benefits and risks: quantification of benefits related to the revision or to the introduction of new activities and possible emerging risks;
- A list of measures to be adopted: a detailed list of the expected organizational/ infrastructural interventions together with the explanation of their schedule;
- Cost–benefit analysis: representation of the emerging and discontinued costs and expected benefits to support the decisions to be made;
- Governance: list of the control activities with the relative programme under the supervision of the project leader and the Lean and Digitize Committee:
- FMEA assessment of possible failure modes;
- Assessment of compliance to regulations;
- Security and risk assessment;
- Preliminary documents of the to-be process architecture;
- Lean and Digitize Committee summary: summary document for the validation of the to-be scenario.

Innovation implies organizational adjustments. It is necessary to progress gradually. After a preliminary analysis of the criticalities outside the organization, the team needs to reschedule the activity logical flow using various tools and techniques:

- Elimination of the activities with no added value that generate waste and do not represent a link for other processes or risk the respect of regulations;
- Rescheduling of actions that present excessive wasting time, discrepancies, unproductivity, batches, queues, inventories, in order to introduce the continuous flow (cells, continuous production lines, etc.);
- Externalization or centralization of low added value activities, which must be kept in the new process;
- Simplification, standardization, optimization and automation of previously manual activity sequences through workflow;
- Reduction of the excessive digitization in some processes.

By means of the as-is map, it is possible to define the aspects that should be improved. These are:

- bottlenecks
- excessive filing
- poor standardization
- useless operations

- necessary activities which add little value
- excessive and poorly controlled digitization
- lack of digitization where it would be possible.

The levers used for eliminating the sources of system rigidity, process variances and waste are the following:

- Lean redesign: it eliminates the waste and helps to remove the system rigidity and the process variability. For example, one might want to move the management process of a retail credit unit of a bank from sequential processing to parallel. It would help to redesign the office layout in order to give continuity of the flow. It is better to eliminate the filing of practices during working hours in order to reduce the work in progress;
- Centralization: administrative activities of low added value developed in various entities may be pooled in back-office centres. In this way, it would be possible to increase the efficiency and free the capacity of branches for higher value activities. Of course, it is necessary to take into account that centralization requires a standardization of activities;
- Externalization: outsource some activities of a very low added value but necessary. In this way the cost would be limited only to the added value, leaving the responsibility of the activities to a third party (for example, the formal control of documents or the keying of data included in them);
- Digitization: if well applied, it eliminates the system rigidity sources, accelerates the processes and eliminates variance. After streamlining and redesigning the process, in many cases it is possible to automatize some action sequences or improve previous automation. The lean office in a bank can be completely automated reinforcing Internet banking applications and creating web-based and advanced ATMs.

The team should not apply these solutions in isolation, since when applied together there well might be synergies. The team should carry out corrective actions of simple implementation immediately to get quick benefits (quick wins).

Once the team has designed the to-be process logical flow (the sequence of the physical and automated activities that characterize the future process) and have implemented the first modifications, the team, together with the Lean and Digitize Committee, must validate the to-be process through the assessment of:

- Possible modes of failure (and related risks) that could block or slow down the to-be process flow;
- The impact of regulation on the to-be process;
- Benefits associated with the reduction of variability and waste.

Preliminary Design and the To-be Process Architecture at a High Level

Having verified and validated the to-be process, the team writes a preliminary document. It will describe the high-level architecture that will govern the process. One can detail in this way the technical and functional characteristics, the respect of laws and regulations of the continuous flow and the interfaces between the organizational, physical and digitized activities.

The Lean and Digitize accelerators are the following:

- Deployment: immediately implementing some improvements accelerates the change and allows immediate results (quick wins);
- Benchmark: observing the Lean and Digitize research from outside the organization may facilitate decisions on the improvement for the phase of process redesign and waste elimination.

The Kaizen Plan

The last activity of the team during the working seminars consists in preparing a kaizen plan. The kaizen plan represents the short, medium and long-term plan (30, 60 and 90 days) for the implementation activities and regular checking of a Lean project progress.

Kaizen planning consists of deciding the sequence of improvement activities designed during the working seminars. It includes the assignment of tasks and responsibilities of each single activity (design, construction, test and launch of the production of the new application, interface, etc.), the project programme and control, and budget assignment.

The team will define the terms and modes of improvement actions according to how difficult it is to implement the solutions found during the seminar. The greater the complexity of the intervention, the greater the scheduled time in the kaizen plan and the greater the checking of the state of progress of the intervention.

It is a good rule to schedule a gradual introduction of improvements. One should start from the simplest and less binding actions to finish with the most complex ones, with bigger benefits, but more risks.

The analyse and process design phase ends with the presentation of the to-be process map, the FMEA assessment, the risks, benefits, TOC (Total operational costs) and the kaizen plan to the Lean and Digitize Committee (or steering committee) and the stakeholders. They must approve the results reached during the working seminar.

The Acceptance Criteria for Tollgate 2 – the Analyse and Process Design Macro Phase

In order to move to the following phase, it is important to answer the following questions positively:

1. Are there any guarantees that the data collected are correct? It is very important that the data are correct because the team will base all the regulations, ideas and analyses geared to the process improvement in them. Wrong data result in erroneous analysis and, consequently, on an incorrect process redesign;
2. Did the team map the process correctly? All process improvement and optimization activities result in elimination of waste, rigidity and variability found in the as-is process analysis phase. If the team did not analyse the as-is process correctly, the

solutions found will not have an objective base and will not be able to solve the problems or obtain the maximum potential benefit;

3. Has the Lean and Digitize Committee and the stakeholders approved the Lean and Digitize proposal? The former has the power to authorize the introduction of the changes. The latter is the one who knows best about the process and are interested in the modifications. If they do not approve the to-be process, there is the risk of not being able to implement the changes;

4. Have the team assessed the modes of failure? The FMEA analysis (or the robust design) helps in checking if the new process is robust. It helps in evaluating the potential risks for the organization in case a problem arises related to the re-engineering process. The lack of assessment of the modes of failure may result in potentially dangerous solutions, even if they might appear to bring good benefits;

5. Has the team completed the checklist from the compliance viewpoint? Completing the compliance checklist means analysing the impact of the norms and regulation on the re-engineered process. The new process might not be compliant, thus eliminating all the benefits and making the improvement useless. Not completing the compliance checklist may cause the implementation to slow down or may block the new process. There would be a negative impact on the cost structure and the customer's satisfaction;

6. Has the team analysed the risks and benefits related to the improvement? Analysing the risks means assessing the modes of failure and the implication of the regulations on the to-be process. Analysing the benefits instead means evaluating the benefits connected with the improvements. By means of the to-be process map, it is possible to calculate the CTQs future values and compare them with the targets. In this way, we can know beforehand whether the process fully meets the customer's satisfaction. Not analysing the risks and benefits may cause the project to fail due to the unforeseen appearance of risks or the gap between the process performance and the customer's expectations;

7. Has the team written the kaizen plan correctly? The kaizen plan is the guideline for the interventions planned for the process improvement. Not using it as a programme for the activities may cause problems for management and difficulties in the governance.

Answering all these questions correctly guarantees the completion of the analysis of the process and allows planning the to-be process. The team should have:

*   Validate all the data collection and analyse the as-is process data;
*   Planned and approved the to-be process;
*   Assessed the risks with possible damages and the legal restraints and the benefits of the redesigned process; and
*   Scheduled the interventions for the effective process improvement.

THE RELATIONAL MODEL AND ACTIONS – THE ANALYSE AND PROCESS DESIGN MACRO PHASE

Figure 3.8 shows the list of activities related to process innovation that must include the technologies. This figure shows the relationships amongst the phases of analyse and process design of the Lean and Digitize method and the connection between the define and measure and analyse and process design macro phases.

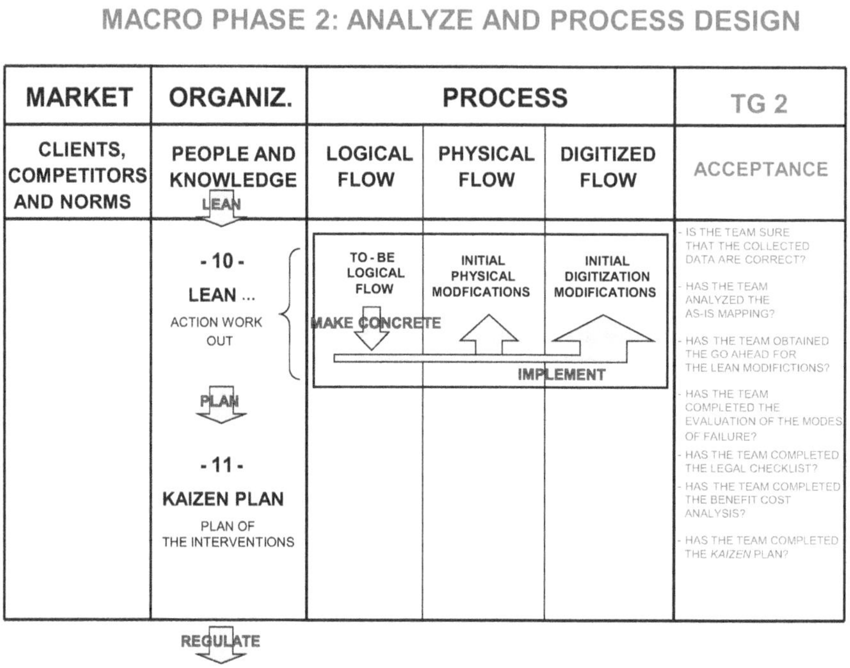

MACRO PHASE 2: ANALYZE AND PROCESS DESIGN

MARKET	ORGANIZ.	PROCESS			TG 2
CLIENTS, COMPETITORS AND NORMS	PEOPLE AND KNOWLEDGE LEAN	LOGICAL FLOW	PHYSICAL FLOW	DIGITIZED FLOW	ACCEPTANCE

- 10 -

LEAN ...

ACTION WORK OUT

MAKE CONCRETE

TO - BE LOGICAL FLOW

INITIAL PHYSICAL MODFICATIONS

INITIAL DIGITIZATION MODIFICATIONS

IMPLEMENT

PLAN

- 11 -

KAIZEN PLAN

PLAN OF THE INTERVENTIONS

- IS THE TEAM SURE THAT THE COLLECTED DATA ARE CORRECT?
- HAS THE TEAM ANALYZED THE AS-IS MAPPING?
- HAS THE TEAM OBTAINED THE GO AHEAD FOR THE LEAN MODIFICTIONS?
- HAS THE TEAM COMPLETED THE EVALUATION OF THE MODES OF FAILURE?
- HAS THE TEAM COMPLETED THE LEGAL CHECKLIST?
- HAS THE TEAM COMPLETED THE BENEFIT COST ANALYSIS?
- HAS THE TEAM COMPLETED THE KAIZEN PLAN?

REGULATE

Figure 3.8   The relational model of the analyse and process design phase

The team develops the Lean and Digitize implementation during the working seminars. Representatives of the organization are members of the team. The purpose of the Lean and digitize process is to trace the process to-be logical flow map, or rather the result of the as-is streamlining through the application of specific techniques and tools.

During the working seminars, the team also need to decide whether to implement the first modifications immediately. They can involve both the organizational, physical and digitization flows and represent the benefits obtainable quickly and with little effort.

At the end of the working seminar the team, with the Lean and Digitize Committee, write the kaizen plan, i.e. the planning of the implementation to achieve effectively the to-be process as represented in the logical flow mapping.

The activities of the analyse and process design phase are:

1. Validation of the collected data;
2. Analysis of the collected data;
3. Detection of waste, rigidity and variation sources;
4. Trystorm: to-be process mapping and implementation of trial modifications;
5. FMEA assessment of the modes and effects of failure;
6. Analysis of laws and regulations;
7. Cost, benefit and risk assessment;
8. Approval of the to-be process, first by the Lean and Digitize Committee and then by the stakeholder;
9. Preliminary design and the to-be process architecture at a high level;
10. Writing of the kaizen plan;

11. Approval by the Lean and Digitize Committee of Tollgate 2.

The most common used tools during the analyse phase are:

- Five whys: the potential causes of the problem are identified by means of five levels of in-depth study;
- Histogram: the team represent data graphically, showing the process centralization, value distribution and the processing capacity;
- Pareto analysis: the team identify the most relevant root causes;
- Box plot: the team describe the data collected without a mathematical analysis;
- Run chart: the development of a phenomenon in time is graphically analysed according to a selected variable;
- Correlation diagrams: identification of possible correlations amongst the variables;
- Test f: verification if two processes have a statistically significant variability;
- Test t: verification if two processes (or a target-value process) have statistically significant averages;
- ANOVA: analysis of the variance;
- FMEA: analysis of the modes of failure;
  - ✓ Model: analysis of collected data and potential solutions with these tools.

The first part of this process design phase follows these paths:

1. Identify potential solutions by means of various tools (brainstorming, TRIZ, value engineering);
   - ✓ Model: trystorm: to-be process mapping and implementation of the first modifications at the pilot stage;
2. Assessing the potential risks of the solution so as not to affect the success of the improvement programme;
   - ✓ Model: benefit and risk assessment;
3. Assigning priorities to the potential solutions by assessing each of them in terms of benefits of the quality of the process, the risks and the effects on the economic and financial metrics;
   - ✓ Model: benefit, cost and risk assessment;
4. Choosing the most convenient solution;
   - ✓ Model: approval of the Lean proposal by the Lean and Digitize Committee and the stakeholders.

The most common and used tools during the process design phase are:

- Brainstorming: creative method for identifying potential solutions;
  - ✓ Model: Trystorm;
- TRIZ: method for customizing potential solutions in case of a complex problem;
- Value engineering: selection and testing of potential solutions, based on functions/costs;
- Design of experiments (DoE): selection and testing of potential solutions;
- Taguchi's robust design: selection and testing of potential solutions;
  - ✓ Model: these tools can also assess risks.

The second part of the principles of Lean Thinking (to identify the value flow–value stream) is:

- Identification of added value activities;
- Identification and elimination of waste;
- Tools: value stream mapping.
  The key points of the third principle (to make the flow run – flow) are:
- The flow runs if there is no wasting time, rejects, unproductivity, batches, waiting lines, inventories (storage and buffer);
- Redesign of the process in order to make the productive flow run;
- The redesign regards the layout and the infrastructure (setting-up time, dimensions and multifunctionality);
- Tools: SMED ***, cells.
  - ✓ Model: use of value stream mapping tool allows in the to-be process logical flow, the elimination of waste and the continuous flow.

THE NEW ELEMENTS OF LEAN AND DIGITIZE – THE ANALYSE AND PROCESS DESIGN MACRO PHASE

The new elements that the Lean and Digitize model introduces to the analyse and process design phase are the Trystorm in the working seminars and in the solutions search outside the organization.

1. The Trystorm in the working seminars: the immediate implementation of the first changes during the seminars accelerates the results and contributes to a gradual implementation of change. Quick actions and quick wins also help giving confidence to the members of the team and the organization staff;
2. Solutions search outside the organization: solutions search outside the organization through the observation of Lean and Digitize experiences can reduce the efforts to find the improvements and generate ideas not found with the team.

The Architecture Design Macro Phase

The results of the analyse and process design macro phase are the to-be logic flow map of the process and the kaizen plan.

The logic flow describes the sequence of activities that will form the future process. These activities will be part of the physical, organization or the digitization flow. There are therefore different interconnected flows, which form a single new continuous flow process connected downstream with the customers.

The functions of the architecture design phase are:

- Design the technical and functional specifications in detail for each activity, elements and service belonging to the physical, organizational and digitization flows;

- Design every interface amongst physical and organizational activities and automation activities, and between the new process and outside the process and possibly the organization; and
- Regulate the process flow so it can be continuous and connected with the end customer.

THE TEST OF BEST PRACTICES – THE ARCHITECTURE DESIGN MACRO PHASE

Table 3.3 shows the main elements of the Lean Six Sigma method and the most used tools regarding the architecture design phase.

Table 3.3   The main elements of the Lean and Six Sigma methods and their tools – architecture design

	Six Sigma	Lean	Lean Six Sigma tools	Lean tools
Architecture Design				PULL: • Kanban; • Heijunka

THE ARCHITECTURE DESIGN

The Architecture Design for the Physical and the Organizational Flow of Activities

Within the to-be process mapping there are sub-processes characterized by physical and organizational activities sequences interconnected at a logical level.

In the architecture design phase, the team must determine:

- what should these activities really do
- their connections
- the physical flow managed
- the organizational flow managed
- how many employees the sub-process requires
- how is the layout organized, etc.

For example, during the working seminars, while the as-is process is analysed, the team might find that production is characterized by many wastes, such as excessive moves, waiting, queuing and inventory (work in progress). The design phase of the to-be process brought the introduction of cell production in order to eliminate waste and achieve a continuous flow. The architecture design needs to establish what this cell should do, its organization and its introduction into the process from start to end.

Thanks to the to-be process design, the team should define:

- The products assigned to the cell;
- The Takt time, or rate of production synchronized with the rate of demand of the products assigned to the cell;
- The work cycle activities of the cell.

The architecture design phase needs to accomplish the following:

- Design, if necessary, new infrastructure and equipment;
- Design the layout of the cell with the location of the infrastructure and the workstations in order to effectively minimize inventories, movements, transportation, obstacles and areas reserved to work in progress;
- Detail the procedures for each single activity of the work cycle;
- Design, if necessary, the machine reconfiguration using SMED techniques;
- Compute the number of employees required so that the time cycle of the cell achieves the Takt time;
- Assign work for the operators (the sub-process physical flow activities involved in the introduction of the cell).

THE ARCHITECTURE DESIGN FOR THE ACTIVITIES (SERVICES) OF THE DIGITIZATION FLOW

Within the to-be process mapping there are sub-processes characterized by digitized sequences of activities interconnected at a logical level.

The architecture design phase should determine and detail:

- The functional specifications of the ICT applications: what most of the digitization flow activities really do (to be designed later as services in the ICT applications);
- The technical specifications: how must the information applications be structured (file characteristics, databases types, details of programs in which the application should be divided, etc.);
- The connections amongst applications: interfaces, infrastructure, etc.;
- The tools for the management of the digitization flow;
- Output: printouts, screens, reports, output files, etc.

The architecture design of the digitization flow helps, during the to-be process design, in making the following decisions:

- Modifying the digitization flows due to problems found on the as-is analysis phase, in order to eliminate the waste related to the information systems rigidity (specific software packages restraints, fragmented networks, complex data or application access, data duplication, low-quality software, system fragility, etc.);
- Digitization of previously manual activities to accelerate the process and make it more stable and precise (data entry, checking, etc.):
- Digitization of activities required for connecting new physical, organizational or automation sub-processes (data transfer from the branches to the back office centre, in case of centralization, or data transfer from/to the external organizations, in case of outsourcing, etc.).

SOA is the best approach to the architecture design of the digitization flow and to the follow-on management of the information systems (Erl et al. 2012). Designing the digitization flow by means of SOA allows having basic applications (called services) to perform single activities or sub-processes. These applications have the following characteristics:

- Modular and complete in themselves;
- Independent of the specific platform and from the operating system on which they can run;
- Independent from the state of other services;
- Easily traceable and available;
- Designed to be connected with other services and to dialogue with them, creating the digitization flow;
- Reusable if necessary.

The applications communicate through the enterprise service bus (ESB), the facility that links the services in a simple, flexible way. ESB manages the data and information flow through a workflow with composition and instrumentation designed to reproduce the continuous flow of the to-be process.

Designing the digitization flow architecture by means of the SOA approach accelerates the future modifications. In fact, SOA:

- Allows easy modification of the modes and the services interaction and combination;
- Facilitates the introduction of new services and the modification of processes according to the specific requirements of the specific business;
- Does not restrain processes to a specific platform, but provides them with immediate and flexible support.

THE ARCHITECTURE DESIGN FOR INTERFACES BETWEEN PHYSICAL AND DIGITIZATION FLOWS

The to-be process is not fully digitize or fully manual. It has a series of automation, physical and organizational flow sub-processes which must communicate between each other. Such communication requires interfaces designed in such a way as to allow, but above all to enable, accelerating the flow at the physical/organizational/automation discontinuity points.

The most common interface between the organizational, physical and digitization flows anticipates the data input in an automated flow. This is often a critical activity because of errors in manual data entry. In order to remediate this critical aspect, in the architecture design phase, it is advisable to design an interface that:

- Acquires data automatically (for example, by using an optical scanner to acquire information present on a conventional support); or
- Has a control system that guarantees the correct input of data (for example, an application for contingency checks of data manually entered in a template).

THE ARCHITECTURE DESIGN FOR THE CONNECTION BETWEEN THE FLOW AND THE END CUSTOMER

At this point, the team have completed the design of the physical, organizational and automation flows and of the interfaces. The last steps correspond to the design of the functional and technical characteristics of the process/customer interface and the regulations of the productive/supply rate according to the demand of the end customers.

The interface between the customer and the process represents the medium with which customers require a product or a service. It should be easy to use and secure, both for the customer and for the organization. Increasingly there are interfaces through Web application design (with all the security devices, such as user identification through a password, firewall, etc.). In this way, the customer can connect securely with the organization and transact automatically.

The selected rule system (levelling the volume and the mix, priority assignation, pacemaker programming, kanban publication, etc.) regulates the productive/supply rate. The system assigns the production and priority rates in order to align the process flow with the end customer demand.

THE OTHER ACTIVITIES OF THE ARCHITECTURE DESIGN MACRO PHASE

In order to facilitate and accelerate the designs of the specific functions and tools it is possible to simulate the future system, trying to replicate with the key users all of the functions scheduled for organizational, physical and digitized activities.

It is also important to:

- Coordinate the change management;
- Develop a training programme for the employees who will operate and interact with the future process; and
- Design the pilot plan, which is the final test before the implementation of the re-engineered process.

The results of the architecture design phase are:

- Documentation of the functional and technical specifications for each activity, service and interface;
- Change management plan;
- Training plan;
- Pilot plan.

The architecture design accelerators are:

- Simulation of the future system through the processing of the programmed organizational, physical and digitized activities: this accelerates the design of the functional and technical specifications;
- Designing the digitized flow using the SOA approach: it accelerates and simplifies possible future project modifications or the availability of the service for similar activities in other processes.

CRITERIA FOR THE ACCEPTANCE OF TOLLGATE 3 – ARCHITECTURE DESIGN MACRO PHASE

In order to move to the following phase, it is important to answer the following questions correctly:

1. Has the team completed the documentation of the functional and technical design and has it been approved? The functional and technical design is fundamental to define how to implement the process modifications. Without the functional and technical design, the improvements will remain theoretical, that is to say, they will not go beyond the to-be process mapping;
2. Has the team planned the change management? Planning the change management beforehand (and starting to implement it) means guiding the staff into a gradual transition from the old to the new to-be process. Managing the change at the last minute could cause too much stress for the staff, due to the sudden change in their tasks;
3. Has the team planned the training? The re-engineered to-be process requires a new way of working and operating. This implies the need for training the staff. Not having planned training can cause difficulties or resistance in launching the to-be process;
4. Has the team planned the pilot? There is a need to test the re-engineered process before the final launch in production. Not planning the pilot process might delay the full implementation of the to-be process.

In order to guarantee the completion of the architectural design, the team should complete:

* The definition of the technical and functional architecture of all the elements of the to-be process and the technical and governance rules;
* The plan of the change management activities for the future process operators and for maintenance;
* The plan for the education and training activities for employees and maintenance;
* The plan for piloting the to-be process.

THE RELATIONAL MODEL AND ACTIONS – THE ARCHITECTURE DESIGN MACRO PHASE

Figure 3.9 shows the architecture design phase of the Lean and Digitize method and the connection between the analyse and process design and the architecture design phases.

The kaizen plan connects with the architecture design. The team must complete the plan in order to make the to-be process. Each one of the improvement actions planned in the kaizen plan starts with the architecture design to regulate:

* The organizational flow: by means of the activities allocated to the cells and the design of the flow coordination rules, in other words, the management of kanbans, the volume levelling and the operations *mix* (heijunka box);

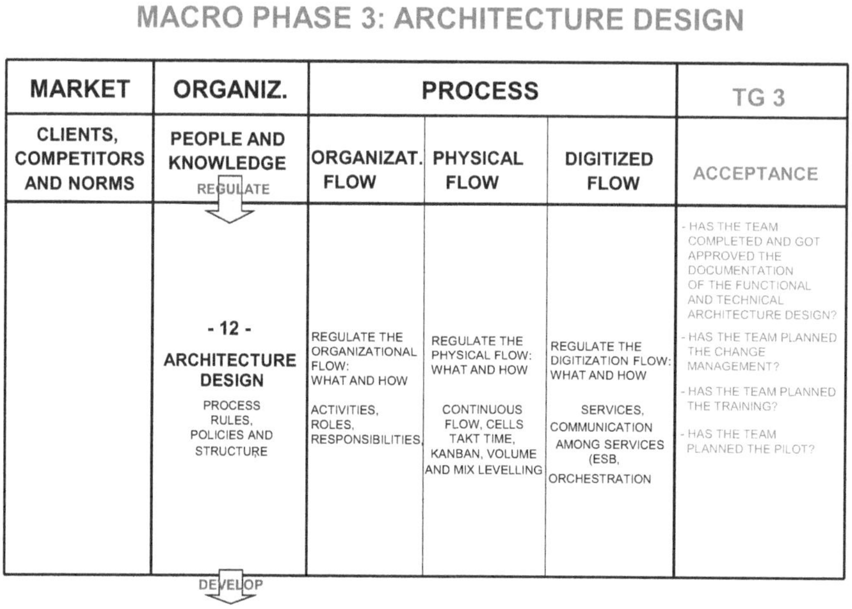

MACRO PHASE 3: ARCHITECTURE DESIGN

MARKET	ORGANIZ.	PROCESS			TG 3
CLIENTS, COMPETITORS AND NORMS	PEOPLE AND KNOWLEDGE REGULATE	ORGANIZAT. FLOW	PHYSICAL FLOW	DIGITIZED FLOW	ACCEPTANCE
	- 12 - **ARCHITECTURE DESIGN** PROCESS RULES, POLICIES AND STRUCTURE	REGULATE THE ORGANIZATIONAL FLOW: WHAT AND HOW ACTIVITIES, ROLES, RESPONSIBILITIES	REGULATE THE PHYSICAL FLOW: WHAT AND HOW CONTINUOUS FLOW, CELLS TAKT TIME, KANBAN, VOLUME AND MIX LEVELLING	REGULATE THE DIGITIZATION FLOW: WHAT AND HOW SERVICES, COMMUNICATION AMONG SERVICES (ESB, ORCHESTRATION	- HAS THE TEAM COMPLETED AND GOT APPROVED THE DOCUMENTATION OF THE FUNCTIONAL AND TECHNICAL ARCHITECTURE DESIGN? - HAS THE TEAM PLANNED THE CHANGE MANAGEMENT? - HAS THE TEAM PLANNED THE TRAINING? - HAS THE TEAM PLANNED THE PILOT?

DEVELOP

Figure 3.9   The relational model of the architecture design phase

- The physical flow: by means of the design of the continuous flow activities from a physical point of view; and
- The digitization flow, through the design of the services, of the communication amongst services (ESB) and the instrumentation (regulation of the digitization flow).

The architecture design activities are:

1. Simulation of the future system, trying to replicate all the planned new functions;
2. Completion of the functional specifications;
3. Completion of the technical specifications;
4. Planning of the change management;
5. Planning of the communication and training;
6. Planning of the pilot implementation.

THE NEW ELEMENTS OF LEAN AND DIGITIZE – THE ARCHITECTURE DESIGN MACRO PHASE

The innovation of the Lean and Digitize method in the architecture design macro phase consists in the simulation of the future system in the design phase and in the use of the SOA approach combined with the process redesigns:

1. Simulation of the future system through the repetition of the programmed functions of computer applications and of physical activities: the simulation (which does not correspond with the functional and technical specifications, testing the project and architecture modifications immediately);

2. The design of the digitized flow using the SOA approach: accelerates and simplifies the possible future project modifications, eliminates the restraints imposed by the classical information systems and brings ICT nearer to the process.

The Build, Test and Deploy Macro Phase

After the architecture design phase, the project proceeds with the macro phase build, test and deploy. In this phase, the team build, test and launch into production the re-engineered process. The activities planned and programmed in the kaizen plan are completed.

THE TEST OF BEST PRACTICES – THE BUILD, TEST AND DEPLOY MACRO PHASE

Table 3.4 shows the main elements of the Lean and Six Sigma methods and the most used tools regarding build and test and deploy phases.

**Table 3.4   The main points of the Lean and Six Sigma methods and its tools –
Build, Test and Deploy**

	Six Sigma	Lean	Lean Six Sigma tools	Lean tools
Build, test and Deploy	IMPROVE: 1. Validating the solution 2. Implementing the solution 3. Measure the efficacy		IMPROVE: • Value engineering • Design of experiments Taguchi's robust design	

BUILD AND TEST

In the build and test phase, the team builds and test the to-be process. The work is about developing the new infrastructure, software and interfaces, according to the functional and technical specifications defined in the previous phase, architecture design. The team should test these aspects individually to verify the development accuracy (if installation actually makes what is required, if the software has code problems or bugs, if the interfaces can link the sub-processes, etc.).

The team can pilot the new process once they have verified the accuracy of the development. The pilot builds and simulates the process on a small scale, according to the process design, in order to:

• Verify the real functionality;
• Assess the CTQs; and in case of malfunctions;
• Make the appropriate modifications.
  There are two particularly important aspects of this macro phase:
• Change management;
• Documentation:

Sometimes, the team does not attach much importance to these two functions. Change management is important. Despite all of the effort involved in the previous phases to consider all possibilities, there might be changes to make in the build and test phase. It is advisable to formalize this aspect. The aim is not to generate bureaucracy, but simply to avoid substantial changes in respect of decisions taken previously and shared with all the stakeholders during the implementation. On the other hand, in the course of implementation it is common to have some changes because:

- Organizations are dynamic. It is always necessary to take changes into account;
- The previous phases may not have considered some aspects correctly.

It is particularly important to document the solution and the work done. It should never delayed or completely forgotten. Process improvement is important, but:

- Leaving clear traces of the changes is also important;
- Documenting the process benefits the operators and maintainers of the process.

DEPLOY

Once the re-engineered process is functioning correctly, it is necessary to go into production for the entire organization. This phase can take a long time. It requires developing the following activities:

- Writing a plan for decommissioning the parallel processes and the activities which are not included in the new process;
- Converting the data of the previous information system, in case they are required by the new applications;
- Developing a training plan for the end users (the employees who will work with the new process);
- Developing supporting manuals for the end users and the maintainers;
- Updating the databases of applications, activities and processes;
- Transferring the responsibility for the maintenance;
- Developing the control plan;
- Verifying the local regulations and possible additional adaptations;

LAUNCHING THE NEW PROCESS INTO PRODUCTION

Launching in production the re-engineered process frees economic and human resources. The organization task is to manage the resources made available in the best possible way, in order to increase the satisfaction of customers, shareholders and employees.

THE RESULTS OF THE DEPLOY PHASE

The results of the deploy phase are:

- Plan to terminate the activities and/or contracts relative to processes which are no longer used;

- Update the databases of data, applications, activities and processes;
- Distribute the supporting manuals;
- Develop the control plan.

CRITERIA FOR THE ACCEPTANCE OF TOLLGATE 4 – THE BUILD, TEST AND DEPLOY MACRO PHASE

In order to move to the following phase, it is important to answer the following questions positively:

1. Has the team developed correctly and in accordance with the functional and technical specifications, defined in the architecture design phase, the infrastructure, applications and interfaces? To develop these in a different way can determine the failure in achieving the planned objectives. It would jeopardize the balance of the overall operation of the process;
2. Has the Lean and Digitize Committee fully approved the pilot tests? The pilot allows verifying the compliance of the project with its design on a small scale. If the new process is not fully compliant, it is possible to introduce the necessary modifications. Not testing the pilot plan could mean having to implement the process modifications on a large scale while the new process is in operation. This circumstance would lead to a great waste of energy, time and money, thus damaging the customer's satisfaction and the profitability;
3. Has the team trained the end users and those employees in charge of maintenance? The end users and the employees in charge of maintenance will be accountable for the process in production and its outputs. If they are not trained (and there are no supporting manuals), the right production/supply flow will be jeopardized. The CTQs and the customers' satisfaction will be negatively affected;
4. Has the team planned for the controls? It is necessary to control the re-engineered process to ensure that it complies with the effectiveness and reliability parameters related to the CTQs. If controls are not planned, the process flow could become ungovernable;
5. Did the team launch the new process in production? The concrete results of the improvement project will show up when the process is in production. Not launching in production would mean that all the re-engineering work has been a pure waste of time, resources and money.

Answering these questions positively will guarantee the completion of the architectural design:

- The infrastructure, applications and interfaces are in accordance with the architectural design;
- A pilot has tested the new process. The pilot was positive;
- The team has plans and programmes for future controls; and
- The process is in production.

THE RELATIONAL MODEL AND ACTIONS – THE BUILD, TEST AND DEPLOY MACRO PHASE

Figure 3.10 shows the relationships between the phases build, test and deploy of the method Lean and Digitize and the interconnection between the macro phases architecture design and build, test and deploy.

There is a connection between the build and test phase and the architecture design, because the development and test activities must follow the process' architecture design.

The organization must implement and test the selected solution, which involves:

- The organizational flows, with the modifications in the activities in the process;
- The physical flows, with the implementation of the new layout, cells, continuous flow lines, etc.; and
- The digitization flows, with the development of applications, databases and systems.

Once the process has undergone the assessment tests, the team launches the selected solution into production, involving the end users and the employees in charge of the maintenance.

The activities of the build, test and deploy phase are:

1. Development of the infrastructure, devices, applications and interfaces;
2. Compliance assessment of applications and interfaces with specifications;
3. Execution of a pilot application;

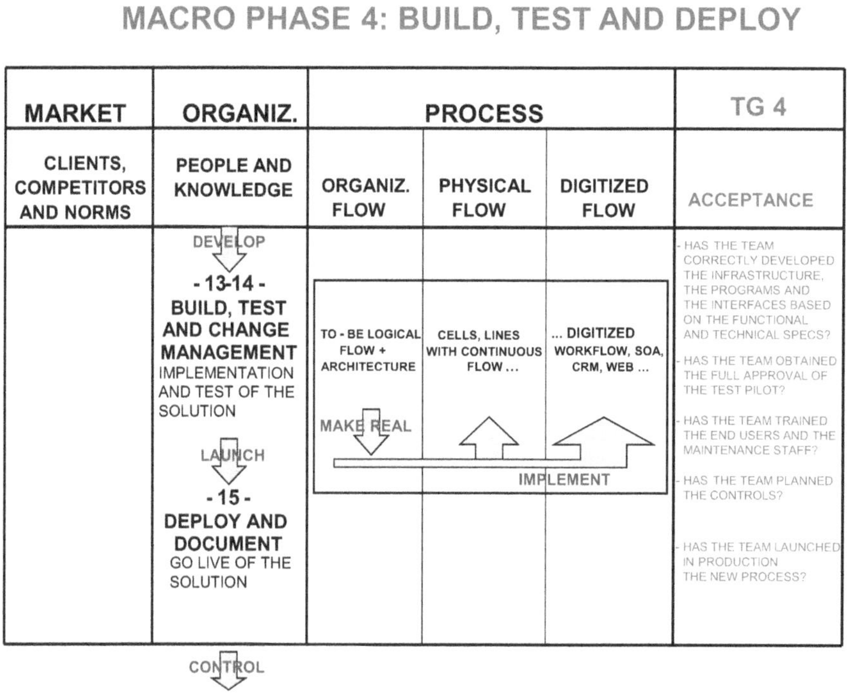

MACRO PHASE 4: BUILD, TEST AND DEPLOY

MARKET	ORGANIZ.	PROCESS			TG 4
CLIENTS, COMPETITORS AND NORMS	PEOPLE AND KNOWLEDGE	ORGANIZ. FLOW	PHYSICAL FLOW	DIGITIZED FLOW	ACCEPTANCE
	DEVELOP ↘ - 13-14 - **BUILD, TEST AND CHANGE MANAGEMENT** IMPLEMENTATION AND TEST OF THE SOLUTION MAKE REAL ↘ LAUNCH ↘ - 15 - **DEPLOY AND DOCUMENT** GO LIVE OF THE SOLUTION	TO - BE LOGICAL FLOW + ARCHITECTURE	CELLS, LINES WITH CONTINUOUS FLOW ...	... DIGITIZED WORKFLOW, SOA, CRM, WEB ... IMPLEMENT	- HAS THE TEAM CORRECTLY DEVELOPED THE INFRASTRUCTURE, THE PROGRAMS AND THE INTERFACES BASED ON THE FUNCTIONAL AND TECHNICAL SPECS? - HAS THE TEAM OBTAINED THE FULL APPROVAL OF THE TEST PILOT? - HAS THE TEAM TRAINED THE END USERS AND THE MAINTENANCE STAFF? - HAS THE TEAM PLANNED THE CONTROLS? - HAS THE TEAM LAUNCHED IN PRODUCTION THE NEW PROCESS?

CONTROL ↘

Figure 3.10 The relational model of the macro phase build, test and deploy

4. Possible changes identified in the test phase;
5. Plan for the decommissioning of the parallel processes;
6. Conversion of the data in the system, in case the new applications require this;
7. Development of the training plan for the end users;
8. Development of the supporting manuals for the end users and the maintainers;
9. Update the database;
10. Transfer of the responsibility for maintenance;
11. Development of the control plan;
12. Verification of the respect of the regulations and eventual specific adaptations;
13. Launching the new process into production;
14. Reallocating the freed resources;
15. Pass Tollgate 4.

THE NEW ELEMENTS OF LEAN AND DIGITIZE – THE BUILD, TEST AND DEPLOY MACRO PHASE

The new element of Lean and Digitize in the phase of build, test and deploy is essentially the greater granularity of the sub-phases as compared to the traditional phases of Lean Six Sigma: improve or develop.

The Verify Macro Phase

Once the build, test and deploy phase is completed, the project ends with the verify phase. This macro phase is necessary to control the process now in production by monitoring its CTQs and by assessing the benefits outside and inside the organization. The Team can close the project. In the continuous improvement spirit, the organization can start the Six Sigma continuous improvement method (DMAIC).

Table 3.5 shows the main elements of the methods Lean and Six Sigma and the most used tools regarding the phases verify, external benefits and internal benefits.

Table 3.5   Main points of the methods Lean and Six Sigma and their tools – verify, external benefits and internal benefits

	Six Sigma	Lean	Lean Six Sigma tools	Lean tools
Verify	'Verify'	Perfection:	VERIFY:	
External benefits	1. Choose the variables to monitor	1. Perfection does not exist;	Control plan Control charts	
	2. Choose the tools	2. There is always some element to	Dashboard	
	3. Assign roles and tasks	improve;		
Internal benefits	4. Document the results	3. Continuous improvement;		
	5. Verify the achievement of	4. Continuous learning		
	6. Close the project			

MONITORING THE PROCESS PERFORMANCES

The use of information to control the process is important. ICT can help in building proper controls into the solution. Computers can capture and report information regarding:

- consumption of resources
- duration of the phases of the process
- characteristics of the process outputs
- general cost of processes.

The real-time display of complete and accurate process information is only appropriate for processes adequately described in terms of outputs, transactions and defects. Other processes and objectives require more innovative and quantitative methods, such as:

- Sampling and researching during the processes;
- Supervision of the customers' processes; and
- Creation of specific computer applications for process monitoring.

It is possible to reuse process information over the long term, to analyse schemes and performances and optimize the design and implementation of a new process.

THE VERIFY PHASE IN THE INTESA SANPAOLO BANK (BORTOLOTTI 2007–2008) ***

Once they have implemented a new process, the Italian bank Intesa Sanpaolo always control its application. Process automation allows control of the relevant KPIs without an increase in costs or labour. Moreover, transaction monitoring can be essential to take strategic decisions.

It is possible to send transactions of administrative documents between branches and the back office. In this way, it is possible to level out the workload dynamically and monitor the performances (time, cost, quality) continuously by analysing the flow.

The digitization of customer care services through online banking and web-based ATMs and their evolutions allow to automatically identify the high transactors in order to focus on the development of actions in relation to the most important and profitable customers.

VERIFY

The verify macro phase requires the implementation of the control plan previously defined. It is necessary to monitor continuously the process by measuring the CTQs. Failure to monitor the process could degrade it and cause important losses due to poor customer satisfaction and, as a consequence, a loss of benefits.

At the beginning of the verify phase, once the new process is in production, it is necessary to implement the possible post-installation changes and the decommissioning plan of inactive parallel processes.

The accelerator of the verify phase corresponds to the automated control systems. These do not require further costs or human resource investments and allow activation of the alarm systems in case of problems regarding the CTQs.

EXTERNAL AND INTERNAL BENEFITS

The project for the improvement of the process has the primary objective of satisfying the customer, the shareholders and the employees, to improve profitability and increase market shares.

The phase of control of the external benefits (market) and internal benefits (organization) is the junction point, with the possible start of new Lean and Digitize initiatives.

The improvement efforts should continue over time, because the market is dynamic: customers and competitors change. If the organization wants to excel, they must look continuously into the future and aim at perfection (Lean Thinking Fifth Principle).

THE ACCEPTANCE CRITERIA OF TOLLGATE 5 – THE VERIFY MACRO PHASE

The Tollgate 5 acceptance criteria do not correspond to activities that need to perform in order to 'exit' this phase. The verify macro phase is continuous over time, in the spirit of continuous improvement. In order to pass Tollgate 5, it is useful to perform the following activities:

- Communications of the results obtained;
- A 'Learned Lessons' Session, so as to use the Lean and Digitize project to prevent future errors;
- A celebration of the project's completion.

At Tollgate 5, it is necessary to answer the following questions confidently:

1. Has the team resolved all the post-installation defects and modifications necessary? Although the pilot simulation can be a faithful reproduction of the actual functioning, once the process is launched into production, there might be the need to resolve some defects and make some adjustments. Not to provide interventions to solve these aspects can cause loss of benefits;
2. Has the team decommissioned the old systems, processes and reports?
3. Does the new process replace some parallel activities or processes that were necessary before the improvement project? Not closing the parallel activities or processes, which have already become useless, leads to an unjustified increase in costs which affects the organization's profitability;
4. Has the team set up activities to monitor the new process over time? The process control is fundamental to keep the benefits obtained during the phase of improvement. Not monitoring the CTQs may mean not being able to detect possible errors which could deteriorate the margins;

5. Has the team installed an automatic corporate performance management (CPM) system? These systems are used increasingly and are particularly useful to follow up the process performances over time.

THE RELATIONAL MODEL AND ACTIONS – THE VERIFY MACRO PHASE

Figure 3.11 shows the relations between the phases in verify of the method Lean and Digitize and the interconnections between the macro phases build, test and deploy and verify. The verify phase connects with the deploy phase because the process, launched into production, must be controlled monitoring the CTQs of the organizational, physical and digitization flows.

The verify phase allows for checking to determine if the process will bring benefits to the customers, shareholders and employees and, accordingly, real benefits to the organization in terms of profitability, quality and market share.

The verify activities are:

1. Resolution of all problems following the entry into production;
2. Close of parallel processes and systems;
3. Measure and monitor CTQs;
4. Costs and benefits control.

In this phase, it is also appropriate to:

• Facilitate wide visibility inside and, if necessary, outside the organization of the results of the project;

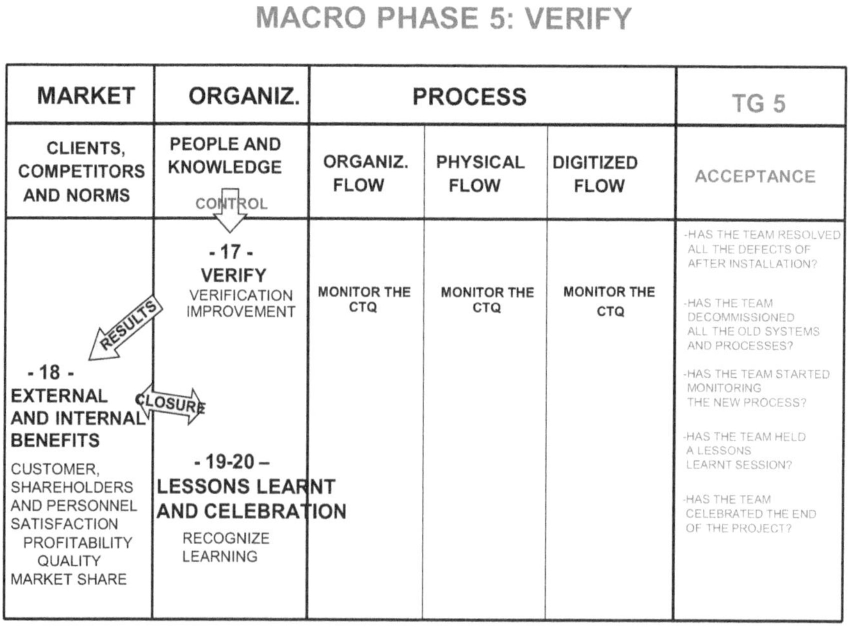

MACRO PHASE 5: VERIFY

MARKET	ORGANIZ.	PROCESS			TG 5
CLIENTS, COMPETITORS AND NORMS	PEOPLE AND KNOWLEDGE CONTROL	ORGANIZ. FLOW	PHYSICAL FLOW	DIGITIZED FLOW	ACCEPTANCE
	- 17 - VERIFY VERIFICATION IMPROVEMENT	MONITOR THE CTQ	MONITOR THE CTQ	MONITOR THE CTQ	-HAS THE TEAM RESOLVED ALL THE DEFECTS OF AFTER INSTALLATION? -HAS THE TEAM DECOMMISSIONED ALL THE OLD SYSTEMS AND PROCESSES?
RESULTS - 18 - EXTERNAL AND INTERNAL BENEFITS CUSTOMER, SHAREHOLDERS AND PERSONNEL SATISFACTION PROFITABILITY QUALITY MARKET SHARE	CLOSURE - 19-20 – LESSONS LEARNT AND CELEBRATION RECOGNIZE LEARNING				-HAS THE TEAM STARTED MONITORING THE NEW PROCESS? -HAS THE TEAM HELD A LESSONS LEARNT SESSION? -HAS THE TEAM CELEBRATED THE END OF THE PROJECT?

Figure 3.11 The relational model of the phase verify

- Take a session on lessons learnt during the project, so as to assure improvements in the management of future projects; and
- Celebrate the successful completion of the project with all the people in the TEAM.

THE NEW ELEMENTS OF LEAN AND DIGITIZE – THE VERIFY MACRO PHASE

The new element that the Lean and Digitize has contributed to the verify macro phase consists in using digitization not only as a process accelerator but also as a method to monitor CTQs. In this regard, the CPM systems and packages can be of great support and of considerable help in guaranteeing a continuous monitoring at reasonable costs and with a reasonable amount of resources.

Automation at the verify phase frees human and financial resources. It also ensures higher accuracy as compared to manual controls.

The Replicate or Roll-out Macro Phase

Based on the success of the first implementation, the Lean and Digitize Committee could decide to extend the new process and the new information system in other parts of the organization or in other organizations of the same group.

The roll-out phase activities are:

- Verification of the validity in the description of the as-is process in the new situation;
- Identification of the variations necessary at the local level;
- Update the to-be process and define the necessary changes;
- Implement the change management plan;
- Go live with the new process;
- Monitor the status of the CTQs.

List of References

Aggogeri, F. and Gentili, E. 2006, *Lean Six Sigma: la nuova frontiera per la qualità. La sinergia tra six sigma e lean production per un innovativo metodo di gestione e miglioramento dei processi industriali*, Milano: FrancoAngeli.

Barney M., McCarty T. 2002, *The new Six Sigma: A Leader's Guide to Achieving Rapid Business Improvement and Sustainable Results*, Upper Saddle River: Pearson Education.

Bertels, T. 2003, *Rath and Strong's Six Sigma Leadership Handbook*, Hoboken, John Wiley & Sons.

Bonfiglioli, R. 2004. *Pensare Snello. Lean-thinking alla maniera italiana. Costruiamo l'impresa competitiva (più produttività – minori sprechi). 5 nuovi casi italiani di successo*. Milano: FrancoAngeli.

Bortolotti, T. 2007–2008 Anno Accademico. Un modello integrato lean six sigma per il miglioramento dei processi. Thesis at the Università di Udine.

Bortolotti, T., Romano, P., Nicoletti, B. 2010, Lean first, then automate: an integrated model for process improvement in pure service-providing companies, *Advances in Production Management Systems*, (Best Paper Award), Berlin: Springer, pp. 579–586.

Davenport, T.H. 1993. *Process Innovation: Reengineering Work Through Information Technology*. Cambridge: Harvard Business School Press.

Defeo, J. and Juran, J.M. 2010. *Juran's Quality Handbook*, 6th edn. New York: McGraw Hill.

Dzierzanowski, J.M. et al. 1989. *The Authorizer's Assistant: A Knowledge-Based Credit Authorization System for American Express*. In Herbert Schorr and A. Rappoport, *Proceedings of the First Annual Conference on Innovative Applications of Artificial Intelligence*, Menlo Park, CA, American Association for Artificial Intelligence, 28–30 March.

Erl, T. et al. 2012. *Service-Oriented Infrastructure: On-Premise and in the Cloud*. Upper Saddle River: Prentice Hall.

Harris, R. and Rother, M. 2001. *Creating Continuous Flow: An Action Guide for Managers, Engineers and Production Associates*. Cambridge: The Lean Enterprise Institute.

Majorana, F. 2008. *Managing a Global Enterprise through a Lean Sigma approach*. Lean Six Sigma and Process Improvement Summit, Amsterdam, 27–30 October.

Nicoletti, B. 2008. Unified content management. *Sistemi and Automazione* 4(April), 38–43.

Nicoletti, B. 2009. *Project Management 2.0, Proceedings of the IPMA Congress*, Rome, 10–13 October.

Read, T.J. 2009. *The IT Value Network: From IT Investment to Stakeholder Value*. Hoboken: John Wiley & Sons.

Smalley, A. 2004. *Creating Level Pull, A Lean Production-system Improvement Guide for Production-control, Operations, and Engineering Professionals*. Cambridge: The Lean Enterprise Institute.

Tartari, R. 2008, *Manuale del Sei Sigma. Verso zero difetti, zero scarti e zero resi!*, 3° rist,, Milano: FrancoAngeli.

Zuboff, S. and Maxmin, J. 2004. *The Support Economy: Why Corporations Are Failing Individuals and the Next Episode of Capitalism*. New York: Penguin.

4 *The Approach to Lean and Digitize*

Introduction

The Lean and Digitize method is an excellent tool in theory and in practice. However, its application requires some precautions. This chapter applies the method in a complete example to show its application. We examine a business case which is particularly relevant for the practice. It consists in the application of the method in the implementation of an enterprise resource planning (ERP) system.

Finally, we consider the precautions to use in the application of the method and the factors for its success.

A Complete Example of Lean and Digitize

This section describes a practical use of the Lean and Digitize method through a simple example of its application (Bortolotti 2007–2008).

Four employees work in of an account receivable office. They must read the invoices one by one and enter the data in the system manually. The stakeholders have noticed that:

- The costs of the existing process are too high (four employees assigned full time);
- There are too many mistakes in the data entry (1 per cent errors or missed data);
- Work has very low value added and satisfaction for the employees.

The objectives of a Lean and Digitize action are:

- A drastic decrease of the human resources assigned;
- Zero defects in data entry;
- Spend as little as possible in implementing the changes.

The team has defined the to-be process in the following way:

- Scan the invoices, sent to just one person;
- Enter the data automatically into the system.

The as-is process is composed of five steps (represented in Figure 4.1):

1. Sending of invoices
2. Reception of the invoices in the office with four employees

3. The distribution of the invoices amongst all four people
4. The opening of each individual invoice
5. Manual data entry in a template
6. Control of the accuracy of the data
7. Sending data to the system
8. Filing of invoices.

The to-be process has five stages (represented in Figure 4.2):

1. Sending invoices (as in as-is, dotted arrow in Figure 4.2);
2. Reception of invoices by one person (the as-is dotted arrow in Figure 4.2);
3. Opening each invoice (the as-is, dotted arrow in Figure 4.2);
4. Scanning the invoice;
5. Filing the invoices (the as-is, dotted arrow in Figure 4.2).

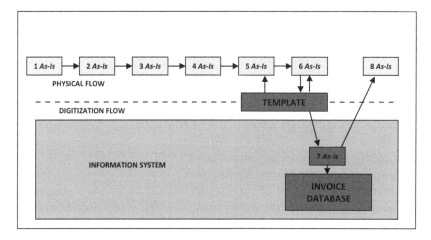

Figure 4.1   An example invoicing process

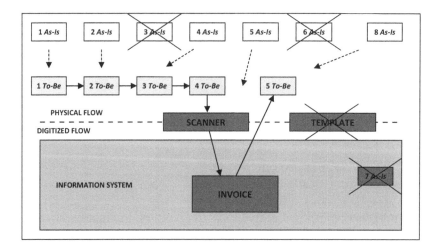

Figure 4.2   The to-be of the case of invoicing process

The stages 3, 6 and 7 in the as-is have been eliminated (indicated with an X in Figure 4.2). The template is no longer in use. Step 5 has been modified (dotted arrow pointing at the scanner in Figure 4.2).

The benefits are the following:

- Decrease in the cycle time thanks to the elimination of:
  - Invoice distribution
  - Control of the exact entered data
  - Sending to the system
- Decrease in the cycle time thanks to the digitization in inputting invoice data;
- More reliability on entering data;
- Better control and no errors;
- Productive capacity freed equal to three out of four employees (drastic improvement).

The achievement of to-be has implied the following:

- The redesign of the office layout;
  - The purchase and installation of a scanner;
  - The setting up of an interface between the scanner and the account receivables system.

Going into more detail, the Lean and Digitize Team has performed:

- The redesign of the office layout:
  - During the working seminar, the process was simulated by changing desks and equipping a workstation with a scanner (not yet able to automatically send data to the system), a computer, a box for receiving invoices and a filing cabinet;
  - Included in the kaizen plan is the task assigned to the person in charge of the process, of the optimal arrangement of the desk and tools so that they are not in the way of other employees in the office.
  - The duration of the actions have been seven days after launching the project;
- The purchase of a scanner and the build of an interface to automatically enter data into the system are complex tasks that require a Leand and Digitize approach:
  - Define and measure: definition of the problem, set up of the team. The list of measures of the project successes;
  - Analyse and process design measure: definitions of the characteristics of the scanning and interface tools. The scanner must allow automatic data entry into the system. Therefore, it has to be able to recognize invoice fields by using optical character recognition (OCR), control that data are valid, block the data entering process in case of reading errors/lack of data/compatibility error of data type/etc., to signal the end of the transaction, etc.;
  - Architecture design: benchmarking of the scanning tools available on the market. Those in charge of the kaizen plan must verify if there are products suitable for scanning according to the to-be process in the market; analysis and choice of the most suitable tool for the demands of the organizational process;
  - Build, test and deploy: contract with the supplier for the customization of the tool to the organization's reality and the interface with the system. Those in charge

must program an application that allows the scanner to send data to the system, the invoice database;

- Verify: launching into production and controlling the tool works well. Execution of the lesson learnt and celebration of the project positive conclusions.
- Replicate: suggesting the extension of the solution to other areas.

On 1 March 2011 the team started to work on the project, discussing the problems with the stakeholders. The various phases had the temporary deadlines shown in Table 4.1.

Table 4.1   Project timeline planning

Phase	Start	End
1. Define and measure	1 March 2011	7 March 2011
2. Analysis and process design	8 March 2011	16 May 2011
a. Lean and Digitize scanning tool plus data enter	8 March 2011	8 May 2011
Working seminar	8 March 2011	17 March 2011
Kaizen plan	18 March 2011	24 March 2011
Architecture design	25 March 2011	27 March 2011
Build and test	28 March 2011	3 May 2011
Deploy	4 May 2011	8 May 2011
b. Employee training	9 May 2011	9 May 2011
c. Layout optimization	10 May 2011	16 May 2011
3. Verify: control of the new process	17 May 2011	Ongoing

The training of the employees only lasts one day because the process is very simple. The control of the new process starts when the process goes into production. It does not have an end. It is necessary to continue to monitor the project in order to pursue perfection.

Ten Technology Keys for the Success of a Lean and Digitize Project

The following is a brief list of the ten technology keys useful to make an agile and lean process and increase the speed, productivity and efficiency:

1. Internet: Web portals and apps facilitate the distribution of information outside of organizations and allow business processes to come closer to customers and suppliers;
2. Wireless: information is entered directly into the database, eliminating intermediate documentation;
3. Digitization of work flow: increases speed, eliminates bottlenecks;

4. Scanning and digitization: digital databases cost a lot less compared to wasted paper; i.e. digital documents are easier to trace and referred to:
5. Content management system: it allows remote collaboration and sharing of information and eliminates the waste of useless shipping and waiting;
6. SOA: it allows an interface between different software systems in such a way that it is possible to communicate and exchange data without human intervention and supervision;
7. Business process monitoring and measurement helps to automatically measure the performance of the old and the new process;
8. Business process management systems integrate several software systems involved in the business process. It allows a lean flow of processes through various departments, functions and administrations;
9. Business system regulation: allows the digitization of manual activities, the cause of waste in many processes. Improves processes and control schedule;
10. CRM plus frequently asked questions (FAQs) online: supports processes, speeds up customer service, eliminates frequent calls.

Benefits of Lean and Digitize

Lean and Digitize brings several benefits to the organizations with respect to the application only of Lean Six Sigma. The benefits are also considerable for the internal organizational processes. The greatest benefits come from interfacing with external organizations, such as the relationship with suppliers or with the distribution channels and the end customers (see Figure 4.3).

Traditionally, Six Sigma has been associated with defect reduction and the operational costs of manufacturing companies. Lean has been associated with cycle time reduction. Digitization is associated with productivity increases.

The following are the benefits obtained in completing Lean and Digitize projects, recorded with organizations that implemented these types of projects:

*   Better customer satisfaction;
*   Decrease in the percentage of process defects;
*   Decrease in the variability of fundamental processes;
*   Improvement of the organizational culture towards the continuous improvement from process performance;
*   Decrease of the process cycle duration and the consequent supplies/very fast supplies;
*   Reduction of operational costs; and
*   Increase of the market share.

These are the results of the Lean and Digitize in some organizations.

*   United Services have reduced the repair and revision time of aircraft by 50 per cent;
*   Collins Aviation Services have reduced the installation and revision time from 22 days to 4 days;
*   The US Army has reduced the time of installation and revision of the helicopter T700/CT7 from 261 days to 93 days.

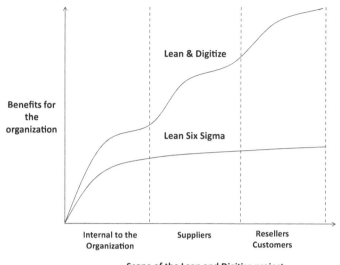

Figure 4.3   The advantages of Lean and Digitize compared to Lean Six Sigma

All of these improvements have been possible thanks to Lean and Digitize projects. In fact, this method allows users to:

- reduce warehouse inventories
- optimize data management
- improve passengers' safety
- improve reliability
- optimize maintenance schedules
- reduce costs
- reduce revision and maintenance time
- increase productivity
- improve capacity.

The Case of Enterprise Resource Planning

INTRODUCTION

An interesting application for the Lean and Digitize method is for the installation and implementation of an enterprise resource planning (ERP) information system. ERPs consist of software packages available commercially that use standard data models and that facilitate:

- Horizontal and vertical integration of many (potentially all) interorganization processes;
- Process efficiency; and

- Monitoring by means of KPIs related to quality, service, timeline and costs.

ERPs were born in the 1980s. In the beginning they supported planning and management of production resources in manufacturing companies. They were initially called Manufacturing Resource Planning (MRP), and later MRP II with additional functions. In this version, they mainly supported production or the supply chain management in the manufacturing organizations. The ERPs represent the extension of the MRP II in other areas of the organizations, such as engineering, accountancy, finance, payroll, staff management and the like.

The initial use of ERPs was mainly in large organizations in the 1990s thanks to a German software organization, SAP. Initially ERPs used client/server technology, but later migrated towards the Intranet/Internet (thin customer) technology.

In time, there were versions of ERP for specific sectors, known as vertical ERP (VERP), such as banking, textile, oil, telecommunication companies, etc.

In general, an ERP has the following modules:

- sales and marketing
- procurement
- supply chain
- operations
- management control
- warehouse management
- project management
- maintenance
- facility management
- accounting and finance, etc.

An ERP on its own cannot improve company processes. The most important challenge is to provide an even better ERP by applying the Lean and Digitize method.

POSSIBLE CAUSES OF FAILURE OF AN ERP PROJECT

The fundamental questions in the implementation of an ERP information system are:

- How to assure the organization benefits through the implementation of an ERP information system?
- Can the implementation of an ERP information system automatically solve all the problems of inefficiency and coordinate all the processes currently fragmented?
- Can multinational organizations process the same ERP for more places, taking into account that each country and region has regulations, processes and ICT environments very different?, and
- If the project is long term, how can one solve the urgent problems, until the final ERP information system is in production?

It is important to ask these questions to avoid the risk of failures in the implementation of an ERP information system.

It is widely known that the main cause of errors incurred in the implementation of the ERP information systems is not technical, but a combination of process and governance problems.

The most common causes of failure are the lack of:

- The commitment of senior management;
- Communication of the initiative throughout the organization;
- The definition of processes' parameters to measure their success;
- Alignment between the initiatives in the business process improvement and ICT;
- An effective improvement caused by the attempt to adapt the process to the ERP information system, or on the contrary, by the customization of the ERP information system so as to adapt it to the old internal processes.

Therefore, technical aspects of the implementation of the ERP information system should not focus on technical aspects alone. They should consider all the other aspects that could be important for success and particularly for process improvement. When neglected, they could lead to a shocking failure. In other words, it is necessary to implement a Lean and Digitize project.

The key aspects to focus on are:

- Meet predefined objectives for the improvement of process performance;
- Improve processes before digitizing them with the ERP information system;
- Write and implement a plan for communication and change management before the roll-out;
- Select the quick win solutions in order to solve the immediate problems;
- Adopt a gradual approach for the implementation to minimize the risks of failure, splitting the project in sub-projects or generations.

Implementation of an ERP Information System

THE PRELIMINARY MACRO PHASE

The premise for implementing an ERP information system is that performances will be optimal only if there is integration and synergy amongst people, processes and technology. It is necessary to integrate the work of people, processes and technology to align them with the specific objectives of the organization. It is necessary to define structure, processes, organization and technologies connected with the new system:

- Strategy: defines the organization's direction, according to the conditions of the market, the strategy and the technological possibilities;
- Structure: defines the organization of the entities and processes;
- Processes: describe the workflows to be followed to implement the strategy;
- Organization: refers to the people who manage the processes;
- Technologies: support the people who manage the processes.

THE DEFINE AND MEASURE MACRO PHASE

In this macro phase, it is necessary to focus on establishing a team and selecting the project manager. These two elements are critical for the success of the initiative.

During the define and measure phase, the team must study the available documentation, in order to understand the objectives and aims – the VoC. The team must translate VoC into a set of factors that are CTQ of the process.

THE ANALYSE AND PROCESS DESIGN MACRO PHASE

The team must then study the as-is processes to understand the rules and to design a high-level map of the status.

In the analyse and process design phase, the team must detail the map of the status with the workflows and information exchanged amongst the different sub-processes.

Then, it is necessary to document the business process CTQs and the critical points. Identifying the critical points allows us to take immediate action to correct some criticality, and to programme a series of gradual and consecutive generations or releases in order to achieve the final to-be.

In this macro phase, one needs to measure:

* the flows of information and of the processing rules (architecture as-is)
* resources
* inventories
* applications and infrastructure
* CTQ performances.

THE ARCHITECTURE DESIGN MACRO PHASE

In this macro phase, the team must study the existing information system in connection with business processes, through discussions (in person or by phone) with the key executives involved in the process.

The team must detect opportunities to improve the processes and the information system. They must determine how and where to conduct the implementation pilot. It is necessary to hold meetings and benchmarks, inside and outside the organization, to find the best solutions. The macro phase must be very interactive, and have all the stakeholders committed to finding solutions and accept change.

THE BUILD, TEST AND DEPLOY MACRO PHASE

In the build, test and deploy phase, the team has to implement a new efficient, effective, economic and quality process. In this macro phase, the team need to start the change management plan to face the questions, fears and concerns of the employees immediately. It is necessary to guide them through a fluid transition into the new business processes and into the new ERP information system. At the same time, the preparation of the pilot needs to start.

THE VERIFY MACRO PHASE

In this macro phase, it is necessary to test the new to-be process through a pilot. The pilot is very important because it represents the first real test of the new process. The pilot is useful for implementing and verifying it on a small scale. It allows modifications or improvements to the process before the ERP information system goes into production.

The activities of the verify phase are to:

- Implement the pilot of the to-be process and of the ERP;
- Collect lessons learnt;
- Update the to-be process and the ERP settings;
- Analyse of the situation of the CTQ performances;
- Implement the change management pilot;
- Celebrate the successful end of the project.

Then it starts the phase of implementation in other functions, or roll-out.

Some recommendations for the success of the project of Lean and Digitize to set up an ERP system are to [hosteddocs.ittoolbox.com]:

- Solve the conflict between production efficiency and customer service. Take the strategic decisions needed, then obtain the approval from the Lean and Digitize Committee;
- Expand the system so as to include suppliers and, if possible, customers or, at least, resellers;
- Maintain the effort to improve the manufacturing process as much as possible;
- Master the supply chain process.
- Some technological tools useful for the project are:
- One solution integrated for the management of quality which supports the effort of doing things well at the first attempt;
- An optimal system to preview and anticipate the customers' demand. By the term system, we mean a software application with possible interfaces with the suppliers and the customers;
- Independently of the type of the operations process, it is advisable to have applications to support customized production: manufacturing to order (MTO), design to order, engineering to order (ETO) and configuration to order (CTO).

Precautions in the Application of Lean and Digitize

The Lean and Digitize method has different positive aspects. They are always valid, even with regard to the implementation of an ERP system. During its application, it is important to take some precautions:

- ICT can provide interesting opportunities for innovation. It can also impose some restrictions on the process design. Organizations should not behave as if they were before a blank sheet of paper. They should recognize the restrictions that the existing systems, both inside the organization and outside, with their suppliers and customers, can impose on new processes, understand the consequences and strive to take the best from it. All the above applies generally, and most particularly with regard to implementing commercial computer packages. The processes considered by the commercial software packages can be more rational and logical than the ones used by many organizations (because they are for multiple environments). Some packages, however, do not fit the specific process viewpoint of the organization. Packages are also designed to support specific functions rather than processes;

- Besides that, take into account that best practices are good, but competitive advantages also arise from being different;

- There are tight connections with customers and suppliers. Their roles are important for the organization processes or very closely integrated with them. Thus, it could be very difficult to impose completely new systems. Nobody can expect that (non-exclusive) customers or suppliers change their internal systems in order to provide better process innovation to another organization. Conversely, as with systems with internal constraints, external systems should also be analysed to establish the process degrees of freedom;

- Taking the system's existing environments as a process limit could seem a constraint in view of a radical innovation. If the organization chooses not to change a certain number of their own systems, the possibilities of process innovation will minimize. When such constraints are rationally analysed, the trade-off will become evident. The analysis of the constraints should not start from the clean systems of the new processes, because later the team will discover difficulties in integrating with the unchanged systems. From the beginning of the project, one should face the difficulty of connecting the process to the existing systems.

PAKISTAN INTERNATIONAL AIRLINES – MAINTENANCE, REPAIR AND OVERHAUL (PIA–MRO): IMPLEMENTATION OF AN ERP (NADEEM AHMED 2008)

Pakistan International Airlines used a Lean and Digitize approach to implement an ERP information system in the area of supervision and maintenance.

The PIA–MRO team identified the following problems and criticalities during the analyse phase:

- Organization:
  - organization by functions
  - lack of planning
  - overlapping responsibilities.
- Processes:
  - lack of orientation to products
  - lack of planning
  - differences between the manuals and what was actually being done
  - the solutions found are too complex
  - long time for supervision and maintenance.
- Information systems:

> - low-quality data
> - manual interfaces
> - duplications
> - isolated, not integrated solutions
> - lack of appropriate ICT support.
>
> The conclusion of the senior management of the division regarding the MRO project was as follows:
>
> *'There is always margin for internal improvements in the organization, and integrating Lean Six Sigma in a program for the installation and maintenance of air transport is the best way to save many million dollars.'*

The Factors of Success and Failure in a Lean and Digitize Project

Based on the Lean and Digitize method and from the experience of many projects, the success factors of a project are the following (please take into account their relative importance and criticality in a specific organization):

- Base the project on a valid idea, with:
  - external consistency (i.e. with the external environment);
  - internal consistency (i.e. with a need within the organization, in respect to the culture, vision and strategy);
- Clearly identify the champion;
- Plan and control in a valid and clear manner;
- Select a strong project leader;
- Establish a good communication plan inside and outside the organization;
- Support the project leader in creating a team spirit, meaning ensuring that individual members of the team (the different resources) see themselves as being part of a team. It is necessary to understand their needs and incentivize collaboration.

The most important factor for the success of the project is the project leader and their leadership skills. Some managers believe that the members of the team of a project should all be exceptional people. If this were true, there would be the danger of conflicts between so many 'first actors'. The excellent project leader knows how to value the people in the team and will find the talent in each one of them.

List of References

Bortolotti, T. 2007–2008. Anno Accademico. Un modello integrato lean six sigma per il miglioramento dei processi. Thesis at the Università di Udine.

Nadeem Ahmed S. 2008. *Integrating Lean And Six Sigma With Erp And Its Extensions To Excel Your Business Processes*. 9th Annual Asian Six Sigma Summit, Process Improvement, Design and Management Know-How for Continuous Business Excellence and Improvement, Singapore, Thailand, 24–25 June.

Websites

http://hosteddocs.ittoolbox.com/wp10-ways-to-use-erp-to-Lean-the-manufacturing-supply-chain.
  pdf.

5 Managing a Lean and Digitize Project

Introduction

This chapter analyses the management of a Lean and Digitize project and underlines the differences in respect to a traditional project.

The Project Management

BASIC CONCEPTS

Project management is the application of a rational model for addressing a range of activities aimed at achieving a goal, usually unique, and in any case predetermined, with quality, time and cost constraints, through the use of different resources (e.g. people, money and equipment) (see Figure 5.1).

Other definitions of project management represent variations on this idea:

Project management is the systemic management of a complex 'enterprise,' unique and of a determined nature, aimed at achieving of a clearly predefined goal by a (continuous) process of planning and control of different resources with interdependent constraints of costs, time and quality. www.laboratorioaltierospinelli.org

The Project Management has as its main objective the implementation of a set of chained actions to realize a project, in respect of cost, time and eligibility requirements and prefixed completeness. Archibald 2003

A complex project is undertaken, single (i.e. not standard), limited in time, aiming to attain a goal that requires planned commitment and coordinated by various capacities and resources: money, men, means, materials and time. Albino 1995

The meaning of time–cost–quality in the management of a project is twofold. You can refer both to the time–cost–quality of the project process itself and to those of the outcome of the project.

Managing a Lean and Digitize project is not the pure definition of a technical solution to a problem: it is the management of all the activities and resources necessary to reach the end result of a drastic improvement in the process.

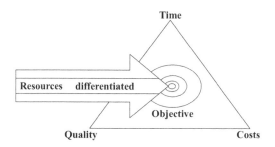

Figure 5.1 A graphic model of the project

The ultimate goal of project management is not, on the basis of activities and resources identified, to establish the start and end dates of the project as a whole. Managing a project must also support the evaluation and control of key elements such as:

- The achievement of its objectives;
- The commitment of resources of any kind related to the project;
- The economics of the project;
- The quality; and
- The contribution of the staff.

Project management is a very old endeavour: think of the pyramids or battles (which in a way are 'projects'). Based on experience both in conducting several projects and the science of management, a set of concepts and methodologies for project management have developed. They are applicable in all situations where you have to carry out unique, and therefore non-repetitive, activities just as in a project of Lean and Digitize.

THE NEED FOR PROJECT MANAGEMENT

Organizations often suffer from a variety of problems, such as:

- poor communication
- lack of resources
- conflicts between sectors
- difficulty in defining medium- to long-term objectives
- conflicting priorities
- limited delegation of responsibilities and tasks
- lack of motivation of the people.

One of the common denominators of these problems is the difficulty of coordinating and balancing the efforts of various groups or individuals within the organization effectively. At the grass roots level, there is often a lack of tools and common methods.

Project management offers a set of tools that can be introduced easily and effectively within any organization to solve these problems. At times, project management is understood as an activity related only to organizations that are working for the mission on 'technical projects' (e.g. organization of a piece of hardware). Surely the benefits of using tools and techniques for managing projects in this sector are considerable. Project management has a much larger scope, since you can apply it to any type: entity, person, or institution, whether public or private.

Project management has a number of characteristics that differentiate it from working in a traditional office. Table 5.1 lists some of these differences.

Table 5.1   Differences between a traditional service and a project

Traditional service	Project
The tasks are (relatively) repetitive	The objective is unique
The resources are (relatively) homogeneous and stable over time	The resources are heterogeneous and variable over time
There is a learning effect, because the transactions are (fairly) repetitive. This allows you to continuously improve the work	A project represents new experiences every time
The type of work is fairly continuous from one period to another	The cycle of life of a project is specific and includes a series of stages, characterized for example as indicated by the methodology of Lean and Digitize
The characteristics are defined on the basis of a timetable linked to the budget of the exercise	The moments of start and completion are defined with dates and a calendar
The service continues to exist even in the case of reorganization	The project can be terminated if the objectives cannot be achieved. In this case, the project ceases
The tasks are known and tend to be slightly different from previous activities	The project is often an innovative task: different from what has previously been done
Work is performed within the limits of the annual budget	The work is completed within the limits of the fixed project budget and deadlines
The activity is relatively simple in the planned expenditures of a period	There are difficulties in predicting time and defined costs
Involves few professional skills and related disciplines within a narrow scope of a defined and stable organization	Involves a lot of professional knowledge and disciplines in different organizations which can change from one stage of the cycle to another
The composition and type of costs are stable	The composition and types of costs are constantly changing
With homogeneous characteristics	With heterogeneous characteristics
Of a stable nature	Of a dynamic nature

Modern theories of project management are applicable to a wide range of activities of an organization. A project, distinct from traditional organizational processes, is the improvement of a process, the launch of a product, the conduct of market research, a marketing campaign, creating a budget, an overhaul of a machine and all activities consisting of a series of operations to be performed sequentially in a limited and defined way. It is therefore an important part of the activities of any organization.

Project management is essentially linked with change and innovation. These issues are growing in importance for organizations nowadays; therefore project management is increasing in relevance.

The management of projects provides the means to obtain long-term effectiveness and duties, even at the personal level. So we urge you to consider the following paragraphs from a personal point of view, taking into account that the life of a person is not a rehearsal.

THE CHARACTERISTICS OF PROJECTS

Projects are a set of activities, usually complex, characterized by an objective (purpose) to achieve within a certain time, with specific technical results and within a given budget.

There are different types of projects. This term refers to situations very different amongst themselves by types of problems and type of business. Some projects may be of a long duration (years) or short/medium (months or even weeks). The word 'programme' designates long-term projects with a broad spectrum. These are sometimes divided into different projects that are more or less interdependent. The shorter projects are in some cases also referred to as tasks – we speak sometimes of a task force. A Six Sigma Design Measure Analyse Improve Control (DMAIC) project tends to be of this latter type.

The issues and tools for managing the programmes, projects and tasks are generally the same and are related to some basic and specific characteristics of such commitments. Organized activities in projects characterize the lives of almost all organizations and, increasingly, also of institutions, public and quasi-public. The projects are born at specific stages of the organization's life (launching a new product, organizational change, merge and acquisitions, etc.) and in specific areas (research and development, marketing, etc.) of any organization.

A possible breakdown of projects is as follows:

- Standard projects. Box solutions due to the composition of components, services and products on the price list or commercial solutions limited to the reconfiguration of already existing customizable systems;
- Customized project. Untraceable solutions due to the composition of components, services and products listed on the shopping list, based on the integration and constructive configuration and/or functional customized applications, services and products.

Modern theories of project management are applicable to a wide range of activities of an organization.

THE ELEMENTS OF A PROJECT

A project consists of the following components:

- An activity is a task or an event which has a temporal characteristic. In other words, it has start and end dates, and/or the need for a commitment of resources to produce defined and measurable results. An activity should have a single person in charge. Using the example of the development of a system, an activity might involve writing or testing an application, having a meeting or participating in a conference call;

• The resources are the elements necessary to execute the activities. Resources are either persons or materials, machines, or the economic aspects associated with the project;

• The allocation of resources to the activities determines the type and amount required to complete that specific activity successfully. This information is necessary to elaborate the budget commitments and costs per each individual activity, per resource. It is also necessary to check that the commitments remain at a level of available resources for that specific project; and

• Logical links between activities establish the relationship of dependency between different activities, so that each of them is planned without any unwanted or impossible overlaps. For example, before you can test an application it is necessary to write it and instal it.

A MODEL OF PROJECT MANAGEMENT

It seems important to analyse the problems associated with project management with an appropriate model. Critical aspects can be represented in three dimensions (3Es):

• efficacy – quality or performance
• efficiency – time
• economy – costs.

Some add an additional E to indicate ethics, underlining the fact that the results of the project and the management of the project itself should be compliant with laws and regulations.

The key moments in the life cycle of a project to Lean and Digitize are:

• define and measure
• analyse and process design
• architecture design
• build, test and deploy
• verify.

The basic components of management are:

• people
• mechanisms and operational procedures (processes)
• technologies and systems.

These three dimensions make up a cube (see Figure 5.2). Each element of the cube must be analysed in detail for each project. In each case, a particular approach must be defined. From that moment on, everything will be a question of consistency with the predefined approach.

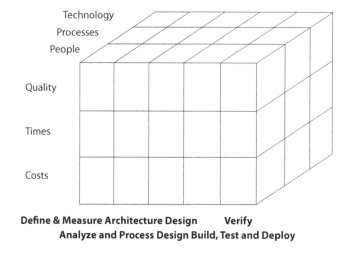

Define & Measure Architecture Design   Verify
Analyze and Process Design Build, Test and Deploy

Figure 5.2   A basic model for project management

The difficulties in project management relate to three parameters (see Figure 5.3):

- The innovation that the project introduces in the product or the process;
- The variety of resources (human, financial, equipment, etc.) associated with the development of the project;
- The relative abundance of resources or the size of the project.

Some experts recommend not undertaking projects in which more than one of these dimensions is high, because of the difficulties that may arise for their successful completion.

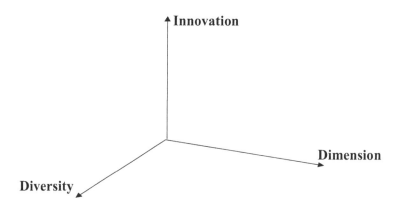

Figure 5.3   Difficulties related to the life cycle of a project

THE LIFE CYCLE OF THE PROJECT

The way in which Lean and Digitize distinguishes the development of the project is by using the following macro steps:

- (preliminary)
- define and measure
- analyse and process design
- architecture design
- build, test and deploy
- verify
- (replicate).

The different macro phases are separated by tollgates. There are different problems in project management according to the specific macro phase of its life. It entails different usage of resources and different needs and methods of control.

Uncertainty on the timing, cost and compliance of qualifying objectives proposed, which normally accompanies the initial stages of the project, is reduced as the project progresses. In the final macro stages, it is also more difficult and costly to recuperate on the delays that the reduced uncertainty makes more visible. The initial phases of the macro project are ultimately more critical because the decisions taken in these macro steps can greatly affect the progress of the project and its success.

The macro phase 'replicate' is indicated in brackets because although in many cases it is an important moment related to the result of a project, it may or may not be considered part of the initial project. It will become active only if the project is successful and it can be extended to other areas.

Examples of the kinds of questions to ask at each macro phase, from the point of view of programme and control, are in the case of define and measure:

- Have the project objectives been clearly identified?
- Is it a single project?
- Have the internal client and developer of the project been formally identified?
- Have the risks linked to the achievement been evaluated against the risks of not achieving the objectives of the project?

A contract exists between the client and the project leader on issues such as:

- time and resources
- responsibility
- date of no return
- risks.

Regarding resources, the relevant questions are:

- Have adequate resources been identified?
- Was an assessment made of essential and non-negotiable resources?
- Was the evaluation approved by the developer?

THE CYCLE OF PROGRAMANDCONTROL

People often speak of two separate topics: programme and control. In reality, it would be more correct to treat the two moments as connected. Some authors have suggested introducing a new word: programandcontrol. The motives are obvious:

- It makes no sense to programme, that is to set goals and do not check on their achievement;
- On the other hand, there is no sense to speak of control before you programme what must be done.

Below, we analyse in details the issues of programandcontrol. These can be summarized in the answers to questions (sometimes identified as the Five W + H):

- Are the objectives of the project well-defined (Why)?
- What is needed to achieve the objectives of the project (definition of activity)?
- Who is responsible to carry out each activity?
- When would the team need to carry out activities in order to meet the objectives and constraints of the project?
- Where is the project located (centralized–decentralized)?
- How to proceed with the project in terms of tools and techniques?

The cycle of programandcontrol requires the preparation of the organizational structure of the project at the lowest level of detail and accountability, with information on their time and costs. Each unit is assigned an account code that makes it possible to estimate costs and control the actual costs.

The next stage is the construction of the grid with the project activities. At this stage, one associates dates and durations (programandcontrol). The project team then estimates costs based on the resources available and builds the project budget. Approval of the plan and authorization at the start marks the beginning of the next cycle of project management: that of control.

THE MANAGEMENT OF SMALL PROJECTS

The method and concepts presented in this book are applicable to any project; no matter how large, medium or small it may be. Critical aspects related to the management of small projects are:

- Integrated management of projects;
- Organization of the methods and systems of programandcontrol.

A small project may not justify the presence of a project leader or of a full-time expert (called Belt according to the Six Sigma jargon). There are then several options:

- Do not have a project leader. Instead entrust the task of overseeing the project to a line manager;
- Monitoring of smaller projects by a Belt.

The possible solutions for the integration of projects are as follows (Nicoletti 1999: 239–278):

- rules and procedures
- planning
- back-up resources
- organization
- information
- lateral relations
- organization/point person of integration.

For details about these solutions, please refer to the specialized texts on project management (PMBOK, 2008) (Archibald, 2003).

Table 5.2 summarizes some characteristics and approaches that are valid for the management of small projects.

Table 5.2   The issues of small projects (modified from Archibald 2003)

	Large projects	Small projects
The role of the project leader	Is given to a leader who has functional responsibilities	Is kept by the line of organization with integrated support staff for planning and coordination. If possible multiple projects are assigned to each project leader
Belt	Is allocated to a master Black Belt (usually part-time) and to the dedicated Black Belts	If possible it is awarded to a Black Belt who follows more than one project
Project team	The size of the project team will vary depending on the situation. If fieldwork is foreseen, a full-time group is assigned	The work is always attributed to functions. During the fieldwork, a full-time group is assigned to each project
Integrated programandcontrol	Each project is planned and controlled on an integrated basis; conflicts between multiple projects are resolved at levels higher than that of project leader. The monitoring of deadlines for specific projects has the utmost importance. Monitoring the use of resources usually has minor importance	All projects must be planned and controlled on an integrated basis under a system of programandcontrol for multi-project operations. Conflicts are resolved by line management. The optimized use of available resources is of the utmost importance. Make sure all deadlines are compatible with the overall constraints on resources. Relies heavily on monitoring priorities

List of References

2008. *A Guide to the Project Management Body of Knowledge: (Pmbok Guide, 4e)*, Newtown Square: Project Management Institute.

Albino, V. 1995. Organizzazione dei progetti. In B.Nicoletti, ed., Manuale delle Imprese. Roma: Dei.

Archibald, R.D. 2003. *Managing High.Technology Programs and Projects*, 3rd edn. Hoboken: John Wiley & Sons.

Nicoletti, B. 1999. La gestione dei progetti. In C. Sirianni et al., eds, *Gestire l'Ambiente*, Milano: Giuffrè, 239–278.

Websites

http://www.laboratorioaltierospinelli.org/giornalonline/numero12/sommario%2012/03_Aspetti_della_progettazione.pdf

Implementing Lean and Digitize

6 Organizing for Lean and Digitize

Introduction

The methodology of Lean and Digitize relies heavily on people and their contribution to the improvement of processes. From this point of view, there are two very important aspects to take into consideration:

- the culture;
- the roles and responsibilities.

This chapter discusses these aspects and emphasizes their relevance.

The Culture of the Organization

When one examines the Lean and Digitize methodology and its management, it is interesting to ask what aspects are truly innovative and substantive. Every organization should adopt theories and models similar to those illustrated. The mere slavish application of these methods is not in itself sufficient to ensure a high level of quality, agility and productivity in the developed solutions. In the improvements in products and processes, it is always important to take into consideration, above all, the cultural dimension and the human organization.

A metaphor for this aspect is an iceberg (Nicoletti 1990). The visible part consists of all those concepts, standards, guidelines and controls common in organizations. Submerged below the surface, however, there is a predominant social base. This consists of the perceptions, attitudes, emotions and aspirations of the people working in the organization. This base is not visible on the outside. It is, however, indispensable; if it were not there the rest of the model would have a very limited effect. Just as in the case of an iceberg, it is impossible to think only of the surface section, assuming it will hold itself up without the larger part, which is immersed in the water.

For any organization and any person truly committed to improving processes, the interdependence and unity of these two dimensions – the structural and social – must be realized throughout the organizational system, not just in theory but in practice, not only at the level of the executives, but in the organization as a whole.

An integrated approach to process improvement has implications for personal and organizational commitment. It must begin in the planning phase and continue throughout the entire project. The degree of quality, agility and productivity the organization should aim to reach, and the actions needed, are not established – nor realistically could be – at the level of the board. This level would be too high. Such a process should ideally be something that helps the entire organization. Particularly important are the front-line operators (the so-called contact personnel). They must be involved at every step of the improvement project. This is the only way to avoid a discrepancy between the attitudes of the organization and those of the individuals with respect to the level of quality, productivity and agility aimed at by the organization. If they are not accepted these principles cannot, and are not, applied to the relationship with customers.

The implications of this approach are significant at the level of personnel management. There must be a willingness to talk openly about the successes and failures in connected to the Lean and Digitize project. There should be a constant two-way flow of information, opinions and experiences. This exchange has a profound influence on the quality, agility and productivity of the result of the project. On the other hand, the way the Lean and Digitize Team address a problem can create a sense of identification with the solution.

Under normal conditions, there is nothing particularly exceptional today in producing a product. Difficulties arise when conditions become unfavourable or abnormal. This means that quality consists of the fact that the service or product is delivered as promised, or better yet, going beyond the expectation of the customer (the so-called 'quality surprise') [Nicoletti 1987], measured by the VoC). This means that staff should be prepared, for example, to extend its service hours. For them to show that availability, management must show an equal willingness to manage their staff well. As an example in this direction, management should be ready for instance to help beyond contractual obligations when personnel have difficulties and personal problems. This is true especially in ensuring that the organization recognizes outstanding performance. The aforementioned example will need to be part of the organization's reward system. Rewards are not necessarily linked with pay. They might be of other types too. Other examples of rewards are helping someone's career in the organization or simply expressing a 'thank you' given by the organization to its employees.

To introduce programs of Lean and Digitize, it is also necessary to identify the needs of the internal customers. To that end, it is important to perform some interviews with a sample of internal customers. In this way one can gather information on the needs of the process, and sometimes on the needs of the product. It is necessary to weight the needs of internal customers with the current performance of the institution. This is useful to identify indicators of process and quality that enable the organization to control the process. This control is possible through:

- The production of visuals available to be seen in each office; or
- Initial display screens on the intranet with status or trends of performance indicators of the process under improvement.

One cannot conclude this section on culture without mentioning an increasing difficulty in organizations. More and more organizations are using virtual project teams. They are located not only in different locations but in different organizations and other countries. In this situation, in the project there is not only one organization or culture of the country where the organization is located – these are multicultural project Teams. The management of these virtual teams is not simple, and we refer the reader to specialized texts to learn more about this topic.

Roles and Responsibilities

Lean and Digitize projects involve many people inside the organization. Some of them have a specific role and a series of tasks to carry out at preset times. In fact, the Lean and Digitize method is very structured and requires the involvement of all of the organization structure. The initiative must start from the top of the organizational pyramid. It is important to have the support of the management, who have the power to act and to impose the substantial changes required for achieving the improvement objectives of product/service/process quality.

The important roles within a Lean and Digitize project are:

- The Committee;
- The champion;
- The project leader;
- Belts: the Master Black Belt, the Black Belt, the Green Belt, the Yellow Belt and the White Belt;
- The process owner;
- The project management office; and
- The project members.

The project leader, the project management office, the functional specialists and the interface staff are the project team.

THE COMMITTEE

The Committee assesses projects and ensures they are in line with the business objectives. A member of the senior management of the organization, be it the general manager or departmental heads, should chair the Lean and Digitize Committee. The Committee is composed of members of the board of directors, the area and process leaders and the champion. It is a multidisciplinary group of business leaders coming from areas such as marketing, engineering, sales, finance, human resources, ICT, organizational, operations and business development.

The committee has the task to:

- Support the Lean and Digitize project;
- Remove possible obstacles;
- Define the implementation strategies, the roles and the structure of the project;
- Prioritize; and
- Allocate the resources.

It is the long-term support infrastructure.

THE CHAMPION

The champion is a role connecting the support infrastructure – the Lean and Digitize Committee – with the operational structure, the project team. The champion is responsible for the economic success of the project and has the task of supervising various activities, acting as a mentor, although not taking part in the operational phases.

> *The Champion's role is strictly relevant to the selection of the projects and the constant review of the DMAIC project phases … The Champion's task, after selecting the projects, is to assign them to a Green or Black Belt and to participate in the definition of teamwork. Tartari 2005: 21–22*

Some of the most important characteristics of the champion are:

- They are generally a member of the senior management;
- They are the link between the Committee and the project team;
- They are responsible for the success of the project before the organization;
- They have the role of mentor; and
- Coordinate the identification, selection, definition and attribution of priority for a project;
- They choose the Black Belt and the Green Belt and assign them projects and activities;
- Then monitor the results.

THE PROCESS OWNER

The process owner works with the champion in the identification of the potential projects and is the holder of the solution provided by the Lean and Digitize Team. Their main task is to use the solution. They should manage the cultural change that must accompany the modifications brought to the process.

BELTS: MASTER BLACK, BLACK, GREEN AND WHITE/YELLOW BELT

The Belt is a person, or a group of people in the organizational structure, that analyse the data and the solutions of problems. This term derives from the same terminology that applies to the sport judo. Another way to describe these persons is as a facilitator.

The Belts are the professional roles that actively participate in the operational phase of the Lean and Digitize projects. They must be knowledgeable of the process to be improved, and the specific techniques of the DMAIC or DMADV approaches. They must be capable of collaborating, communicating, working in a team and managing and conducting meetings.

The main activities are to:

- Participate in the project choice;
- Help in managing the team;
- Plan the project;
- Coordinate the DMAIC or DMADV phases;
- Define and train on the technical tools to be used; and
- Manage the communication.

The role of the Belt resembles that of a trainer or facilitator, or external social consultant, which in the past was associated with:

- Training the staff that takes part in the improvement initiative;
- Providing the team with the necessary methodological support in order to ensure that the team applies the Lean and Digitize method and tools correctly.

External consultants would initially assist the Belts. They would start to work independently once they obtain their self-sufficiency. At a still later stage, they would manage the training of new Belts.

The assignment of the Belts to a specific project should be oriented to those already known for their attitude, capacity and professionalism. All mature Belts should be qualified to train the employees that participate in the improvement group. In the Lean and Digitize organization, there are various levels of Belts which differ in experience and capacity.

- Master Black Belts have the task of training the other Belts and supporting the more challenging and strategic projects from the point of view of their economic return and impacts;
- Black Belts dedicate 100 per cent of their time to supporting Lean and Digitize projects and training other staff;
- Green Belts dedicate a large amount of their time (about 50–60 per cent) to Lean and Digitize projects. They may also act as the person supporting projects that are not particularly complex. They can also be team members in projects supported by the Master and the Black Belt;
- White and Yellow Belts form part of the group as team members. They carry out less important tasks. Their participation also serves for their direct training in their area (learning by doing).

THE PROJECT LEADER

The project leader is the most important role for the project's success. The management of the Lean and Digitize project is usually a complex activity, not only because of the objectives to be reached but also because of time limits, quality objectives and resource availability. The operative decision must ensure the following conditions:

- Each project must have only one point for integration and responsibility: the person in charge of the project;
- Each team should plan and control the project on an integrated basis, performing a cross-section and including all the contributions of the various functional areas of the organization, together with the phases of its life cycle.

Once the project has been identified and a project leader has been assigned, the decisions are at what level and in which area they should be placed in the organization and how to structure the project.

The project leader must have a position that allows establishing a dialogue at the same level with the people in charge of the various functional areas. They should report to high levels in the organization either of the entity in which the project is carried out or higher in case of a project that relates to the entire organization.

Project leaders have different tasks according to the macro-organizational solutions adopted. In a weak project structure, the project leaders do not have hierarchical responsibility over the resources. They carry out activities of coordination, planning and control of the resources, acting on behalf of senior management, who are ultimately responsible for the improvement, costs and quality of the project.

In a project structure the project leader has, for the duration of the project, the authority of and the responsibility for the assigned resources. The Lean and Digitize Committee must perform the role of assistant, coordinator and global controller. In this way, there is less ambiguity and project control problems, but there may be some inefficiency, for example due to the duplication of functional resources on various projects.

The project leader is also required to manage the relationship with the Committee, the champion and the process owner. They should negotiate the conflicts that may arise amongst the various people engaged in the process. The objective should be to avoid negative consequences over the organization and the project. In a matrix structure, the demand for specializations and coordination of functions and projects would have equal weights.

The functional managers must trace, manage and develop the functional resources and make them available for the different projects as and when needed. The project leaders must employ the resources available, coordinate them, programme and control the project activities.

Clearly, there are two lines of authority:

- One based on the resources and the functions; and
- The other based on the objectives of the Lean and Digitize projects.

A strong coordination at the Committee level should ensure the balance between the two lines.

In a matrix organization, the project leader also tends to have the features of a negotiator with the various net components.

THE PROJECT LEADER'S ROLE

The project leader has different names according to specific organizations. Titles include project head, project leader, programme manager, team leader, and so on and so forth. These names have slightly different meanings.

The profiles of a project leader and a technician are substantially different. Table 6.1 shows some of these differences.

Table 6.1   Differences between the profiles of a technician and a project leader

The technician	The project leader
Looks for the best solution from the technical point of view	Looks for the factual/sellable solution
Points towards precision	Points towards achievement
Works with objects (components, etc.)	Works with people
Focuses on procedures	Focuses on results
Works with immutable laws	Works with rules linked to specific situations
Seeks specialization to improve	Seeks de-specialization to improve
Is successful on their own	Is successful through others, as well as on their own

The main responsibilities of the project leader are:

- Support in defining the objectives;
- Plan and control the project ('planner');
- Agree on the modes of implementation with the various functional services (lines) for the achievement of the work package according to the specifications, time and the expected costs;
- Coordinate all the project resources – people, money, infrastructures, etc.;
- Monitor the progress of the project in relation to the objectives by measuring the results with respect to the technical specifications, the costs and the time, drawing on the resources made available to the organization;
- Referring on the progress and the difficulty of the project;
- Duly inform the Committee each time that the project seems not to reach the technical objectives, the budgeted costs and the planned timeline;
- Recommend the project termination if it is not possible to reach the objectives within the contractual obligations.

The fundamental role of a project leader is to work as an interface amongst the so-called four C's:

- customers
- collaborators
- chiefs
- colleagues.

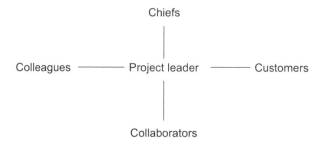

Regarding these interfaces, the project leader tends to have the following main roles:

Interface	The main role
Customers	Communication
Collaborators	Collaboration
Chiefs	Conduct
Colleagues	Coordination

Each of these relations has specific characteristics:

Interface	Characteristic
Customers	Critic
Collaborators	Continuous
Chiefs	Conspicuous
Colleagues	Complex

The project leader must have the behavioural ability (soft skill):

- To be the contact point with the customer, the Committee, functional management in the project specific environment (interfaces);
- To assess the contributions of the single resources (continuity, initiative and responsibility) and notify the line managers of them.

In a matrix structure, the resources assigned to the functional guide of the project frequently report to the technical resources line managers. They have the following roles:

- To plan the demand on resources in the long/medium term and the subsequent actions. Have the resources available and take action to start training;
- To make the decisions about allocating resources amongst the various projects, according to priorities, the sector leaders and the interested project leaders;

- To plan and control the correct use of the resources assigned temporarily to the projects and their professional growth;
- To follow, from the management point of view, the assigned resources for all the operations of common administration;
- To suggest reward/punishment actions;
- To assign directly to collaborators less important or complex activities that do not require a specific project from the organizational point of view;
- To set goals (according to department strategies) for the resources, verify the scope, contribute to an assessment based on results and point out the areas of improvement.

The project leader should be able to handle various tasks:

- technical
- managerial
- interpersonal.

Table 6.2 shows the competences of the project leader for each particular aspect.

Table 6.2   The competences of the project leader

Technical	Managerial	Interpersonal
Techno-economic extraction	Contract administration	Negotiator
Experience in specialized areas	Good understanding of programming and control tools	Conflict manager
Understanding of the basics to deal with specialists	Experience in the use of coordination mechanisms	Leadership expert
	Confidence with the IT system	Creator of team spirit

In fact, it is impossible to find a project leader that is great in all these skills! It is best to choose a project leader according to the characteristics of the project. In order to understand the exact characteristics of a project leader it is useful to have the 'model of project difficulty' as a reference guide. According to this model, the difficulty linked to the management of a project depends on three parameters:

- The degree of innovation of the project;
- The diversity of resources connected with the development of the project;
- The dimension of the project;

Some researchers think it is inappropriate to undertake a project that has a large element of more than one of these dimensions large. In such a situation, it is likely that the project will fail, anticipating the difficulty of finding a project leader skilled in all three of these aspects.

Organizations usually find that the best choice of a project leader depends on the specific characteristics of the project. This would mean that:

- In the case of a project with a high degree of innovation, the chosen project leader should be strong in technical aspects;
- In the case of a project with the large dimension, the project leader should have strong ability as a manager;
- In the case of a project with a large diversity in its characteristics, the best project leader would be someone who is skilful in personal relations.

Even if these three elements seem very different, they are equally important in the success of a project.

Project characteristics	Management skills
Innovation	Technical
Dimensions	Managerial
Diversity	Relationships

So far we have talked about the image of the project leader as responsible for the achievement of the desired results. This does not mean that the other people involved in the project are less important: each of them has a very important role in every project. In particular, it is necessary to focus on customers and collaborators:

- Regarding customers, their assistance in 'setting the correct objectives for the project' is very important;
- Regarding collaborators, their contribution in terms of knowledge is very important, in their own area of competence.

THE PROJECT MANAGEMENT OFFICE

Wikipedia defines the Project Management Office (PMO) in the following way. In a business or professional enterprise, it is the department or group that defines and maintains the standards of process, generally related to project management, within the organization. The PMO strives to standardize and introduce economies of repetition in the execution of projects. The PMO is the source of documentation, guidance and metrics on the practice of project management and execution. In some organizations, this is known as the Programme Management Office (sometimes abbreviated to PgMO to differentiate); the subtle difference is that programme management relates to governing the management of several related projects.

Traditional PMOs base project management principles on industry-standard methodologies. Increasingly influential industry certification programs such as ISO9000 and the Malcolm Baldrige National Quality Award (MBNQA) as well as government regulatory requirements such as Sarbanes–Oxley have propelled organizations to standardize processes. Organizations around the globe are defining, borrowing and collecting best practices in process and project management and are increasingly assigning the PMO to exert overall influence and evolution of thought to continual organizational improvement.

Ninety per cent of projects do not meet time/cost/quality targets. Only 9 per cent of large, 16 per cent of medium and 28 per cent of small company projects were completed on time, within budget and delivered measurable business and stakeholder benefits (Johnson, 1995). There are many reasons for such failures. As a KPMG survey of 252 organizations indicated, technology is not the most critical factor. Inadequate project management implementation constitutes 32 per cent of project failures, lack of communication constitutes 20 per cent and unfamiliarity with scope and complexity constitutes 17 per cent. Accordingly 69 per cent of project failures are due to lack of and/ or improper implementation of project management methodologies.

Establishing a PMO group is not a short-term strategy to lower costs (Santosus, 2003). Surveys with companies indicate that the longer they have an operating PMO group the better the results achieved to accomplish project goals (which might lead to lowering costs).

PMOs may take other functions beyond standards and methodology, and participate in strategic project management either as facilitator or actively as owner of the portfolio management process. Tasks may include monitoring and reporting on active projects (following up the project until completion), and reporting progress to senior management for strategic decisions on what projects to continue or cancel.

A PMO can be one of three types from an organizational exposure perspective: enterprise PMO, organizational (departmental) PMO, or special-purpose PMO.

The responsibilities of the project management office include:

* Working as a focus point of information for internal control and update of the Committee, the champion and the process owner;
* Controlling the time, cost and quality in the project;
* Ensuring that each required job is documented and assigned to the key staff;
* Ensuring that each job is authorized and agrees with the contract specifications.

The main responsibility of the project leader and the project management office is to integrate the work of various functional areas of the organization. Coordinating, planning and controlling are a continuous full-time function and cannot lie outside the project management office in a large project.

THE PROJECT TEAM

The project team, also called in some cases the 'progress group', are the members of the project contributing to the improvement project activities.

The Lean and Digitize Committee assigns each team to work on the solution to a problem. This could involve only one or more areas in the organization: an example is the setting up of a customer care unit. In this workshop, the improvement group needs to optimize the information supplied to the clients, mainly in situations of non-quality.

The project team is comprised of the project leader, the project management office, the functional specialists and the staff who interface with the rest of the organization. In general, the functional specialists contribute to the project in specific phases. Their effort varies according to whether they are full- or part-time members of the project.

A typical size of a Lean and Digitize project is around 10 members. Sometimes the project team exceeds that number. The members could work either full- or part-time in the project. In case of projects of large dimensions, however, it is almost indispensable to have full-time assignment of functional experts coming from any main areas of the organization.

The project team must always be interfunctional. Representation of all the functions related to the process under examination is essential.

The team has a time assigned to find a solution to the problem: in general from three to six months. For very complex problems and for very simple problems the time allocated could be quite different. Meetings of the project team should take place during business hours. The group participants learn the methodology of data analysis and of problem solutions during the training courses.

Belts assist in the team activities. The team is only responsible for the project. Belts are only responsible for the correct application of the Lean and Digitize method and the right selection of the tools to use.

The Lean and Digitize Team, as a whole, is an operational group that:

- Identifies the solution;
- Submits it to the Lean and Digitize Committee, which must approve it;
- If the solution is approved, then it is developed;
- The same team members supervise the implementation of the solution.

In general, to test the improvement intervention, it is necessary to have a pilot. A successful pilot would give the go ahead to roll out the solution to all interested areas.

THE COMPOSITION OF A PROJECT TEAM AT THE INTESA SANPAOLO BANK (BORTOLOTTI 2007–2008)

The programme 'Lean banking and projection of a new operating model' has involved all the main structures of the Intesa Sanpaolo bank.

The operational services management was responsible for the design and realization of the operating model and improvements and set up various working groups in order to align the operative process.

Teams have been composed selecting the most suitable people for the various functions, in order to e better managthe change, with all the competences and knowledge available.

The background of the team members, competence areas and roles/tasks was:

- Domestic banking (branches in different areas of italy, forming part of the retail and commercial bank staff and organization network): definition of the requirement of intervention and service degrees, commercial and initiative implementation;
- Governance of the resource (ICT, organizations, acquisitions): implementation of competence intervention;

- Credit competence centre: support for competence;
- Administration: support for competence and the legal aspects;
- Credit risk centre: support for risk management.

The personnel management organization were responsible for the part of the project related to the general coordination of the activities and the management of the conversion of the resources made available by the improvement process. They formed several teams with the scope of managing the 'machine for reconverting the now available productivity'.

The background of the team participants, competence areas and roles/tasks was:

- Domestic banking: definition of the productive capacity requirements;
- Value government: planning and control of the budget alignment with regard to the available productive capacity;
- Governance of resources: recruiting, validation, training and reallocation of resources.

The different groups interface continually, interchanging ideas, plans and results.

Structure and Roles

THE STRUCTURE

It is appropriate that a strategy oriented towards Lean and Digitize become operational with a new structure in order to avoid conflicting messages

In order to make everybody responsible for quality, it is not advisable to create a specific quality function, but rather a light structure mainly in charge of supporting the initiative of the various workshops and solving the controversies that may arise.

The introduction of the Lean and Digitize method should be gradual. Initially, it must look after a limited number of operative actions. It is possible to subdivide it into the typical phases of a Six Sigma project (Alitalia 1992):

- The first phase is necessarily of experimentation, information and training for those who must work with the new technology. The units involved form the Lean and Digitize project team, with the aim of developing improvement activities within an established time.
- In the second phase of the project, a growing number of people should participate in the improvement team for the divisional and interdivisional project implementation, all of which is possible thanks to the participation of Belts. In this phase, the aim is that the organization works not only in a series of parallel functions (staff, management control, commercial, assistance and other departments) but as a set of processes oriented towards a common result. Each organizational function, which develops a precise role, has links to another department in the production chain (what Joseph Juran called the quality 'spiral' – Juran 2005). In this, each department/function is, at the same time, supplier/customer of the former and the latter (including, of course, the management);
- Eventually, in the last phase, they should work to systematize the utilization of all the acquired methodologies. At the functional level, each operative unit must

automatically achieve their own objectives coherently with guidelines issued by the corporate offices. The name of this part of the project is policy deployment (Galgano 1991). This term implies the process of communication and diffusion of the management strategies in all sectors of the organization. It is a cascade process. The people that receive the strategies of the senior level need to translate them into simpler terms, and in concrete actions, for the use of their own collaborators. These, in turn, translate them in the lower level. In this way, it is possible to express the strategies in detail to support concrete actions.

THE RESOURCES

In a Lean and Digitize project in any organization, the resources, and in particular, human resources, are of prime importance for the improvement of quality, agility and productivity (Berthold 1991).

TRAINING

The basic principle of the Lean and Digitize method is that there should be no need to control process improvement once introduced: they should be correct the first time they are issued. If this is true, people become the most important element in producing with appropriate quality. Hence, there is a need to increase the human capital of the organization. This requires appropriate training of the resources working for the improvement of processes. These actions must not be casual or occasional, but must be the object of careful planning, and they must not limit themselves to scorecards or to the employees of the quality department. Training should cover all the entities that need to improve. For training in Lean and Digitize, it is appropriate to perform a detailed analysis of the training needs at different levels.

Organizing training activities requires quite a lot of attention to practical problems and, in particular, care in choosing the instructor and the teaching material.

Training activities are expensive: therefore it is appropriate to choose, during and a posteriori, a method for controlling and assessing the results even though such actions are not easy or immediate.

The seminars on Lean and Digitize are an important part of the improvement programme (Pellicelli 1987: 1–466). They aim at developing the abilities and attitudes of people in the projects. They must aim especially at developing the ability to work as teams and at encouraging the search of solutions and decision-making without conflicts.

The recurring theme in ideas, objectives and techniques used in the seminar is that the organization desires to develop a better attitude and capacity for communication. For example, Scandinavia Airline System (SAS) trained a group of instructors who were supposed transfer their knowledge and experience to other collaborators (Carlzon 1987). It was a two-day seminar, and the staff participated in groups of 50; in total about 6,000 collaborators of SAS attended this seminar.

The training must start at the beginning of a Lean and Digitize Project, because it plays a very important role in the development of the project. The training plan considers different levels (Nicoletti 1987: 229), and the objective is to provide information in the organization about the logic of the project, the progress and future activities. This is essential for spreading the quality culture, which in an organization pointing towards quality, agility and productivity, must permeate all of the organization. This action is normally on two levels:

- An activity involving the managers. This aims at a self-diagnosis of the possible improvements of the process;
- Inside every sector of the organization, a series of meetings should take place in order to present the basic principles of the project and the future programmes.

The training should include information regarding the project and the Lean and Digitize method. It should also include how to use the tools in a Lean and Digitize project.

External training consultants should manage at the beginning these activities. Later on, internal trainers to the organization, known as Belts, should act as trainers. In this way, it is possible:

- To reduce the high cost of consultant trainers;
- To manage the whole project completely inside the organization, with the extra benefit of reducing the costs, but above all of gaining credibility for those who are involved in the project.

At the start of the project, the external trainers aim not only at instructing the staff about the Lean and Digitize tools, but also at training the Belts in the method. The training course for the Belts consists of various phases:

- In a first phase, the Belt must take part in a training course from three to five days;
- In a second phase, they should be part of an improvement team;
- Many go straight to the third phase. In this phase, the training course takes place during three days and provides:
  - A first day on classroom management methodology; presentations, use of slides, etc.;
  - Then a part of the course is on the presentation of instruments to experiment immediately in the field.

The training on the Lean and Digitize method should be gradual. Only those who must personally apply the method receive training. For instance, in an initial period when an improvement group deals with the improvement project, the content of the training focuses on the tools for data analyses and problem solutions.

Team members who do need to apply the tools directly should not be part of the training classes, saving in costs and time. This also implies that the training for Belts should be gradual, first regarding the tools for the analysis of the problems, and secondly the other tools for implementation. This does not allow the external consultant to quit the project before the initial phase: the consultant must intervene to train internal instructors and the managers of the organization about the Lean and Digitize method frequently used in the organization.

A frequent suggestion is that the Belts should provide the participants' training in an improvement group. The typical training course specifies that each participant of the improvement group should attend from three to five days. The structure of the course is:

- Half a day is for the basic elements of the Lean and Digitize culture: the meaning of quality and lean thinking, the new priorities for making decisions, the improvement process, etc.;
- The other days are for teaching use of tools for data analysis and problem solutions.

An example of specific training for the team is the training on daily routine work (DRW). Belts or external instructors could provide training on DRW. The training course would last three days, with an introductory morning on the basics of Lean and Digitize.

External instructors would provide training related to the Cause and Effect Diagram with Addition of Cards (CEDAC) system (Nicoletti 1987) exclusively to CEDAC leaders. The training programme requires two days. In turn, facilitators of CEDAC develop the sensibilization activities in the unit where the tools are applied.

For the other tools to be used (quality function deployment, policy deployment, and process management), the training is also delivered by external consultants. Very few groups of team members would use these tools. Training of Belts takes place only when a large number of people use the tools.

The external consultants should provide documentation to support the organization in the use of Lean and Digitize tools. Both internal instructors and staff would use the manuals.

Manuals usually consist of two parts:

- The first part, the same as with all manuals, should be dedicated to the basic concept of Lean and Digitize;
- The second part should be specific to the Lean and Digitize method: a basic course of problem analysis and solving, the policy deployment, the CEDAC diagram and the DRW (Nicoletti 1987).

MOTIVATION

All of those involved in Lean and Digitize projects agree that their experiences have been positive. They emphasize the positive results achieved in the improvement groups (in terms of quality, times and costs), in the management of processes, and in other methods (Bisignani 1992).

The reasons why there have been difficulties in some cases are manifold. The project development was not monolithic, that is to say senior management did not manage the project. In a Lean and Digitize project based on decentralization, the accountability and participation of all people requires the commitment of everybody.

The first step must be the self-diagnosis by those in charge of the different areas of the organization, in order to:

- identify the problems
- set the objectives and
- set the plans for improvement.

Self-diagnosis is very important because the analysis of the problems of the organization and thus the selection of the objectives and the initiatives is the key element of the project. In the majority of the organizations, the objectives selected have been interesting both for the people and with regard to the competitive advantages of the organization. They were challenging objectives. In other areas (about 30 per cent), they do not get it right and delineate unexciting objectives, mostly intended for the short term. In these cases, the teams did not obtain substantial improvements for the organization and no breakthrough took place, which is precisely the objective of a Lean and Digitize project.

In some areas, the potential of Lean and Digitize is at the maximum. This allows not only excellent results in the short term (decrease of some costs) but also strategic results for process improvement that are fundamental in order to adjust to the changing international scenario.

In the operational units with disappointing results, people did not catch the potential of process improvement projects, or at least they did not exploit it. People scarcely participated, because those in charge were themselves not comfortable in introducing changes.

The cultural change should involve the entire organization: this is crucial for the success of a Lean and Digitize project. This change is not easy. Many organizations tend to resist changing. This is what happens in some organizations are too tied to the past. It causes a slowdown in the project: it is not convenient to take a poorly coordinated path towards quality, agility and productivity. For this reason, in some organizations it is appropriate to slow down the implementation of Lean and Digitize projects in order to overcome the contradiction and homogenized culture inside the organization. This is fundamental in this kind of project. This will not cause adverse opinions on the project: Lean and Digitize and the cultural change require time to complete.

The key factor in the Lean and Digitize method is to be a catalyst to turn the potential aptitudes and competences acquired by training into visible quality (Fontana 1989).

To listen to the radio programme that you want, you need to tune to the right frequency. If you do not tune, you may have the most sophisticated set of equipment, but it will be useless. The same applies to people. Ultimately, a Lean and Digitize project is an issue of 'tuning'. In other words, it is difficult to motivate people into spontaneously generating process improvements, day by day. On the other hand, it is necessary to create an environment in which collaborators are ready to offer the best of them, and in which a real sense of dedication and commitment is cultivated. This is motivation.

Is a situation of limited resources compatible with process improvement? The connection is indirect. The scenario of today is much more challenging: it is necessary to fight stagnation and recession in many sectors. Increasing margins has become necessary for everybody, everywhere, every time. This fact has led to many organizations striving to hold in costs by rationalizing e.g. upstream procedures: making the process in every sector flow, while increasing the use of automation and ICT networks to process information more efficiently.

List of References

Alitalia 1992. *La qualità totale*. Doc. Alitalia.

Berthold, G. 1991. *Qualità totale e risorse umane. Direzione del personale*. Nov–Dec.

Bisignani, G. 1992. L'industria europea del trasporto aereo. *The Quality*, 3–4, April–July.

Bortolotti, T. Anno Accademico 2007–2008. *Un modello integrato lean six sigma per il miglioramento dei processi*. Thesis at the Università di Udine.

Carlzon, J. 1987. *Moments of Truth*. Cambridge: Ballinger Publishing Co.

Fontana, F. 1989. *Lo sviluppo del personale*. Torino: Giappichelli.

Galgano, A. 1991. *La qualità totale*. Milano: Il Sole 24 Ore.

Johnson, J. 1995. *Chaos Report*. Standish Group. Available from http://www1.standishgroup.com/sample_research/chaos_1994_1.php.

Juran, J M. 2005. *Quality, and a Century of Improvement La qualità nella storia. Dalle civiltà antiche al Total Quality Management*. Milwaukee: ASQ PressTorino: Sperling & Kupfer.

Nicoletti, B. 1987. *La gestione della qualità*. Milano: Franco Angeli.

Nicoletti, B. 1990. *Swissair in Casi di Organizzazione* edited by F. Fontana, M. Lacchini and B. Nicoletti. Torino: Giappichelli.

Pellicelli, G. 1987. *Casi di management*. Milano: EtasLibri.

Santosus, M. 2003. *Why You Need a Project Management Office (PMO)*, CIO.com, July.

Tartari, R. 2005. *Sei Sigma +, La fabbrica delle idee, Guida al recupero della redditività e della competitività con il metodo Six Sigma Plus. Ampi esempi applicativi in Excel®*. Milano: Franco Angeli.

7 *Project Communication*

Introduction

Communication is one of the most important aspects in any activity involving people. It becomes particularly relevant when it comes to Lean and Digitize projects because they act on processes and potentially on different departments of the organization. Ideally, a Lean and Digitize project should have a brand, bearing in mind that any important project of the organization could have a 'story' associated with this brand (Ray, 2009).

The programmes of quality and lean improvement require a particular support in order to pass from the programme itself to action. Marketing of the new initiative should have a strong emphasis, both inside and outside.

After a brief reference to outside communications, this chapter will focus on communication. Outside communication is also important but does not apply to the Lean and Digitize project teams; marketing or commercial areas are in charge of it.

External Communication

It is also important to communicate changes for improving processes outside the organization. The market should know about the decision of the organization to further improve quality and leanness. This communication may be implicit in actual changes, but it must also occur through the channels for external communication. These can be the traditional communication channels, such as press releases, presentations, events and so on, or modern channels, such as the Internet, social networks, etc.

The external communication is necessary also to justify the collection of VoC – the Voice of the Customer. It is also important as a means of promotion on the market, to communicate the efforts to improve.

Communication happens either through direct advertising or else through promotion. The latter must be consistent with the image that the organization is endeavouring to convey to the market. The organization should also plan and hold, when appropriate, events and publications for customers or prospects. They must show the changes already implemented, the improvement actions and the plans for the future.

Internal Communication

A relevant task is to communicate the new strategy of Lean and Digitize to everybody in the organization. Every employee should participate by making suggestions to improve the level and the efficiency of the organization. Regular and frequent reports addressed to all employees should keep them informed about:

- Which are the objectives of the initiative;
- What is happening with the project;
- Which results have been accomplished and will be celebrated; and
- In which areas everyone's contribution is expected.

The informative action when introducing a Lean and Digitize project should be coordinated, during the realization of the project itself, with a number of initiatives and events intended to keep people informed about project developments and accomplishments. These initiatives could be meetings involving executives, managers and officials held in each area, at the beginning and the end of each year.

The operational base should not be kept informed about the project developments through this kind of initiative, for these reasons:

- The annual periodicity does not fit the project;
- Large organizations have many people working for them: to inform the structure through meetings with 50 employees at a time would take years;
- Difficulties due to having people working in different locations.

The project team should use all the communication media of the organization in order to keep people informed about the results once achieved. This tool reaches all the people, including the operational bases. Written communication is the only tool to keep all people informed, so it is important to leverage and spread it as much as possible.

The project team should publish in the internal institutional magazines or intranet articles and news about the experience gained in the project and the results achieved. In every sector, the team should define an internal personalized communication plan and support it with specific tools.

Illustrated communication tools are typical of one-way communication. The large number of people scattered in different locations within the organization might make it difficult to implement an interactive way of communication in which people have the opportunity to not only get information but also provide information. There are now, and there will be in the future, more new and interesting tools that allow this kind of interactivity and collaboration (Nicoletti 2009). Improvement teams, on the other hand, should guarantee the interfunctional communication essential to provide collaboration and communication.

Aleksandr I. Solženicyn (1974) wrote: 'Quality is the soul of the work.' Promoting process quality reinforces people's sense of belonging to the organization.

INFORMING THE EMPLOYEES' REPRESENTATIVES

Is it appropriate to inform/include the employees' representatives in a Lean and Digitize project? It would seem appropriate to inform the employees' representatives, but not include them directly, because their functions are different from those of the project. The organization should provide formal information to employees' representatives at the very beginning of a Lean and Digitize project (Various Authors 1991, 1992). For this purpose, it is appropriate to organize informational meetings with the participation of all the representatives. At these meetings, the organization should provide information about the project, as well the impact, the involvement and participation of the people.

The consensus of the representatives can be hostile or supportive – full or partial. A mature representation tends to agree that quality and leanness can be an opportunity to benefit both the organization and its personnel. People have a key role in the quality and leanness improvement programme.

The participation of the representatives in a Lean and Digitize project is limited to the following aspect exclusively: representatives should not always be involved but informed about the strategic decisions of the organization (Tixier, 1990). This information must also cover whatever is necessary to convey a full understanding of the requirements of the socio-economic scenario and the economics and management compatibilities related to the context.

As regards relations with people, it is also advisable to introduce, contractually, some aspects connected with the quality, the leanness and the digitization of the processes (Bernini, 1992). For instance, it could be appropriate to adhere to the principle of conditioning the payment of productivity bonuses to the contribution of the labour factor (in terms of quantity or quality of the services provided) and the situation of the economic productive cycle of the organization (Parrotto, 1992). These decisions aim at encouraging the participation of personnel in the actions for improvement. This is an important contribution because quality, leanness and digitization are key factors that determine the difference when it comes to the customers' choosing the products and services of the organization (Armaroli, 1992).

The organization must assert the full autonomy of decisions relative to strategic management. The representatives can participate in some initiatives regarding process improvement and quality, but not the strategic decisions regarding the project. In general, any decision of the organization is a responsibility of the management team. This is the situation unless, as is true in some countries, there is participation of the labour unions or the labour representatives in the organization's board. In this situation, the personnel representatives have the levers to participate in this kind of decisions.

This does not mean that the representatives of the employees are not interested in the Lean and Digitize projects, albeit with different motivations. The main reason is the attention and interest that labour unions have ion the key issues of a modern business strategy. This interest is not academic and does not aim at replacing the managers in charge. The labour union is convinced that they cannot be merely a functional agent of the redistribution of wealth, thus being relegated to marginal and secondary roles regarding the deep change processes in progress and becoming in this way unable to defend, but only partially, people's interests and expectations.

Therefore, as quality and slenderness have proven to be the ineluctable dimensions of an organization which intends to be competitive in the market, the representatives can not and do not want to neglect the market or the organization demands. However, they have a critical eye with regard to the problems introduced by the quality, leanness and digitization. They do not consider that they have one single and precise solution, but that there are different interests and projects in the organization which have to be pondered, and, whenever possible, agreed.

An example of the employees' representatives reaction regarding a Lean and Digitize Project and a new operational model at the Intesa Sanpaolo Bank (Segreterie di coordinamento di credito 2006)

THE LEAN BANK PROGRAM

At the meeting with the Work Organization Commissions of Sanpaolo Imi and Sanpaolo Banco di Napoli, the company illustrated the project 'Lean Bank' to the unions in the following way.

The three-year plan 2006–2008 points out the increase of benefits as the main factor of team growth (+8.5 per cent on an annual basis): in order to achieve the goal, some new assumptions have been made and the time devoted to the commercial activity has been increased, thanks to the decrease of administrative activities.

The Plan foresees that in three years, the need of 2,600 resources (1,100 for covering the turnover and 1,500 to increase the front office) will be covered by acquiring 1,200 employees and reconverting 1,400 administrative activities. These 1,400 resources will be regained, as well as an almost equivalent amount of time/labour over more employees, through the 'Lean Bank' project.

The project consists in leaning and digitizing the operational processes and improving the quality of the commercial processes, with integrated interventions on digitizing procedures, process automation, branch layout, modifications in the labour organization, selective pricing policies, etc., by means of different workshops (that is to say efficiency improvement-specific projects) with the overall objective of regaining 3,000 FTE (full-time equivalent): this amount of time/labour should then turn into 1,400 resources to be converted and in the recovery of time/labour over more employees equivalent to approximately 1,600 FTE, as above.

The workshops are developed with the usual scheme of design, experimentation in pilot branches, procedure modification and roll out (i.e. spreading the new process in the whole network). We are currently in the phase of operational design and of experimentation in the pilot branches of most of the planned workshops.

The workshops are:

- Lean office: migration of the deposit area from the traditional pay desk to:
  - advanced ATMs, migration of withdrawal from an ATM, spreading of remote channels, and
  - payment electronic tools
- Credit process: decrease administrative activities, elimination of:
  - rework, simplification of procedures by introducing automatic renewals
  - overdraufts: introduction of the automatic authorization mode on predetermined criteria, simplification of the inquiry operation, automation of transfers.
- Commercial back office: simplification of the processes of contract opening.
- Simplification and automation of the processes of conditions management.
- Back office and treasury: automation procedures and paper reduction in processes

- Foreign operations; automation and centralization for transfers, cheques, receipts and payments in Italy, standardization, automation, centralization of the operations of the treasury.
- Printouts, mailing, information and archives: reduction and rationalization of printouts, revision and centralization of mailing to clients, unification of informative channels and progressive elimination of archives.

The Lean Bank programme has an ambitious objective: 'Let us promote growth by recovering efficiency.'

List of References

Armaroli, V. 1992, 'La qualità del contratto per una organizzazione più efficiente', *Notiziario del Lavoro*, n. 58, Dic..

Bernini, R. 1992. L'organizzazione SIP, il piano qualità, *Dialogo*. Dicembre.

Nicoletti, B. 2009. *Project Management 2.0, Proceedings of the IPMA Congress*, Rome, 10–13 October.

Parrotto, R. 1992, Contratto collettivo, qualità totale e nuove relazioni industriali, *Notiziario del Lavoro*, n. 58, Dic.

Ray, R. 2009, Un vantaggio competitivo creativo per un project management innovativo, *Project Management per Innovare*, Milano, 22 October.

Segreterie di coordinamento di credito. 2006. Falcri – Fiba/Cisl – Fisac/Cgil – Uilca, Sanpaolo Banco di Napoli, Torino–Napoli, 2 February.

Solženicyn, A.I. 1974. *Arcipelago Gulag*. Milano: Mondadori.

Tixier, P. 1990. Sindacalismo e qualità. In Laboucheix V., ed., *Trattato sulla qualità totale*. Milano: FrancoAngeli.

Various Authors. 1991. *Sindacato e Qualità Totale. Un possibile accordo, a cura della FIOM-CGIL Regione Lombardia*. Milano: FrancoAngeli.

Various Authors 1992, *Qualità Totale e sindacato partecipativo*, Roma: *FIM-CISL*.

8 *Information Systems*

Introduction

Information systems to support Lean and Digitize are important. The use of suitable tools is vital for the success of a project. Information systems can provide data and documents, analysis and simulations. They are of such high value that it is appropriate to use the best tools available. Use of ICT is important for both the design and the operation of the process, for project management and in supporting the work of the team and operational units.

The use of Lean and Digitize when not supported by valid tools tends to require a big commitment in terms of time and resources. There should be interconnections between the method and the management of information of the project. The use of the Lean and Digitize method should be as automated as possible for a successful project.

The Information System

A system is a set of elements with a common objective. The theory of systems uses a model to describe systems of any kind. A system has three main features, as shown in Table 8.1.

Table 8.1   General model of a system

	Objectives	Each system has an objective/s that should be clearly defined
Systems	Structure	The system has subsystems or applications
	Processes	Within a system automated processes take place

The resource 'data' is the recording of a code agreed by a social group, the measure or identification of certain attributes of an object or event (Maggiolini, 1981). It therefore consists of numbers, words, codes or the like. Alone it holds no meaningful use.

The resource 'information' is an entity that reduces the state of uncertainty and, within an organization, allows the correct use or value of resources. The information also consists of numbers, words, codes or the like. Unlike the data, information permits decision-making. One possible definition of information is 'a meaningful excerpt from a data set' (Maggiolini, 1981).

The information system of the organization is a group of people, equipment and procedures, whose job is to produce information needed to operate and manage the company (De Maio et al., 1982). An information system does not necessarily imply the use of a computer (or computers): where the volumes of transactions are small and there is the possibility of a direct perception of the situation (Camussone, 1990: 156).

The information system is a cross-business sub-system that covers all processes that use the resource information:

- processes that collect information
- processes that manage and process; and
- processes that return information.

The organizational structure determines where the processes should take place. The information system manages all information, structured and unstructured. Initially information systems processed structured data (data necessary for the processes are useful when the process is standard). It is easier to computerize structured processes. The first computers also involved simple, non-integrated processes (or at least they were treated as independent).

Support of functions was the basis for the computerized system. Such computerization is just a new version of the old structure of manual information systems. It does not take into account that computerization can streamline the use of human resources without the involvement of people in the process.

A computer system is an information system that uses, partially or fully, the computer data. From this point of view, the computer system is a subset of information systems that the organization uses.

Later in this section, we interest ourselves primarily in digitized information systems. Some considerations could be applicable to non-digitized information systems. For this reason, in this chapter we shall speak in general about information systems.

From an ICT perspective, you can essentially distinguish three possible types of support from information technology to a Lean and Digitize project:

- Supports the conduct of analysis and improvement of process and operations;
- Tools for improved management of the project;
- Software that supports the work of a group, also called groupware.

Below we examine each of these three possible supports.

The Computer Support for Process Improvement

A business process management suite (BPMS) is the set of applications that can support the analysis, improvement and operation of processes. It consists of an integrated set of software technologies that allow the control and management of business processes. A BPMS involves business users throughout the process of improving the project life cycle; from planning to implementation and monitoring and optimization during the normal life of the process. Instead of stressing the reduction from the dependency of people through automation, a BPMS seeks to enhance the coordination of people and information, in addition to systems, as resources vital to the organization.

The BPMS uses explicit process models to coordinate the interactions between people, systems and content, as equally important aspects of a project and an implementation of Lean and Digitize. A BPMS is driven by a model and is coupled with the physical resources used at runtime and the design process, allowing considerable flexibility. During the operation of the process, the BPMS acts as a 'super-workflow' manager, coordinating (or orchestrating as they say in the jargon of a BPMS) activities in the process from start to finish, including all of the resources involved, the people and infrastructure.

A BPMS represents a holistic technological approach for managing the entire process; from design to operations to the monitoring and ongoing optimization of the work. A BPMS must support a number of functions:[1]

- Modelling and analysis of business processes, including all aspects of the workflow to manage, to identify the best process possible. This includes the tasks, roles, decisions, approvals, collaborations, flows, rules, policies, forms and other objects of information in the organization, events, goals and scenarios;
- Process simulation and its optimization using real-time data values, historical and estimated;
- Interchangeability, so that changes in the model can quickly be included in its physical implementation and vice versa;
- Coordination of different models of interaction between users participating in the process and systems required to complete the process from beginning to end. Some information may be on the outside of the organization yet interacting with it. The models of interaction can be from person-to-person (H2H), from system-to-system (S2S), person-to-system (H2S) from person to information content and interdependencies of content;
- Access to various forms of business content (structured and unstructured information) for handling and management in the context of the process (Nicoletti, 2008);
- Handling by the users and managers of the business rules;
- Collaboration of the group in the context of the process (in real time and offline);
- Monitoring, analysis and reporting of activities and corporate events, using data on transactions: work completed and active transaction in progress (in real time and offline, potentially for the predictive analysis);
- Visibility of the capability of the process and its use, with a forecast of possible saturation points in the process (bottlenecks);
- Management of all components of the process through their life cycle (such as access control, version control, meta data descriptions, etc.);
- Simplified management but secure in access (friendly interfaces);
- Verification of compliance with respect to the service levels of the process – service-level agreement (SLA).

A BPMS is more suitable for processes that balance the needs of people, systems and information. In these processes, the management of interactions and interdependencies amongst all three of these components is crucial to obtaining the desired results from the process. A BPMS (in the 'classic' scenario of use) is particularly important for processes that have frequent changes in time and cross more boundaries (such as physical boundaries,

---

1   D:\My Documents\Quality\BPM\Magic Quadrant for Business Process Management Suites, 2007.mht

organizational boundaries, the boundaries between structures, system boundaries, the boundaries of information, etc.). These situations require a higher degree of coordination of human activities, information and transactions in respect to established internal business processes.

The features that make the processes appropriate for such systems are:

- The interfaces outside of the organizations make them vulnerable to disruption by external forces such as weather, currency fluctuations, consumer preferences, market pressures, the actions of distributors, price competition, changes in regulations, geopolitical events, availability of core competencies and the like;
- The discovery of such workflows has a greater chance of success, making their performance visible and controlled. The experience derived from the execution of the process is used as input in the next operational iteration of the project;
- A collaboration of people with a strong impact on results (as in design, engineering, diagnosis and management of difficult cases).

A BPMS enables its users to see and directly manipulate resources in a coordinated way. The explicit model of the BPMS, used in the design and implementation, makes it easier for the operations managers change the sequence of work between individuals and/or changes in the rules followed by the process with a simple change of parameters. Explicit process models are much easier to change for process designers in comparison to traditional applications, which use logic included in the programme code and then require the intervention of specialized programming for its modification.

For all these features, the BPMS tends to be more effective in service organizations such as retailers, financial services, insurance, telecommunications, transport, public services, higher education or the media. These types of organizations are more sensitive than others to external forces of change. Recently there has been a growing interest in this type of software, even in manufacturing companies such as producers of consumer goods and pharmaceuticals. In fact all organizations should invest in BPMS to improve the agility of the enterprise and promote staff involvement in process improvement throughout the life cycle of the process.

Because a BPMS represents a paradigm shift from the traditional or simplistic approaches for automating business processes, users of these systems expect BPMS providers to make available on their systems not only the support for the design and management of the operational environment, but also the content of business processes. In this way you can accelerate the learning of the organization and the implementation of new process models.

Even today, you still cannot find software solutions in the market that include all these features. Your best case scenario is to reach from 70 to 80 per cent of the overall solution.

Market Definition

Nowadays the software suite of BPMS allows organizations to manage the life cycle of a process on a single platform. The BPMS software is able to put together the information from the right people with the right data. The result is to allow more informed decisions about the completion of a process.

The BPMS combines features classified in the past as separate technologies:

- workflow
- integration of applications; and
- business intelligence.

THE WORKFLOW

The workflow software manages the interface between people and ICT systems. This feature plays a major role in the macro steps of define and measure and verify and in the automation of the stages of the life cycle of the process on which the team is working. The workflow software automates business processes, playing an intermediary role in the flow of information from an operator or a system to another. The workflow uses messages, e-mail, online forms, or other documents for such intermediation. The workflow integrates with existing systems of calendar management (individual or project) or other collaboration tools.

Another important feature of workflow is providing the capacity to take decisions. A typical example of this feature in the case of a credit management system is that it must be able to route a request for credit based on the amount requested automatically.

Most of the workflow programs also incorporate graphical interfaces to design and build in a terminal workflow process using simple visual tools (such as drag and drop). In this way, it becomes possible to change the process flow to even non-technical staff using simple visual tools. This ability is very important in BPMS, as it allows interested parties, businesses and ICT to develop and model business processes in collaborative form.

Since workflow software contains many features of the BPMS, some producers of the workflow software have positioned their products as BPMS. In reality the workflow software itself does not address the full feature set of BPMS, and does very little to help the organization to achieve the full functionality of BPM.

In summary, the workflow allows:

- Design driven by the model and environment of development: the modelling environment is appropriate for both the drag and drop, included with wizards and visual process modelling, development tools of the models and architectures for all components of the process, including the design process, customer interaction, interaction through rules, user interface, the interaction of the system and electronic forms. Features such as search, version management, partitioning the repository, publication and subscription services should be included. Finally, there must be a possibility of rapid implementation of customized transactions;
- Execution processes and availability of an 'engine' for state management: this permits us to orchestrate the sequence of models of interaction of multiple processes and maintain the state of process instances, activities and distance between people and systems based on meta data and the process stream that have been modelled. The features to support are H2H, H2S and S2S interactions, case management and compensation operations;

- The management of business rules refers to the ability to abstract and execute company policies and decisions/instructions according to the underlying applications and allow more flexibility to process changes. This includes rules based on events, rules based on inferences, testing and correction rules, the rules of simulation/what-if analysis and models for the rules.

THE INTEGRATION OF APPLICATIONS

In order to support the life cycle of BPM successfully, the BPMS must integrate with other applications of ICT, present or future. In large environments, this feature should allow you to connect to a variety of applications resulting in a number of substantial benefits.

The name of the component to support application integration is enterprise application integration (EAI). This avails itself of two basic tools:

- The application programming interface (API) which provides a set of tools that programmers can use to exchange information with the applications;
- The adapters or connectors, which provide ready connections between applications and databases.

Often in the past it was necessary to write custom code to provide this type of connectivity. It was necessary for the update and maintenance of this software. When you need a strong integration, the resulting workload can be a heavy commitment for ICT resources. These resources might not always be available, especially for unplanned requests.

One of the challenges of EAI is that large organizations need more than one EAI platform. For this reason, the best BPMS products ensure that their BPMS software integrates easily with other applications, especially those most widely spread, such as SAP, Oracle and Microsoft.

In summary, the BPMS must ensure easy connectivity of the system: these tools enable system architects to:

- Publish and subscribe the system services;
- Choreograph the interaction of the service; and
- Set the bidirectional connections to various business applications, back-end through connectors of prepackaged systems, such as enterprise java beans, technical adapters, enterprise service bus, data transformation tools and application adapters.

THE BUSINESS INTELLIGENCE

In order to analyse and optimize a business process, one must have quick access to critical data (internal and, where possible, external to the organization) and, above all, have the ability to extract useful information for decision-making. The BPMS should incorporate a technology that can provide analysis of processes in a comprehensive format.

A BPMS should allow the management of business events, business activity monitoring (BAM) and the management of business intelligence (BI).

Business intelligence is, in short, the art of extracting useful information from large databases and presenting information so that it is comprehensive in terms of business.

Business intelligence systems often offer dashboards for monitoring processes, with a display of metrics of critical information and alarm notification via messages, e-mail, text messages or whatever, due to certain events or if the results are outside of specifications. These also provide financial analysis that enables stakeholders to identify under-performing business segments. Business intelligence often uses KPIs to monitor the status of the organizations versus specific goals.

There are instruments for monitoring and reporting of business to govern and alert managers on current behaviours and changes in the operations of the organization. The functions should include listening to events, alarms and thresholds to trigger:

- Online/reporting analytical processing of business intelligence
- Providing dashboards with KPIs
- Monitoring chart of processes and tools for the discovery of the process.

The name of these functions is corporate performance management (CPM).

A BPMS needs to integrate all these features to help users to constantly monitor and improve their business processes.

System Management

In addition to the features described so far, a number of software vendors also have products that support areas of system administration. They are important for coordination between people, systems and information. From this point of view, the BPMS must allow:[2]

- The management of documents and records, with the option to store the storage, indexing, the collection and monitoring of various types of content (the data being both structured and unstructured) in and out of context of a process stream. Specifications must include the management of folders, indexing of images and documents, the management of structured and unstructured data, document archiving, as well as security management of access or custody of documents;
- Collaboration during the design by providing development tools for business users and ICT to help close the communication gap between groups. The tools must provide the ability to collaborate so that groups can get the job done quickly and can discover and recommend changes in system components to optimize system performance. This area must include the management of shared work waiting lines, project portals/sites, development based on roles, instant messaging/blogs and bulletin boards of the user community;
- The recording of all process definitions, components, templates, rules and process data from other systems accessible by users and retrievable by other automated applications. The BPMS must support the search, version management, partitioning of the repository, the publish and subscribe services and provide fast exits of all software components created and orchestrated during the operation;
- The setting and maintenance of systems and user access, as well as providing monitoring tools to govern the state of executable systems. These include deployment

---

2   D:\My Documents\Quality\BPM\Magic Quadrant for Business Process Management Suites, 2007.mht

tools for role management, security management, control of system management, Lightweight Directory Access Protocol (LDAP) integration and active directory;

- Simulation and optimization online and offline, using data values in real time, historical and estimated to identify and propose opportunities for process optimization. The simulation tools must have a tight integration with the development environment to allow rapid transitions between more than one environment. This functional area must support the predictive analysis (financial and risk), concurrent processes and simulation of rules, a repository of simulation, optimization algorithms and rapid transition between development environments and production.

A BPMS supports these features of pre-integration of various technologies to deliver a unified experience of the product. The platform architecture must allow users to interact easily and smoothly through the improvement process of the life cycle – from analysis to design, implementation, monitoring and review – with greater collaboration between business and ICT.

There are two particularly important features, detailed in the next two sections.

Digitization

The BPMS should help in the analyse and process design and architecture design macro phases. In accordance with the methodology of Lean Six Sigma, if you use automated tools for defining the new process the computer tool must be able to:

- Represent the stages of the process graphically;
- Describe the exchange of materials and information between the various stages;
- Be able to understand and outline the flow rate, the consumption of time and resources, and the level and/or information present in every step of the process;
- Provide the implosion or explosion of the process stages in a hierarchical fashion, so that changes are permitted on the level of detail;
- Provide a user interface, preferably graphical and interactive;
- Perform simulations in a reliable manner and deliver results in graphical form in real time;
- Identify bottlenecks and fundamental clamps of the process;
- Be compatible with the construction of a model for data and procedures for the application of tools to support software engineering (so-called systems computer-aided software engineering cases).

For the success of a radical innovation of processes, it is necessary to limit the scope of the objective to improving the individual process and its interfaces. It may also be necessary to limit the construction of a data model to some subsets of the entire process.

An application that provides the opportunity to build a model and simulate a variety of situations can play a more important role than limiting itself to printing the diagrams. The team can use models that describe the entire process.

The application of model building of processes must meet four criteria:

- Be fast and easy to use;

- Allow comparison between the new and old models;
- Provide a process model that is not only descriptive but also analytical;
- Allow the conduct of subsequent changes in the process design.

Aris from Software AG is an example of software that can support these functionalities. Its basic modules are:

- Strategy platform: it is the module that allows the team to define business strategies, implement them in business processes and continuously monitor the target systems;
- Design platform: this module can model, simulate, optimize and publish business processes and manage ICT architectures;
- Implementation platform: the third module is designed to execute process models in ICT systems, configuring SAP systems, manage business rules and create service-oriented architectures;
- Controlling platform: this module allows one to dynamically monitor business processes in progress, implement systems to manage the performance of the project team and establish a single system for managing unique compliance throughout the enterprise.

GE has been active in this field. Thus, for example, GE Fanuc has developed a system referred to as QuickStart which reduces costs through automation and Lean work and automation, with a good handling of exceptions. The system can reduce variations in performance, cost, and at the same time digitize both manual and automatic processes with a tool that captures data on processes and their traceability and quality to reduce errors and eliminate waste and delays (ww.gefanuc.com).

The Prototypization

Usually the construction of a prototype of the new process partially overlaps with the design activities, which means the project could begin as soon as the process begins to take shape. ICT can accelerate and increase productivity in the construction of a prototype. Addressing prototypes in the field of process flows, the real-time simulations are very useful. ICT can facilitate the construction of prototypes on information systems of the new process in two ways:

- Using the CASE systems, which allow the immediate translation of models in applications, albeit simplified;
- With high-level languages, which with relatively few instructions allow the team to create prototype applications.

SERVICE-ORIENTED ARCHITECTURE AND BUSINESS PROCESS MANAGEMENT

Digitization applied in an unchanged organizational context has marginal and not substantial benefits. It is ineffective from a competitive standpoint within the market, especially if mature and saturated. Every competitor has access to the same technologies and can offer the same products/services.

Another aspect to take into consideration is the increasing complexity of processes and systems. The development of communications infrastructure enables the interconnection between organizations through dynamic processes, not fixed permanently. Digitization is not relative to one individual system in a defined location, but includes more and more pervasive processes that spread across distributed systems that can be geographically and legally far apart.

The main problem that limits the benefits of automation of traditional management is their inflexibility when faced with processes that are increasingly dynamic. The solution is not an adjustment of the process to the rigid architecture of information systems. The team must seek a flexible system that does not constrain the structure of the process, but instead supports and facilitates it.

Business-oriented architecture (BOA), the new approach based on SOA and BPM, brings the two worlds of Automation – Organization closer:

1. SOA focuses on creating a flexible and scalable architecture;
2. BPM aims to the optimize the processes.

BOA may be considered as the last (until the time of writing this book!) evolutionary step of automation and information systems and a great support for Lean and Digitize projects.

The Service-oriented Architecture

The SOA is not only a new technology, it is an entirely new way to build systems (Salunga, 2008). SOA is a paradigm, an approach to management and maintenance of extended systems (Erl et al., 2012). These systems are by their nature heterogeneous, with goals, implementation time and differences in characteristics. They use different platforms, programming languages, rules and policies. The reason for this heterogeneity is that information systems have a long life cycle. During this period, there may be many introductions of new technologies to the market, new systems and new processes.

Extended and distributed systems also have different managers, different groups, departments, divisions, companies, budgets, schedules, relationships and interests. They may have redundant information or have platforms under maintenance. SOA seeks to overcome these differences and problems.

OASIS (Outcome and Assessment Information Set), the organization for the development of standards of information structured, defines SOA as follows:

[Service Oriented Architecture is] a paradigm for the organization and the utilization of distributed resources that may be under the control of different ownership domains. [It] Provides a uniform to offer, discover, interact and use the ability to consistently produce the desired results with measurable preconditions and expectations. it.wikipedia.org

The SOA approach consists of element management: service, workflow, infrastructure, architecture. In particular:

1. The service represents an application, a feature or component of a process. It can

participate in one or more processes and must be implemented by any technology available on any platform;

2. The workflow is the tool for managing the process flow;
3. The infrastructure is through technology that allows joining services in a simple and flexible. In technical jargon, this is called ESB;
4. The architecture is the set of policies that manage distributed systems, which may be heterogeneous, with different properties and under maintenance.

The SOA approach allows the team to:

1. Easily change the ways and the combination of interactions between services;
2. Facilitate the introduction of new services and modification of processes in response to the specific needs of particular business reference;
3. Not bind processes to a specific platform but ensure their immediate and flexible support.

The information system that underlies the SOA architecture is not a new technology but a pool of reusable system functions: the above-mentioned services.

In the following paragraphs, we detail the elements that characterize the SOA:

- the architecture
- the services
- the workflow; and
- the infrastructure.

THE ARCHITECTURE

The most important key feature of SOA is the architecture. The solution needs to meet the policies, roles, responsibilities and standards of SOA. As processes change, in some cases very quickly, the organization should handle them with strict and rigorous rules. The definition of flows and the language of communication must be unique.

The architectural decisions need to drive specific implementation decisions to avoid disorder. This involves:

- Classifying the different types of service;
- Deciding when to decouple;
- Reducing the number of data models of the interfaces of the services;
- Orchestrating the calling sequence of the services and exchange of information, to trace the desired and planned process stage in a Lean and Digitize initiative.

THE SERVICES

The basic components for building a SOA system are the services. They are reusable applications designed to perform one or more processes. They can reside on multiple computers within an internal network or connecting more cooperating systems – a local area network (LAN) or wider area network (WAN) (in the latter case we also talk about cloud computing – processing in the cloud).

The SOA architecture is able to combine more services and to use them so they can manage the flow of automated production processes to which they belong.

An important aspect of SOA services is their close correlation with the mode of operation of the organization. They are not just pieces of the programme. It is possible to assemble services in such a way that they become a complete process using the technology of orchestration. The latter allows one to guide the flow of services and ensure the correct execution of the process, based on rules and policies (www.caffeconbea.it).

The services are functional pieces. They can carry out tasks:

- Simple, such as saving given data; or
- Complex, such as a whole sub-process for taking customer orders.

The services are also loosely coupled with each other and transparent at the level of organization. The end user does not necessarily need to understand the operation on a technical level, but only at the logical level. Decoupling is the key to independence and scalability. These elements are essential if you want to release the processes from ICT technology. Minimizing dependencies allows you to implement changes. In this way, it is possible to limit severely failures of systems and frequent interruptions of processes.

The service is:

- An application defined and independent within the intranet or internet. It provides a functionality for production processes;
- A traceable component: through the interface. The service can be searchable and dynamically retrievable.
- A service must be sought according to the interface and invoked at runtime. The definition of service based on its interface makes the latter (and thus the interaction with other services) independent of the manner it was realized by the component who implements it (Polini, 2007);
- Self-contained: modular but complete. Each service must be well defined, comprehensive and independent from the context or status of other services;
- Independent: the standard interface allows independence from implementation, referring to both the programming language used for the component, as well as the platform and the operating system on which it is running;
- Loosely coupled: linked to other features limited to only a few components;
- Available: through the publication of its interface on a service directory or the service registry, the service is accessible in a transparent manner.
- Being available on the network makes it accessible to those components that require its use and the access must be independent from the allocation of the service. The publication of the interface must also include information about ways to access the service (Polini, 2007);
- 'Coarse grain', meaning it must have few functionalities and a low number of transactions that do not require a complex monitoring programme. It is preferable to have multiple services that interact via standard mail. This feature facilitates the reuse and modification;
- Communication skills obtained through messages written in a standard format usable on many platforms (platform-neutral);

- Designed for composition: the goals of reusability, scalability and modularity lead to benefits only if the services are easily composable. By using the composition, the team can create processes, combining their calls to services, operations on the results, with external data enrichment and manual operations performed by users.

Comments on some of these service features are in the section on BSE infrastructure.

THE WORKFLOW

An important methodology for SOA is the workflow. The workflow is a set of techniques and tools for supporting the automation of operations and re-engineering of processes. It also helps in the dematerialization (the transformation of paper documents into electronic documents handled by the computer) and the automation of certain phases of the process.

The dematerialization process management is important because the documents are key elements in all processes. The dematerialization is a key element when the objectives are:

1. Reduce the time spent by the resources for such activities as data entry system;
2. Relocation or outsourcing within the country or abroad for some work phases;
3. Reduction of materiality.

The workflow, as information technology, was introduced in the 1990s. It includes both technical process analysis and software technologies, specifically targeted to automate the process flow. The techniques of workflow analysis specify:

1. The set of tasks to be performed;
2. The order of execution of tasks and conditions under which these tasks should/could be performed, even automatically;
3. The synchronization of tasks;
4. The flow of information.

The workflow systems are software that automates the processing of tasks, the flow of execution of tasks and their synchronization. The workflow is important as a tool for re-engineering, especially for initiatives for improvement (Bracchi and Motta, 1997).

The workflow allows a series of features that makes possible the automation of processes, such as automatically:

1. Capture data or documents;
2. Send e-mail, SMS or other types of messages to certain addresses;
3. Load replies.

It is possible to use the workflow to manage processes that cut across multiple geographic locations. For example, through an intelligent optical character recognition (OCR) tool, after having scanned documents, the workflow can load data related to these documents. The workflow will automatically compile a form and send it to another party.

The Enterprise Service Bus Infrastructure

The enterprise service bus (ESB) is the infrastructure of SOA: 'the neuronal and circulatory system'. This substrate allows the use of technical services in a productive environment. The ESB connects services following special routing rules. It transforms the data when there is the need to mix them. In other words, it guaranties interoperability. It allows the call to different services by distributed systems, integrating different platforms and languages. It makes easy the distribution of processes across multiple systems.

> *Interoperability is the ability to communicate between services and their users. It is assured by standards that constitute the basis of the infrastructure on which to build. Can be enhanced by software mediation. These tools add a further level of decoupling, ensuring standards where not present and perform operations of common interest. itlab.wordpress.com*

The ESB is also responsible for managing the security and reliability, the monitoring and recording (logging), the inventory and the organization of services.

The ESB has the following properties and tasks:

1. Connectivity: connects the services simply and in a flexible manner;
2. Pervasive: connects the distributed systems and entities;
3. Messaging: forwards messages between entities in a synchronous and asynchronous mode;
4. Routing: street posts through 'intelligent' algorithms;
5. Interoperability: allows interaction between services and users;
6. Standardization: transforms the data in case of heterogeneity;
7. Security: monitoring of services, transaction integrity;
8. Monitoring: handling of exceptions;
9. Logging: management of registration and connection;
10. Inventory: mapping of services.

Three entities manage the communication between services:

1. the service consumer
2. the service provider; and
3. the service registry (see Figure 8.1).

The service provider makes available the service. The service consumer needs to be visible in order that the entities, which want to use it, be able to find it: i.e. it must be published ('Publish'). To this end, the service provider notifies the service registry, the third and final entity involved, of the information relative to the service, such as the URL and access mode. The service registry stores this information ('Bind').

When a service consumer needs access to a service it requests the URL and mode of access related to the service registry ('Find'). If the service is accessible and running, once information availability is exchanged between service registry and consumer service, the latter may communicate directly with the service provider and use the service.

No steps described can occur without the ESB infrastructure.

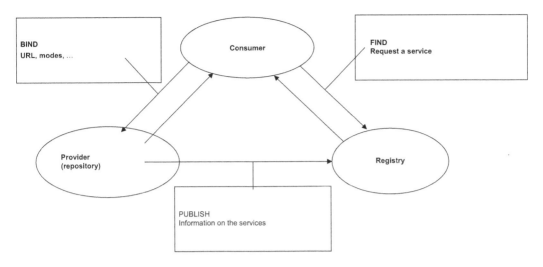

Figure 8.1   The connection between a process and an SOA outline

The Implementation of Service-oriented Architecture

When a computer system becomes obsolete, you can choose whether to purchase/implement systems/next-generation platforms or upgrade the existing structures:

1. The first solution requires know-how of the new computer system;
2. The second solution is viable only if it is possible to reuse the facilities already in use with some modifications and adaptations.

The implementation of SOA is particularly advantageous when the organization has one or more of the following problems:

1. Merging departments;
2. Acquiring/dismissing;
3. New products/processes;
4. Misunderstandings between ICT and non-specialists;
5. Justifying the ICT costs (savings) or recognizing the ICT value contribution;
6. Implementing fully the potential of ICT (reuse, efficiency).

The SOA is interesting only in the presence of these features:

1. Distributed systems (different jobs, countries, offices or factories);
1. Complex and heterogeneous systems;
2. Different owners (physical or logical);
3. Locks are not integrated, closed, monolithic, vulnerable, fragile, imperfect;
4. Redundancy (no consistency).

When the system is homogeneous, simple, consistent, there is less sense in adopting the SOA solution because it introduces a higher level of complexity without affecting the objectives significantly.

> *The service-oriented architecture is particularly well suited for organizations that have a moderate complexity of processes and applications, since it facilitates the interaction between the different realities permitting, at the same time, the business activity to develop efficient processes, both internally and externally and increase their flexibility and adaptability. www-05.ibm.com*

The adoption of SOA requires close collaboration between ICT and the organization. This collaboration must go beyond the departmental/organizational barriers. The solution should involve the entire organization, beginning with senior management.

It is interesting to examine the relationship between the architecture of SOA and BPM. The traditional architecture of ICT imposes rigid structures, independent and mutually incompatible. The high cost of these structures requires the organization to structure its processes following the constraints of specific software packages. The utilities must navigate in networks, databases and separate applications to perform specific operations, with a consequent waste of time and therefore money.

> *Thanks to SOA, users no longer have to access multiple systems to find the data they want and integrate the results manually. The data on the activities of business processes are provided as a service integrated into a single application on a single screen and with a single login. it.sun.com*

The SOA integrates ICT modules in a flexible way. Otherwise, they would be:

1. closed
2. monolithic
3. vulnerable
4. fragile.

SOA supports:

1. shared services
2. collaboration
3. compatibility
4. integration.

Implementing the SOA also allows maximum use of existing technology without requiring additional costs for purchases of new packages and platforms. Thanks to reuse, there are substantial savings and returns on investment.

> *The SOA and WS (Web service) technologies, linked to these, are the solutions which the organizations created due to the following problems: realize fully the potential of ICT: justify the cost of ICT: provide to the non-technical staff a clear understanding of what ICT does, how it does it and its intrinsic value. www-05.ibm.com*

However, SOA is not always advantageous. There must be special conditions that maximize the benefits that SOA generates, limiting the possible disadvantages.

Business-oriented Architecture

The BPM and SOA individually provide considerable advantages. There is the maximum benefit in a synergistic approach called business-oriented architecture.

Many of the ICT systems in the initial phase are sufficiently compact, stable, and do not require the SOA to support the BPM. However, with the initial success of BPM initiatives there is an exponential growth in connecting services, applications and databases.

If the system grows, it grows alongside its complexity. It will be increasingly less manageable if we use the traditional approach to information systems. The SOA simplifies and makes the system agile (see Figure 8.2).

An organization should adopt a rational approach to its SOA to enjoy the benefits of flexibility, reuse, and adaptability that SOA provides. The organization can gain bigger benefits by applying the architecture according to a Lean and Digitize initiative. In this way, it can greatly improve the return on investment (ROI) and have a direct impact on the organization.

Similarly, Lean and Digitize provides real value to the process, but the SOA eases the integration and provides components to manage the technical services related to the process. It increases reuse and improves the governance of processes (Figure 8.3).

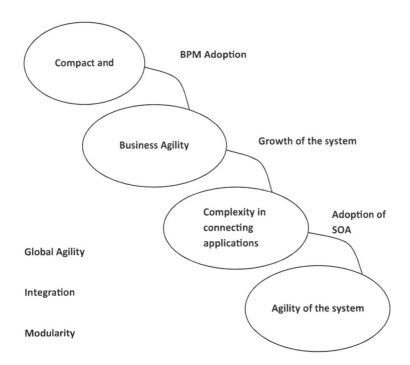

Figure 8.2   Graph of states adopting BPM and SOA

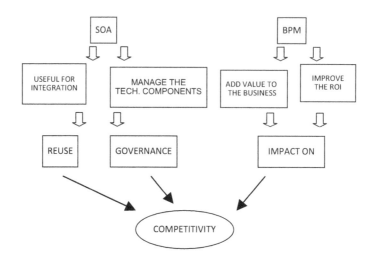

Figure 8.3   The impact of SOA and BPM on business competitiveness

The SOA:

1. Provides the technical basis for process improvement;
2. Refines the data structure and services;
3. Provides the tools that the project teams will use to build applications for improving organizational processes.

The BPM provides the tools that enable users to improve the process, to go directly from design to active management of the process, and finally, to the analysis leading to the optimization of business. The BOA combines the flexibility of the SOA-based information system to the value of the process given by the BPM approach.

The BOA manages the organization, the use of the services, provides tools for the design, active management, the analysis and the optimization projects (see Figure 8.4).

The result is:

1. Lower costs of design and management;
2. Improved productivity;
3. Increased customer satisfaction; and
4. Better image and economic return.

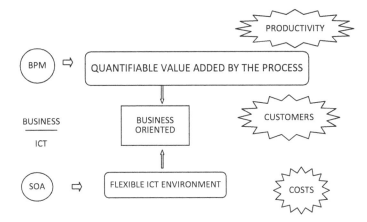

Figure 8.4   A diagram of business-oriented architecture

Table 8.2 is a summary of the development of the ICT to the BPM.

Table 8.2   ICT and processes (Smith and Fingar 2003)

The infrastructure of the organization	Automation	Process management
Office environment – e-mail, PC, portals, etc.	Data processing, automation of the current way of working	Support for the organization's strategy
Source of lower cost	Standardization	Translating the actual demands of the organization
Allows the organization to communicate and share information	Provided tracks	Improved understanding
	Scalable supports with the organization	Provision of the return on which to take action
	The reduction of resource requirements	Allows differentiation
	Provision of reports to managers	
Requested by all	The type of organization determines the needs	As the organization grows, it runs and maintains the market position

The next 50 years of ICT will move increasingly towards process optimization versus the automation of the last 50 years of ICT.

CIMB GROUP: BUSINESS PROCESS RE-ENGINEERING (THEYVENTHERAN, 2008)

The CIMB[3] (Commerce International Merchant Bankers) Group is a bank present in many countries around the world: Bahrain, Brunei, Hong Kong, Indonesia, Myanmar, Republic of Mauritius, Singapore, Thailand, United Kingdom and the United States. It has headquarters in Malaysia, where it is the second-largest bank in the country.

From 2003 to 2006, the CIMB Group doubled its profits from 782 to 1,504 million Malaysian dollars and improved the market value of its capital of 13,936 to 24,721 million Malaysian dollars. These results come from the development of three strategies:

1. Become a 'universal bank';
2. Expand the market through innovation; and
3. Aim for operations excellence.

CIMB wants to satisfy all the demands and needs of customers with its products and services, in every region and every nation.

The vision of the Group is to be the: 'Southeast Asia's most valued universal Bank.' In other words, the Group aims to be the logical choice for customers for banking, the preferred organization for the employees, and the most profitable opportunity for the shareholders.

The strategic transformation

The transformation of the CIMB group's strategy led the transition from systems-oriented to products and services, to systems focused on individual customers.

The initial situation, the 'as-is' of the CIMBA group at the launch of the business process re-engineering initiative showed a scenario where the bank aimed at pushing new products and new services. The Bank designed these products and services within the group and/or by following the choices of the direct competitors in order to increase profitability and improve customer loyalty.

This strategy brought satisfactory results, but did not lead to the complete satisfaction of all customers. In fact, it lacked a detailed knowledge of the real needs of every single customer.

The bank decided to migrate from a product-centric approach to a customer-centric approach. The aim was to interact proactively with each customer in order to deliver the various products and customized services.

The first step in this direction for the CIMBA group was to understand the new trends in the financial services market. The bank was able to identify some of the most important emerging trends by analysing the requirements of existing and potential customers. They were:

1. The ability to access banking services anytime and anywhere (online access);
2. A personalized offer (particularly in regards to financial advice);

3   http://www.cimb.co

3. Get fast, reliable and efficient services (no waiting lines, comfortable environment, etc.).

In short, customers want and demand from a bank a specific solution to all their financial problems.

These requirements involved:

1. The development and enhancement of online and telephone channels as alternatives to bank branches;
2. Strengthening of financial consulting and customization of products and services;
3. The revamping of the processes of service allocation, thereby reducing waiting times and offering different options and secure transactions;
4. The offer of solutions customized to individual problems thanks to in-depth knowledge of the financial requirements of each customer.

Once they had completed the market analysis and trends, the CIMB Group moved on to re-engineering the processes.

The business process re-engineering (BPR) approach

The approach of re-engineering processes went through the following steps:

1. The preparation of BPR: establishment of a project team consisting of resources from different functions, setting goals for the customers and development strategies;
2. Mapping and analysis of the as-is process: development of the as-is process map, Pareto ABC analysis, identification of waste and activities that do not add value;
3. Design and validation of the to-be process, analysis of cost benefits;
4. Implementation of the re-engineered process: developing a roll-out plan, implementation of the pilot, beginning of training and execution programmes of a full roll-out;
5. Continuous improvement measurement of performance, reviews and continuous process improvement;
6. Changes in information systems through process redesign.

Initially the information system included:

1. Mortgage system: credit origination, credit score, disbursements;
2. Core system current accounts, deposits, loans, financial system;
3. Access points (contact): website, call centre, telephone and ATM.

Figure 8.5 shows how the infrastructure linking the three main systems was messy and complex. It lacked a central system that could regulate the communication between the different modules of the information system.

The issues connected with the infrastructure of the information system as described in Figure 8.6 are:

1. fragmentation
2. complexity
3. interdependence and
4. duplication.

These factors affected the development of products customized for each customer negatively.

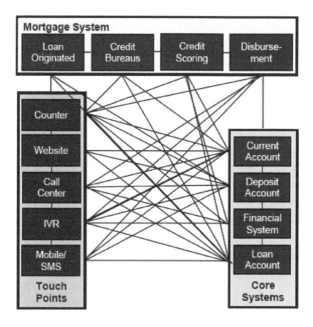

Figure 8.5 **The infrastructure of the information system built on the product-centric approach**

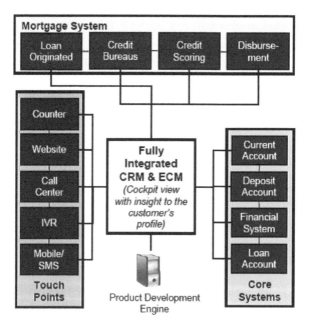

Figure 8.6 **The infrastructure of the information system built on the customer-centric approach**

The transition from a product-centric to a customer-centric approach forced the CIMB group to introduce the CRM and a data warehouse at the level of the entire organization. The new data warehouse and the CRM allowed CIMB to centralize all products data and to provide a single access to the data of each customer, as shown in Figure 8.7.

The solution adopted, based on an integrated CRM and ECM and on a single data warehouse at the level of the organization, allowed to solve the major problems of infrastructure complexity, fragmentation processes, the interdependence of systems and components and of data duplication.

This new system, connected to other major systems, allows the bank to manage customer profiles in such a way as to have unique data that is always up to date.

Using a single platform, a single data warehouse and a unique infrastructure through a SOA is to have reusable applications. The bank can reconfigure the applications with minimum effort, being sure of user-friendly access and high-quality data.

The Benefits of BPMS

The BPMS helps to optimize and measure the return on investments in a BPM project. The tools to measure the business value of an intervention to improve processes are an essential part of the software. Moreover, the BPMS is modular. This provides the flexibility to use only the modules needed in a specific implementation. The result of all these aspects is that the implementation of a new BPMS brings returns in a relatively small time frame.

A typical goal for improvement projects is the reduction of costs in the short term. For example, the support of a BPMS at a process such as the approval of an application for insurance leads to greater productivity. Other benefits such as increased customer loyalty, achieved by a faster service, require more time to be able to demonstrate and then measure. However, the analysis tools of a BPMS provide feedback to business managers for the evaluation of significant correlations between the introduction of the system and improvements in the organization.

Table 8.3 shows some examples of media that IBM's Websphere BPMS allow to provide to Lean and Digitize projects.

Table 8.3   Examples of support of BPMS at different stages of a project of Lean and Digitize (Skalle et al., 2009)

Macro phase	Aim	The contribution of the BPMS
Define and measure	Understanding customer needs and its requirements. Validate the business opportunities and identify constraints. Quantitatively define the critical requirements of the customer, the necessary data, the key events in the process, the metrics and the KPIs	Process models and dashboard of KPIs provide the backdrop for the new processes that affect them. Metrics and dashboard of default KPIs allow to design and implement critical measurements
Analyse and process design	Analyse the current process and alternatives to the high-level process. Determine which of these best meets the critical success factors	• Alternatives of process can be modelled and analysed to determine which best meets the requirements of customers and business, at the same time minimizing the risks. • Archives of existing processes and service components can be revised during the project. The appropriate components can be selected and reused in the new process to speed up the time of implementation and further improve the ROI
Build, test and deploy	Detailed design, develop, test and install a solution	There are several ways in which the BPMS can help the project team of Lean and Digitize, such as: • A scalable and robust engine to manage workflow and the interaction of systems. This feature should include exception handling, actions to bring the problem to higher levels and situations where it is necessary to go back into the process, in case of failure; • Capacity available in the system integration to securely access data and functionality of existing applications and use in the workflow process; • Management of business rules and policies expressed in clear terms and controllable by the business users; • Components (files, screens and reports) that can be customized to address specific requirements
Verify	Verify that the KPIs are satisfied and that the solution introduced is sustainable	Availability of metrics and KPI dashboard defaults that allow the verification of the achievement of project objectives in time, and system flexibility in allowing adjustments as may be necessary

The Software on the Market

In terms of products available on the market, Gartner evaluates vendors using a so-called Magic Quadrant. It is based on two measures:

- Ability to execute, that is the ability to support product implementation and maintenance;
- Completeness of vision, intended both as availability of product features and capacity for developing the product systems with a clear view of the future requirements of the market.

Gartner also labels vendors according to the quadrant in which they are located:

- Leaders. Vendors with a high ability to execute and completeness of vision;
- Challengers. Vendors with a high capacity for execution but who do not yet have a completeness of vision. As such, they are potential challengers for the leaders;
- Visionaries. Vendors with a completeness of vision but with limited implementation capacity;
- Niche players. Vendors focused on niche markets, either as functions or vertical.

We suggest searching on the Web for the different players in the market by using the above classifications.

Market Overview

The BPMS market is entering a stage of maturity. By the end of 2011, the BPMS market reached nearly US$2.0 billion of software revenue. It began to have the characteristics of a mature market, that is, with proven technology, stable vendors, the consolidation of vendors and rapid adoption by a growing number of customers. The BPMS market is the second-fastest growing segment of the middleware market: Gartner estimates that it had a compound annual growth rate greater than 24 per cent from 2006 to 2011. Although spending on BPMS has grown rapidly in recent years, only 20–30 per cent of the implementations support cross-functional processes in the organization. Many improvement initiatives are limited to simpler processes. Consequently, they under-utilize the full power of a BPMS.

The Computer Support of Project Management

THE INFORMATION SYSTEM

The management of projects is an important way of monitoring the development of the innovative products or processes of an organization. It also enables effective communication of objectives, responsibilities and project status to all individuals and groups involved.

The organizations should not underestimate the aspects of information processing and communication in the life of a project. The use of tools is essential to the success of a project. The tools can process data and provide charts, analysis and simulations that are particularly useful. On the other hand, the use of a proper methodological approach not supported by a valid tool tends to require more time and resources. The two aspects, one methodological and the other connected with information management that is as automated as possible, are important success factors in project management.

In this section, we will focus on the support of project management by information systems. An information system in support of project management is a set of data, information and procedures, aimed at the project planning, project monitoring and decision support for meeting project goals within the constraints of time/cost/quality.

For sizeable projects, structures and systems for collecting and processing data should be standardized within an organization.

As with all the automation of management activities, it is important to digitize the processes only after having clarified the organizational and physical conditions to use.

THE PACKAGES FOR PROJECT MANAGEMENT

There are several packages that support project management. They try to simplify the daily work of project management in the broader context of corporate planning. With them, the planning, management and reporting are easier and therefore it is easier to meet deadlines and budget. Any project linked to planning and a budget necessarily requires an accurate plan. The project requires good management skills to identify and correct any possible problems before they can reflect badly on time and on budget. Moreover, the project requires timely communication to keep the project team consistently focused on the activities and deadlines. In short, the project requires the support of a computer package to manage projects.

With a computer package for project management, project team members can more easily handle:

- Lists of activities and the organization of their daily commitments;
- Building of programs, also viewable in graphical formats;
- The periodic summary of the activities planned.

We can summarize the above considerations as follows. A computer package for project management represents an effective software tool for managing project activities. It must offer a number of advantages:

- Ease of use. Over time, besides adding new features, ease of use of packages for project management has improved. It has now reached significant levels of sophistication compared to only a few years ago. This has been due, for example, to the use of graphical interfaces, different 'windows', the use of different ways of interaction, etc.;
- Extensive use of graphics. Informational packages for the management of projects make extensive use of advanced graphic tools and provide the user with a wide range of functions;
- Integration. Informational packages for the management of projects are available in many platforms: Windows, Macintosh, Linux etc. Furthermore, they should integrate

with other office automation packages normally available in the company, such as bulletin boards, word processing, spreadsheets, etc., thanks to the support of advanced technologies such as Object Linking & Embedding (OLE), Dynamic Data Exchange (DDE), and Open Database Connectivity (ODBC);

- Programmability. Packages for the management of projects should include programming tools capable of guaranteeing an adaptation of the product to the user-specific requirements and to integrate their use with other complementary add-on software.

These aspects are discussed in more detail below.

THE FEATURES

Thanks to modern management ICT tools in support of project management, the project members may, for example:

- Constantly check the progress of projects with respect to medium- and long-term corporate objectives;
- Choose on an informed basis, through benchmarks and economical evaluations, which projects to approve, postpone or cancel;
- Integrate multiple projects in a general dashboard capable to follow the overall pace of business activity (project portfolio), but also allow them to review the details of a specific project.

The project leaders, area managers and the like, can in turn:

- Set and communicate objectives for their group teams and management;
- Automatically produce a periodic list of things to do for each person involved in the project;
- Easily integrate the individual information collected from individual resources within a report that summarizes the progress of the whole project;
- Identify with precision timing delays, their causes and the corrective actions necessary;
- Produce regular reports for management effortlessly;
- Share resources with other project leaders, limiting the possibility of conflicts and misunderstandings;
- Evaluate the expected performance of individual resources.

Project team members can:

- Consistently have an accurate list of tasks in a given period of time;
- Quickly produce reports summarizing the work done during the period for the benefit of the project stakeholders;
- Understand the expectations of the management of the organization and its executives.

THE CLASSIFICATIONS

There are several possible criteria for the classification of information tools to support project activities. The benchmarks may be elements such as:

- purpose/type of activity
- type of projects
- functions performed
- operational aspects of project management
- type of hardware
- cost.

One possible classification of information systems in support of project management is in Table 8.4.

On the Internet, it is possible to find an evaluation of these and similar packages, classified according to Gartner in the Magic Quadrant (mediaproducts.gartner.com).

SYSTEMS FOR MAINFRAMES, MINI AND PERSONAL COMPUTERS

The initial development of systems for the support of project management was in support of programming and control. Initially, this support was available on dedicated mini computers, with the characteristics of being:

- Multi-user;
- Multi-project;
- With connections such as transfers of media files on computer or transfer files with different purposes.

Other versions developed for servers and personal computers soon became available, with:

- Server, to consolidate data management at the level of the entire organization;
- Personal computers, to meet the needs of individual users with a modest investment or for use in decentralized locations.

There are already examples, and they will likely increase over time, of project management software available on the Web – examples of software as a service (SaaS).

Table 8.4   A classification of information systems of support for project activities

	Formalized	Not formalized	Data and information
Not automated	It is official	It is private	Develop, deal, store, exchange
Automated	It is official	It is private	Cooperation: • Coordinate, • Collaborate, • decide, co-decide
		Operational-management modules; Synthesis modules; Decision modules; Support modules for communication/cooperation	

Technique/ objective	Hardware			Characteristic
	Personal computer	Client/server	Server	
	Traditional			
Monotecnique	Pertmaster Promis Control		Cypher	
Multi-techniques: + integrated	Superprojects Ms Project Open Project	Sas System Artemis Primavera	Sw Metier Primavera	
Environments: • Integrated	Project planner; Epiware – project and document management		Ca-Superproject	
Support documents/ time	For comment/notes Personal Information Manager (PIM, Ecco)	Hypertext		
Decision support				
	Not traditional			
Environments to support collaboration	Notes, Exchange, Share Point	Cardinis, Coordinator (Chaos)		
Collaboration tools	Seavus Project Planner (add on di MS Project)			

The Structure

It is not easy to list the basic requirements of an information system to support project management. Some aspects are certainly relevant:

- From the functional point of view:
  - Manage the cycle and the functions connected with the project;
  - Program and control even a large number of activities or multiple projects simultaneously;
  - Manage structural and logical relationships between different activities;
  - Be able to produce timely, complete and updated reports and graphical presentations;
  - Able to simulate the consequences of errors, changes in the nature, duration, cost and management policies ('what if' techniques), obtaining timely results;
  - Have an online help and the possibility to access it, if possible, by typing a question with words not in code;
  - Include reporting standards or formats for different levels of users and be able to produce reports relative to the Quality Certification according to UNI EN ISO 9000 or CMM standards;
  - Be easy to use even for non-technical users;
  - Provide the opportunity to apply the principles of work breakdown structure (WBS) and active-responsibility matrix;
  - Allow you to subdivide the projects into coherent jobs and tasks with the criteria of planning/programming;
  - Periodically verify and account with administrative and accounting data;
- From the interface point of view:
  - Interact and be able to collect data from other systems in such a manner as to make it possible to directly exchange data with other applications through adapters or connectors;
  - Have the possibility to connect with other computers and business operating systems by standard protocols, allowing the use of corporate data when these guarantee the necessary speed;
  - Easily exchange data with spreadsheets, slides, reports and other documents created in applications of integrated packages, whether this is Microsoft Office rather than Open Office or similar, further facilitating the sharing of project information;
- From the technical point of view:
  - Easiness of use by the end use but with the possibility to use macros for the development of customized features:
  - The creation of different representations of the WBS;
  - The preparation of reports and graphical representations (CPM diagrams, Pert, histograms, Gantt charts, etc.);
  - Manage directly or through connectors interfaces to relational databases (Oracle, DB2, etc.);
  - Have some powerful components: such as Visual basic for applications, OLE automation, object libraries, messaging application programming interface (MAPI) support, vendor independent messaging interface (VIM) support, ODBC

support, and support for e-mail packages in order to contribute to the creation of business applications that are mission-critical;
- Implementing systems and procedures for data acquisition to ensure timing and degree of resolution required;
- Own an effective graphic representation geared to management;
- Include specific modules for managing security access and preservation;
- Have tools for the management of workflows. For example, have interfaces with an e-mail tool Messaging Application Programming Interface (MAPI) compatible, so that you can work online with the utmost efficiency for:
  - Sending updates to members of the working group via e-mail trough a distribution list;
  - Instantly communicate and delegate new tasks with the function of task assignment;
  - Collect information on the progress of activities and maintain an update on deadlines;
  - Enter data on the individual project components;
  - Exchange data and information with other applications: send documents and show the custom activities and updates of the project to the members of the work group and other stakeholders.

There are some important elements in the structure of information systems for project management. It is appropriate that the system integrates with other systems of the organization, such as ERPs. A high percentage of the information is transferred to/from the system by company databases or from other central information systems of the company. The updates might be relative to the loading of only some accounting and/or non-accounting data. Furthermore, a common interface with ERP (SAP, Oracle, Microsoft, etc.) is very useful in order to support for instance the control of the project, the final evaluation and eventually the third-party billing if based on the progress of the project.

Moreover, the system may be stand-alone. In this case, the system is isolated or connected to a limited extent in corporate databases. The project team loads the majority of the data. This mode is prone to possible errors or delays in the loading of data.

The Market

The information systems to support project management often suffer from some drawbacks which tend to stem from their origins. The systems were born to support the needs of projects in very large organizations. This type of project tends to be very large (even well over 10,000 activities). They require the processing of large volumes of data, especially about costs, concurrent update of data, etc. A tool for such projects must have a remarkable capacity to process large volumes of data as well as to be flexible in order to support the decisions of the project leader.

The difficulty of use, the extreme specialization of information systems and not least the direct impact on the organization are the basic reasons for which on some occasions project management information systems have failed to establish themselves akin to other packages such as word processing or spreadsheets.

The market situation is evolving significantly. The Information Systems Publishers Association, an organization that brings together all the major manufacturers of computer systems worldwide, recorded a growth in the sales of packages to support project management of almost 50 per cent per year between 2007 and 2011.

Currently the packages for project management are of two types:

- Low end; and
- High end.

Vendors with a long tradition in the production of information systems for project management provide high-end products. In some cases thses products can trace their origins to 10 years ago or more. The products are normally available in client/server platforms.

Characteristic organizations with a tradition in supplying office automation tools normally offer the low-end products. This is the case, for instance, with Microsoft.

In some cases, the product has been a workhorse for years (in the case of CA and HP) but was not the company's most important business area. In other cases, packages are provided by vendors who specialize in supporting project management, for example Artemis or Cardinis. All have been available for some years and have significant advantages in terms of ease of use.

The reasons for the difference between high- and low-end packages lie in their functions. High-end products have very advanced functionality and are suitable for complex projects such as those found in large engineering companies.

High-end packages may appear to be less user-friendly for some project leaders and people sometimes use the low-end packages also for complex projects. However, this means they under-utilize the capabilities of information technology in support of project management.

The packages available in the client/server versions are interesting because they allow maximizing the investment in hardware, giving a station with more 'authority' in terms of responsibilities to the project leader who actually needs it.

Finally, oit would be very reductive to limit the discussion to the information systems of project management themselves. This is a complex task and in many ways still under development: entire areas have not yet fully been explored from the point of view of automation. There may be surprises in the future in terms of functionality. From this point of view, it is particularly important to ensure that the package selected to support project management is able to interface easily and efficiently with other applications available to the organization (e.g. the ERPs) and is provided by vendors robust enough to support the future development of the packages.

While an information system for project management is in itself complete in that it makes available different tools to project leaders, this is not always sufficient to meet the needs of the organization. In particular, when the project management involves operational work, there is a need to reduce the burden of repetitive tasks and to redistribute to various resources the workload arising from the management of these tasks.

In other words, two elements are important:

- Integrate the information system of project management inside the corporate information system to reduce the need to re-type data (management of projects generates is a large amount of information);
- Develop packages that can automatically generate repetitive projects' plans.

Advanced Tools and Integration with Other Applications

The versatility of modern software tools for project management and their ability to integrate with other programs allows their use for a virtually infinite number of activities. The informational packages for project management can often be used in combination with other software products (such as Microsoft Excel and Microsoft Visual Studio), even for the creation of complex applications.

The Conditions of Use of Packages

The usual requirements of technological innovation projects that push towards the use of information systems are:

- Complexity of the project:
  - many activities
  - many interrelationships between activities
  - many organizations who are often involved in conducting the project
  - many locations in which the working groups (virtual team) are located.
- Complexity of products of the project:
  - difficulty in complying with the technical specifications (quality of components);
  - difficulty in complying with operational costs.
- Criticality of delivery times:
  - penalties set by the customer;
  - missed production.

When faced with all of these critical aspects, the integration processes in the organization of automated systems for project management should include:

- The diffusion of the culture of project management and its operational tools through seminars that discuss problems, difficulties in carrying out the project, the levels of applicability, etc.;
- A critical review of the criteria and the process of planning and control of projects by the managers;
- The extensive and coherent application of the principles of the WBS;
- The definition of comprehensive data collection;
- The link with corporate information systems, where possible, to meet the criterion of the uniqueness of the data management and reducing administrative efforts to keep them updated;
- The definition of objective criteria for measuring advancement;

- The timing of reports on work in progress, standardized and finalized at the different levels of responsibility;
- The necessity to train the personnel of the project in the utilization of the system;
- The need to avoid the confinement of the system within the area of ICT personnel;
- Continuous monitoring and attention on the part of management. It should consider the inclusion of these systems at the level of other priority projects in the organization;
- The continuous attention of the management to limit the intervention of the ICT personnel only to the stages of setting up the systems.

The Responsibilities

The information system for project management should seek to use data from other business functions, such as the administrative and accounting functions, to their maximum. On the other hand, other departments in the organization use data inputted into the project management system by project team members. The project is as such responsible for the databases it manages directly (advancement activities, forward orders list, list of projects, etc.).

The project team should periodically run a quality control of data (especially if there is a project management office).

The responsibility of reporting remains with the project team that sets the frequency, content and distribution, in agreement with all entities involved.

The regular meeting of the project is the only place where users should notify any inaccuracies or defects in data collection or processing.

The main barriers to the diffusion of information systems for project management are:

- The costs in versions for mini and mainframe computers can be substantial. On the other hand, there are limitations in processing capabilities in stand-alone personal computer version;
- There is still also some immaturity of management and organizational structures, and therefore under-utilization of advanced digitized tools.

The Future

The evolution of information systems for project management is towards the support of the entire cycle of project management in an integrated way. From this perspective, the development of project management packages in recent times has been remarkable, thanks to the more extensive use of telecommunications networks and the Internet.

Another line of development of information systems for project management follows advances in project management theory. More and more organizations are adopting a lateral type of approach to the organization to address the problems of organization and automation in information management. This is the process management. From this new perspective, information systems of projects tend to coincide increasingly with the information systems of process management, and as such with the management of the organization as a whole. This development is not surprising: as mentioned previously, more and more organizations use project organization as the natural form of organization for the improvement of processes.

The Computer Support for Teamwork

THE DEVELOPMENT

The term computer-supported cooperative work (CSCW) originated in the US in the mid-1980s to identify a new field of research investigating the use of information technology to support teamwork. The opportunity was a conference held in Austin, Texas, in 1986, in which the main issue discussed was the need to establish tools and techniques to support cooperative activities in distributed environments. In other words, the research was on systems able to develop and support collaboration between work teams characterized by high autonomy and not subjected to strict disciplines of conduct.

A few years later, in 1989, the inaugural lecture given by William Wulf at the National Seminar on Cooperation made it very clear that the problems of CSCW were already evident in scientific circles and the road towards a new discipline:

> *In the years to come remote collaboration will not only be possible but necessary. The interaction with remote tools will become indispensable both for their often remote locations and their shared use, as well as because often the operational environment can be harmful to humans.*
> *Kouzes et al., 1996: 40–46*

The same meeting proposed a neologism to replace the original acronym CSCW with the word groupware. Since then, groupware is used to indicate tools and informational methodologies that allow users of networked workstations to:

- Communicate in different ways: From the exchange of messages written explicitly (electronic mail) to the tele-presence of voice and video on a computer screen (instant messaging or chats);
- Share multimedia documentary databases (text, data, images, video, sounds);
- Use the same application programs, whether it involves a simple spreadsheet or a complex drawing such as those for computer-aided design;
- Planning the processes where users take part;
- Agree on decisions at various stages of the process, by using tools that facilitate comparison and generation of ideas.

Figure 8.7 shows the areas of groupware in comparison with other systems.

Groupware finds applications in extremely diverse fields. Table 8.5 shows some of the possible uses of such systems.

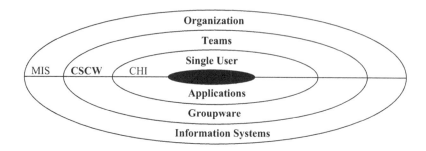

Figure 8.7   Groupware in comparison to other information systems

Table 8.5   Some possible fields of application of groupware

Sector	Application
Banks	Documents Trust management and banking practices Support of financial analysis Comprehensive assistance to the customer
Public administrations	Coordinated management practices Information services to citizens Management deliberations Elaboration of internal regulations Interconnection with other administrations
Distribution companies	Management orders to vendors Management orders for customers Cost analysis Definition and management of sales budget Development of marketing plans
Manufacturers	Design and product development Definition and management of sales and revenue budget Development and coordination of marketing projects Contract management Offers to clients Management orders to vendors Managing trade negotiations Management of manuals and technical documentation of the product
Insurance companies	Management policies Definition and management of production budget Development and coordination of production plans
Professional studies	Planning of work and presence in the office Client management Contract management Joint development of 'critical cases' Consultation with external databases

In 1986, when, for the first time, people started to talk about groupware, technologies such as the Web were not yet mature to support CSCW. There was however a proposal for a classification of the areas of the new applications of interest. We believe that it is still valid. The product categories include (Kouzes et al., 1996):

* Messaging systems to provide for exchanging conversations, keep track of them and supporting the users in asking questions and providing answers, even with a time lag;
* Computer conferencing systems (bulletin boards) allowing remote voice or video conferences. In this way, users are able to share work with each other, and update on reciprocal results during a work session;
* Calendaring systems, enabling the sharing of calendars, appointments and diaries. They facilitate a cooperative scheduling of appointments;
* Shared filing systems to access and browse common databases;
* Co-authoring systems providing suitable services to create cooperative and shared documents;
* Screen-sharing systems with the ability to display the contents of another user, and vice versa. In this way, it is possible to transfer to another display your content, eventually integrating data with voice and images;
* Group-decision support systems (GDSS) supporting resolution by the group of ill-conditioned or ill-structured problems, both in distributed environments as well as in face-to-face work;
* Advanced meeting room created specifically to better support the work group in face-to-face environments. These are characterized by advanced integrated equipment in the workroom (megascreen multi-user, server, etc.);

This taxonomy, at that time a thing of the future though today fully available, derived from the analysis and logical aggregations of the demands and needs of CSCW systems, coming out of the diverse activities of organizations. There were areas from which the most convincing demand for such systems arose, and from which stemmed a multitude of initiatives. Unfortunately, there are further developments that need to take place:

* large projects and initiatives
* engineering and scientific research
* coordination and development of new ideas and proposals
* robotics and artificial intelligence
* development of tools and collaborative software applications.

It is possible to add to this list the projects of Lean and Digitize initiatives. The support central system, developed in-house by GE, is an example in this direction.

The remainder of this chapter examines:

* The state of the art in groupware; and
* The framework of reference in this field.

Groupware is evolving more and more, and even greater developments will come in the coming years. Web 2.0 is an example of a fertile application field for groupware (see Chapter 11, The future of Lean and Digitize).

THE MAIN FEATURES AND AREAS OF APPLICATION

Advanced workstations, networks, broadband and shared multimedia computer files are all components of distributed computing. They are prerequisites of groupware. These technologies are now available and relatively cheap. However, the existing technological feasibility is not in itself a sufficient reason to justify interest in groupware. Parallel to technological developments, there is more evidence of new requirements in the labour market and the economy that are difficult to solve with traditional approaches.

A first instance, arising from the globalization of the economy and increased competitiveness, is the need to:

* Minimize time for the evaluation of business opportunities;
* Define strategies;
* Develop products or services, and as such minimize the reaction times of the organizations; and, as discussed in this book;
* Improve internal processes and interaction with organizations in the outside world with the Lean and Digitize approach.

The minimization of time to deliver solutions is possible through two routes:

* Faster Execution of each activity necessary for teamwork;
* Parallelize the execution of various activities as much as possible.

Efficiency is not enough to guarantee low response times. Processes need to be flexible (lean but also agile). They need to be able to adapt quickly to increasingly rapid and frequent changes of context. Organizational flexibility is the fundamental requirement today.

To guarantee that the structure copes with this requirement, there is a need to move from the traditional organizational design by functions to that by processes. This entails, essentially, working with multidisciplinary teams. At the same time each of them needs to take into account all aspects of a process. They replace the rigid hierarchical structures of the past. The new organization needs to have reduced inertia: it must be able to decompose and recompose as needed.

As a methodology and a set of tools for groups working, groupware can play a key role in this new organization. Groupware has assumed a more precise identity in terms of functionality and application areas over the years.

Three aspects are essential in teamwork:

* Communication is the cornerstone of teamwork. A groupware system uses a wide range of communication, from e-mail to tele/video conferencing, available at various levels of sophistication;
* Coordination uses rules, explicit or implicit, which allow different components to operate together in synergy. Typical groupware tools are, to this end, the automatic group calendaring and software packages to support project management;
* Collaboration implies sharing work that changes from situation to situation.

Table 8.6 identifies the main groupware features in relation to the three typical areas of cooperative work.

Table 8.6   Groupware features relating to different areas of cooperative work

Functionality	Area		
	Communication	Coordination	Collaboration
The exchange of electronic messages	x	x	
Emulation of face-to-face meetings	x	x	
Planning of processes		x	
Joint development of solutions	x		X
Joint development of documentation	x		X

ELECTRONIC MESSAGING

In the context of so-called messaging, e-mail is the tool that has the most widespread use due to some of its most distinctive features:

- Operates asynchronously, and is therefore able to support communications needs of different types;
- Provides an excellent level of interoperability in synergy with all productivity tools found on personal computers;
- It has, thanks to messaging, a wide flexibility of use because it does not require compliance with strict working procedures, while still allowing you to assign priority to communications and to respect confidentiality.

This ease of use implies difficulties sometimes. A first case concerns a conversation mediated by the computer, based on the engine provided by electronic messaging. It may be difficult for the users to maintain a continuous dialogue, properly associating sent messages to those received. All the more so if several partners are involved.

Another case concerns the exchange of documents. The difficulty stems from the fact that when there are several partners, each of them able to modify the documents exchanged, it can be difficult to know which is the updated version. To overcome these difficulties, there are tools capable of managing these problems automatically.

There is also another problem with e-mail; its excessive use. This creates problems of information overload, and distracts people from the work they are doing.

A variant of e-mail is IM (instant messaging or chat). This has the advantage of informing the user of the presence of the other party on its computer. They tend to be even more destructive on the operations of people. Their diffusion, especially in the version short message service (SMS) in cellphones, has been incredible and overwhelming,

Recent statistics indicate that it takes 20–30 minutes for a person to refocus on what they were doing after the interruption of a phone call, e-mail or a chat.

THE EMULATION OF FACE-TO-FACE MEETINGS

Teleconferencing is a synchronous communication. All members of a workgroup can communicate by voice, seeing each other and exchanging documents of every kind and nature.

There are two categories of teleconferencing:

- Those which can be established between two or more meeting rooms equipped on purpose; and
- Those which you can carry out by remaining in your workplace and using a personal computer equipped with a videocam.

Desktop conferencing uses the screen of a personal computer. It represents a natural evolution of the computer equipment already present in the office and implies the availability of a broadband network infrastructure and signal compression techniques.

The Planning of Processes

One of the objectives of groupware is the integration and harmonization of individual contributions to achieve a common objective. Automatic planning system processes (a workflow nanagement system) can help in this direction. They can be of various types. Typically, they allow reciprocal updating of the various participants on the state of progress of the work of the group. In addition, they are able to intervene when certain situations take place via an event management system (EMS). These can be, for example, the arrival of a deadline or a request of contribution to resolve a problem in the flow of the activity.

The requests of intervention generated from these types of tools can be geared not only to the members of the work group, but also to machines, or better yet, to the software supports that make up part of the system of groupware. In other words, the verification of an event can cause the automatic intervention of other computerized procedures.

This intertwining of human and technological contributions constitutes an interesting alternative paradigm for the development of the applications. It exemplifies well the spirit of developing the world of groupware.

The organizational aspects on which such supports can work are:

- Increase in the distribution of human resources in the territory: the organizations will depend less and less on the persons being 'always' in contact (emergence of virtual work groups or the virtual team). There are organizations with top-level coordination, operating on a worldwide scale in an extremely effective manner. The consequences will be an inversion of tendency in respect to the current urbanist approach to the construction of centres or offices;
- Progressive loss of importance of the typical managerial roles: in today's organizations, everyone develops some management functions besides the operational ones typical to their role. What distinguishes the managers from the others is that their task is essentially to direct other people's work. Groupware decreases the importance of this type of centralized management in favour of one that is more distributed;

- Increase of organizational reactivity and of the capacity of replies to the change: this is in regard to predictable changes, for which organization structures already exist. There is a need to improve the reaction to unpredictable changes;
- Reduction of the need of transferring people and things;
- Potentially, a smaller dependency on paper: even if it does not mean its total elimination.

The Joint Development of Documentation (Co-authoring)

Most of the documents in an organization results from the work of several authors. There are groupware applications that support such tasks. These systems help in regulating access to documents shared by various co-authors and keeping them updated on changes. To reach this objective it is necessary to combine the management of multimedia databases with advanced e-mail techniques.

An alternative to these shared documents consists of the so-called 'Wiki' documents. They are born from the collaboration between different users. The most striking example is that of Wikipedia, the universal encyclopedia on the Internet, in which an extraordinary number of people have collaborated voluntarily. Wikipedia has reached 15 million of entries relatively few years.

Joint Development of Solutions

Groupware systems support the analysis and solution of complex problems of various kinds by several people, each contributing according to their specific expertise. The objective is to improve the decision-making process through the comparison of different viewpoints in order to arrive at an optimal definition. Prerequisites for reaching joint solutions are the sharing of the context by the members of the group. This means starting from the same objectives and general constraints, and proceeding using models and simulation tools.

The sharing in the context means, in computer terms, accessing common databases and knowledge bases and the use of the same decision support tools.

However, while starting from a common framework, the various members of the group might, in principle, propose different solutions to the problem, since each person might follow their own criteria, derived from specific experiences and expertise.

At this point it is important to analyse and compare the various proposals in order to reach an agreed solution. This means following a process of convergence, which on the one hand points out the differences while on the other it enhances the knowledge base through a common intercomparison. The class of general tools for groupware useful for this task is called a group-decision support system (GDSS).

Various groupware functions can integrate with each other in the development of a Lean and Digitize project (see Table 8.7).

Table 8.7   Groupware features that integrate well with each other in reference to the development of a Lean and Digitize project

Development of a Lean and Digitize project		
The exchange of electronic messages Emulation of meetings Face-to-face	The exchange of electronic messages Emulation of meetings Face-to-face Joint development of documentation	Joint development of solutions Joint development of documentation
Define and measure	Analyse and process design, architecture design	Build, test and deploy, verify

Starting from a specification, in terms of deadlines and objectives, the team agrees, using the capabilities of message exchange and emulation of face-to-face meetings, a work programme which includes the definition of individual commitments. During the development phase the programme is updated automatically, following the actual state of play, using the planning functions. During the development work, the team uses all the tools for the joint development of solutions, integrating them with those of communication. Finally, the project ends with a document that contains all the technical and economic details developed by the team by using the groupware features.

The Success Factors of the Information Systems to Support the Lean and Digitize Initiatives

The success factors for groupware systems in support of Lean and Digitize initiatives are:

- The acceptance and support of the users;
- Ease of use. It is essential that these systems have a user-friendly interface;
- The ability to integrate with existing calendars, alert systems and other user-friendly features is a critical factor. The key to the buy-in is to minimize the interactions that do not fall naturally into the group workflow. In essence, the process must provide more benefits to the end user in comparison to previous ways of working;
- Integration with the existing application environment is important to minimize the changes associated with the introduction of new solutions brought by the Lean and Digitize project. Organizations tend to have very complex legacy infrastructures. The ability to integrate the new software resulting from the Lean and Digitize project with existing applications should be a major concern. This critical factor of success involves the improvement of the existing process rather than a radical change with the total deletion of existing applications;
- Compliance with standards is a fundamental prerequisite to guarantee long-term sustainability of a solution;
- Service-oriented architecture (SOA) has become an increasingly popular approach to reduce the complexity of ICT applications. Many organizations are working on SOA

initiatives. The ability to 'play ball' in an SOA environment is therefore essential in order to develop projects of Lean and Digitize in organizations;

- The viability of the vendor or developer of the software is a major concern when choosing a software product and its implementation. This requires a significant commitment by the vendor to continue to develop and support technology. Few vendors offer the full range of functionality in their suite software. Even fewer have a proven record of accomplishment of investing and supporting their products in the long term. It is necessary to consider the viability of the vendor in the future. A large number of software companies are bought and sold each year, often leaving their clients without an effective support or a clear line of development of the packages bought. This includes:
  - Ensure availability of adequate and continuous support;
  - Reduce the risk that the platform of Lean and Digitize becomes obsolete.
- Last but not least, it is important the ability to reduce the total cost of the process, the total cost of operations (TCO).

ICT has the potential to help organizations to design, implement and improve business processes. Since these processes include a substantial flow of information, Lean and Digitize relies heavily on ICT. The execution of a project by Lean and Digitize is no small challenge, but the potential benefits are significant and far-reaching:

- Continuous quality improvement in core business processes;
- Business agility through the ability to implement fast processes that take account of the changing conditions of the context and the organization. This can be greatly improved thanks to the establishment of a centre of excellence that makes available to the whole organization the knowledge of Lean and Digitize;
- Better monitoring and control of factors that affect the KPIs and the financial performances; and
- Creation of an overview of the company information system to bridge the gap between the business and the ICT.

Many of the efforts to implement Lean and Digitize rely on ICT components. The software features are substantial and only software vendors and appropriate systems integrators can provide a complete solution thanks to:

- A large and sufficient number of resources; and
- A commitment to long-term investments in effective platforms and support to their customers.

List of References

Bracchi, G. and Motta, G. 1997. *Processi Aziendali e Sistemi Informativi*. Milano: FrancoAngeli.

Camussone, P.F. 1990. *Informatica aziendale*. Milano: Egea.

De Maio, A. et al. 1982. *Informatica e Processi Decisionali*. Milano: FrancoAngeli.

Erl, T. et al. 2012. *Service-Oriented Infrastructure: On-Premise and in the Cloud*. Upper Saddle River: Prentice Hall.

Kouzes, R., Myers, J. and Wulf, W. 1996. Collaboratories: Doing Science on the Internet. *Computer*, 29, 40–46.

Nicoletti, B. 2008. Unified Content Management. *Sistemi and Automazione*, 4, April, 38–43.

Maggiolini, P. 1981. *Costi e benefici di un sistema informativo*. Milano: Etas Libri.

Polini, A. 2007. *Note per il corso di Ingegneria del Software*. Online: Università di Camerino Dipartimento di Matematica ed Informatica. Available from http://www1.isti.cnr.it/~polini/downloads/WS_Unicam.pdf, accessed 25 January 2010.

Salunga, A. 2008. *What Process Experts Need To Know About SOA*. Forrester Research. Available from http://www.forrester.com/Research/Document/0,7211,45534,00.html, accessed 15 March 2010.

Skalle, H. et al. 2009. *Aligning Business Process Management, Service-Oriented Architecture, and Lean Six Sigma for Real Business Results*. Armonk: IBM Redbooks.

Smith, H. and Fingar, P. 2003. *Business Process Management, The Third Wave*. Tampa: Meghan-Kiffer.

Theyventheran, D. 2008. *Business Process Re-engineering for Customer Centricity*. Fintech Asia, Singapore, 28 February.

Websites

http://www.caffeconbea.it/2008/03/03/soa-reference-architecture-a-che-cosa-serve/

http://it.wikipedia.org/wiki/Service-oriented_architecture

http://www.gefanuc.com/workflow

http://www1.isti.cnr.it/~polini/downloads/WS_Unicam.pdf

http://itlab.wordpress.com/2007/09/10/soa-service-oriented-architecture-definizione-e-considerazioni/

http://www-05.ibm.com/it/ol3/number14/ol14_soa.pdf

http://it.sun.com/practice/software/soa/

http://www-05.ibm.com/it/ol3/number14/ol14_soa.pdf

http://mediaproducts.gartner.com/reprints/oracle/article75/article75.html

9 *Lean and Digitize in Manufacturing*

Introduction

This chapter examines some possible areas of application of Lean and Digitize in manufacturing. We will not include services processes in manufacturing organizations (such as finance or information systems): Chapter 10, on the application of Lean and Digitize to services, will cover this.

In manufacturing organizations, there are three key processes:

- product development
- order management; and
- logistics.

We will now examine each of these three key processes, focusing in particular on the last one. Logistics represents one of the areas with higher probability of return on investment with a Lean and Digitize project and could benefit from projects for process improvement and digitization.

Product Development

There are several possible applications of the Lean and Digitize method to the processes of product development:

- The Lean and Digitize method supports design and rapid prototyping of many products and their components, both dual and multidimensional;
- The simulation technology allows designers of processes and products to simulate the project execution in an increasingly complex and more realistic environment;
- In the research and development process of complex products, those responsible must be able to ascertain the status of development of a product or of a project in the project cycle. The support of Lean and Digitize in this regard can be quite relevant;
- Key moments in the process of design of a product are analysing and deciding when to:
  - supply additional resources
  - launch a product into the market or
  - abandon a development project.

- Tools for analysing decisions which compute the return on investments in product development at various stages of its life cycle can provide the data necessary to make these decisions;
- For many organizations, a key application of product development is interorganizational communication. Designers must be able to exchange ideas and documents for new products, as well as daily messages on the progress and improvement projects for existing or future products.

Order Management

A number of organizations need to improve the process of moving from an order or customer's proposal up to the collection of revenues. The objectives to achieve are to:

- Speed up delivery to the customer;
- Increase satisfaction in the management of the order;
- Reduce costs and resources used by the process.

The role of Lean and Digitize in the process improvement stems from the need to coordinate order management across multiple entities and to speed up communication. There are at least six applications that, according to Davenport (1993), can transform the fulfilment of orders:

- Customers often find it difficult to select products from large, complex, or overly technical catalogues. Companies with product lines of this type can use expert systems or databases of variants of products to make available applications that help the choice of products matching the requirements of a customer;
- An ever-present problem with order fulfilment is to analyse and forecast customer demand. Some organizations prefer to anticipate the demands of their customers instead of making products to order. This has been possible for a long time at the aggregate level. Now, with the proliferation of customer identification codes, organizations are trying to forecast the demand at the micro level, based on the analysis of past purchases. Enterprises quote the price of individual products using complex systems and data from previous bids. The long-term direction for these applications is to design a marketing strategy tailored to individual customers and the decline in advertising and promotions for mass market (mass customization);
- Based on order taking over the phone, the applications of the Lean and Digitize method re-launch direct communication with the customer (vocal or through messages). It offers significant opportunities for process innovation. At the simplest level, the ability to send voice messages or SMS can benefit communication amongst customers, the sales manager and sales staff. In telemarketing-oriented environments, this application can identify the customer (via an automated identification number) at the beginning of the call, displaying the customer's history on the screen of the operator. The operator can transfer the call to other parts of the organization if this is useful. The support of digitization is particularly important in moving from a pure service to a sales effort being in contact with the customer (the so-called S2S Service-to-Sales approach);

- Electronic commerce (e-commerce) can be simple or complex. The simpler applications include electronic catalogues with access via the Web by the customer. The more advanced versions include offer systems, negotiations and fixed pricing with the possibility of automatic cancellation. Many organizations have implemented e-marketplaces on the Internet for a wide range of products and services;
- Electronic data interchange (EDI) is an ICT application for order management. It represents a relatively 'primitive' form of communication between organizations, as it generally involves simple transactions of purchase and delivery such as billing and bill of lading. It tends to be of the batch type and not real-time. The opportunities for innovation are a combination of EDI with process changes that automatically generate the request for re-supply;
- The composition of texts on the processing unit with the possibility of revisions is becoming increasingly common. The process of managing orders can benefit from the composition of the text in automated proposals. A growing number of organizations have developed applications that allow sales staff, automatically or computer-assisted, to answer customer queries in a structured dialogue and to issue customized proposals. This application becomes more common when organizations simplify their selling processes through Lean and Digitize projects.

Organizations are only now beginning to appreciate the potential of the Lean and Digitize method for process innovation in order management. In so doing, they not only transform their processes, but also impact on the processes of their customers and, above all, of their suppliers, as discussed in the next section.

The Logistics Processes (Nicoletti 2009, 2011)

There are various definitions of logistics. Each of them differs in the breadth of vision. According to Wikipedia, logistics is:

> *The management of the flow of materials and services between the point of origin and the point of use in order to meet the requirements of customers or corporations.*

> *Logistics involves the integration of information, transportation, inventory, warehousing, material handling, and packaging and often security. Logistics is a channel of the supply chain that adds the value of time and place utility. Today, it is possible to model, analyse, visualize and optimize complex logistics processes by plant simulation software. This can involve anything from consumer goods such as food, to ICT materials, to aerospace and defence equipment.*

When it comes to industrial logistics, the term 'industrial' emphasizes that the point of view is that of the manufacturer and/or supplier of the product, rather than the point of view of the end customer.

Industrial logistics is composed of two parts (see Figure 9.1):

- The supply of materials and components with the objective of ensuring their availability for production (inbound); and
- The delivery of products and their spare parts to the customer (outbound).

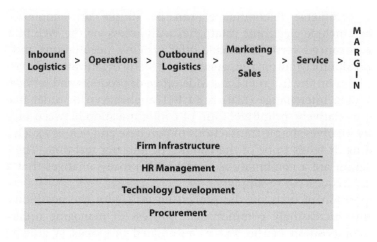

Figure 9.1   Logistics is part of the value chain of the product (Porter 2008)

In Italy, it is estimated that logistics, as a system of services for the organization of production lines, stock management, warehousing and distribution systems of products, has a total value today of about €200 billion. In the system of manufacturing organizations, the average incidence of the costs of logistics is equal to 7.3 per cent of total costs. This figure rises to 9.8 per cent for smaller organizations of 20–49 employees (www.censis.it).

From the viewpoint of economics, the importance of logistics is growing:

- In the logistics industry, consolidation is growing (OTM-SIG, 2008);
- There is an increasing globalization in the markets. It involves the movement of parts and products throughout the world and, increasingly, from emerging markets. Emerging markets are a threat from the point of view of competition in products, but also a great opportunity. Keep in mind that their technological maturity is often limited. There is a need to extend the life of the plants and to improve their productivity;
- Many organizations are increasingly outsourcing an important part of the manufacturing of products. This implies the increasing importance of logistics, in this case inbound;
- Today the time-to-market, i.e. the speed with which a product is available to the customer, together with the quality of products, is increasingly amongst the first requirements for competing in the markets;
- Industrial logistics is a key factor in ensuring the flexibility and immediacy of response to the market by the suppliers. It is also important for the use of continuous and reliable products over time, by the provision of spare parts. This is an optimization along all the life of the products

For all these reasons, logistics is probably one of the most advanced industrial sectors in the world. It is also a business segment that would benefit from process optimization.

From the point of view of the application of the Lean and Digitize method logistic is of considerable importance, for example to ensure just-in-time delivery.

In summary, the importance given to the logistics industry by the manufacturers of products was modest in the past. This attitude is changing. The concern for customer satisfaction leads to a re-valuation of the contribution of logistics and its employees. The functionality of logistics services is now of major importance for:

- Customers, whose increasing dependence on machines, from equipment to systems, has accentuated the need to always guaranteed the timely delivery; and
- Manufacturers and suppliers, where the importance of the logistics industry in the supply chain is increasing for efficient, effective and economical delivery.

To match these changes in the environment, the logistics industry is changing. Change is not easy because logistics is a complex function from a management point of view. The logistics industry is now subject to different stimuli:

- On the one hand, there are changes in machine technology (electronics, new materials, etc.).
- On the other hand, competition is becoming more intense.
  Under these conditions, one needs to keep in mind:
- A number of aspects to ensure the effectiveness, efficiency and economics of industrial logistics; and
- The changes in the processes needed to meet these new challenges.

A Lean and Digitize project needs to start from the VOC. A survey on the VoC in organizations with logistics problems revealed that customers want:

- Excellency in the technology of their products, but also in the logistics part of the delivery of the products they purchase;
- 24/7, 7/7 delivery of products without unscheduled delays;
- Continuous monitoring of the delivery of their products or spare parts;
- 100 per cent security and safety (zero incidents).

These assumptions about the development of logistics services represent an interesting perspective. Customers are moving very cautiously when, through the efficiency of the logistics services, the productivity of the organization is at stake. Many factors, including psychological ones, contribute to the choice of a logistics service industry:

- security and safety
- understanding the urgency factor
- the need to contain costs.

In response to these needs, industrial logistics services must change. In the development of the logistics industry, the customer could be the main beneficiary if there are changes in their attitude: less dependent on the supplier, more cooperative, but also more independent, in evaluating new offerings that organizations could find in the market. Organizations must review the basic logistics services in the mechanisms of intervention, in substance and in the rigid original structure. The new process needs to take into account the profound changes in the customers' approach in regard to traditional approaches.

INNOVATION IN LOGISTICS

It may be interesting to delve into some of the trends in the field of industrial logistics where strong support can be provided by an approach such as that of Lean and Digitize. From this point of view, in the following paragraphs we analyse the potential process improvements for industrial logistics and integration services of the product from the perspective of the customer.

Innovation is essential in a world of rapid and turbulent change. It is possible to link innovation in industrial logistics to changes in product technology, to the process and of the organization. The basic decisions are what to provide and how to grant the work. The most relevant question that logistics managers should ask themselves with respect to innovation is that of the need to define clearly the services provided to the sectors and markets that they intend to serve. Product innovation has no limits on the types and a variety of services offered. The possibility of introducing these innovations, taken for granted that there is a need for the organization and the market for them, depends on the type of services that logistics organization intend to provide.

Amongst the specific processes of logistics in transportation organizations are managing orders, inventory, materials management and service delivery. Amongst the generic applications relevant to logistics processes, we mention the following applications:

- The key to logistics processes is knowledge of the location of materials or of vehicles. With sophisticated applications and communications technologies, it is increasingly possible to determine rapidly and accurately the location of the business units – either individuals or goods. Sometimes the computers are used to choose possible alternative routes for vehicles and goods;
- In addition to locating objects, systems should be able to recognize and identify them accurately and quickly. Hence a number of technologies such as barcodes, and more recently radio frequency identification devices (RFID) (Finkenzeller, 2010)), for potentially identifying every piece or set of pieces (for example, a pallet);
- It is important to optimize the use and management of resources in key processes, whether physical inventories of goods, human resources or financial assets. Organizations must always keep in mind the location, availability and better use of those resources.

An organization that intends to use the Lean and Digitize method as a lever for the change of process needs to explore the processes and existing digitization applications in detail. This can help the process improvement team to understand how information technology can provide support for innovation.

In order for an organization to improve a specific application, it would be good to first determine the performance of the same application in another organization. Benchmarking of the potential innovation is important: it involves understanding how Lean and Digitize supports the logistics processes in other organizations. This is not about copying, but learning from the experiences (and if possible mistakes) of others.

The Development of Lean and Digitize for Logistics

THE OBJECTIVES

The use of the Lean and Digitize method to support the improvement of logistics has three fundamental objectives:

- Increase the effectiveness of the logistics system to respond to the objectives of the customer and the organization;
- Improve the efficiency, increasing productivity and thus reducing resource requirements;
- Increase the margins of the service, by helping to improve revenues and reduce costs to benefit both their customers and the logistics operators.

A study done by the OTM SIG group (2008) demonstrates the need for such improvements:

- Ninety-two per cent of customers consider that the support of information technology represents a key element in the offering of services of their logistics providers;
- Thirty per cent consider that the innovation in information systems, made available from their logistics providers, has also increased their internal use of ICT in the processes and operations inside their entire organization;
- Only 32 per cent of customers interviewed believe the current installed base of ICT of their logistics providers is satisfactory.

Table 9.1 shows some of the problems reported by customers with respect to the logistics services provided to them.

Table 9.1   Problems in information systems of outsourced logistics services

Outsourced logistic services	% of customers who indicated problems
Lack of integration between internal systems of logistic service providers	53
Inability to provide adequate visibility of orders/shipments/stocks	52
Inability to bill correctly for services provided	31
The time required to introduce a new customer	22
Inability to provide quick quotes for special services	21
Inability to accept electronic orders	18

If you use the Lean and Digitize method for the improvement of processes, in logistics the transformation project must include three phases:

- Improving the process through the use of the method and tools of Lean Six Sigma;
- The implementation of those aspects that do not require digitization, such as new organizational models, elimination of unnecessary steps and so on;
- The digitization of the aspects of the process that require digitization.

THE INTEGRATED APPROACH OF LEAN SIX SIGMA IN GENERAL ELECTRIC (GE) (ECKES 2000)

GE Corporation

GE is a diversified company that operates in several macro-areas in technology and financial services. It is present in over 100 countries and employs over 300,000 workers (www.ge.com). In 2007, it had a turnover of US$172 billion, achieving a profit of US$22 billion.

Methodological approach to Lean Six Sigma

GE started to use Six Sigma in 1996. Since then, the approach has evolved and in 2004, GE integrated Six Sigma with the Lean Thinking: the Lean Six Sigma method.

GE implements the Lean Six Sigma projects following the classic pattern Define – Measure – Analyse – Develop – Verify (DMADV). GE added to this approach the tools included in Lean Thinking: the five principles, the seven wastes, the five S's and so on.

Recently GE has also approached process improvements in a Lean and Digitize way.

Setting up an improvement project

A Lean and Digitize project begins with the setting-up phase of the project. Voices of external or internal customers are the base used to decide the issues that the improvement project should address. Based on the voice of the customer, the first aspects considered are:

- which process should be analysed
- its boundaries
- the level of detail
- the end result that needs to be attained; and
- the timeline.

The team draws a project charter

The next step is the mapping of the process selected: applying value stream mapping or the Supplier Input Process Output Customer (SIPOC). GE calls these meetings Action Work-Outs (AWO!): this means: 'let's work together' or 'let's get together'. The word 'Action' calls for 'action'. An Action Work-Out therefore means teamwork and immediate action (Ulrich et al., 2002). Initially, it is used to draw the as-is of the value stream of the process. Points of contact are rightly outside the process, such as customers, suppliers and the various functions involved.

Once mapped the process, the team compute the following measures:

- the defect rate

- the throughput time
- the cycle time; and
- the inventory.

These measures represent the main parameters of the process.

The measure of defects is in Sigmas

The total cycle time is equal to the sum of the individual cycle times of all the phases that are part of the process. Initially the team computes the cycle time. Later, the team analyses the inventory and the volumes of each phase for a given period. Analysis of the inventory and volumes should follow these specific steps:

- At day zero: implementation of the process and calculations of the inventory for each stage;
- After a month: implementation of the process and calculations of the inventory;
- After another month: implementation of the process and calculations of the inventory.

In practice, one often finds itself analysing processes with a cycle time of several months. This prevents the analysis of the parameters in a limited time. To avoid this, it is necessary to analyse historical data, if available, in the existing information systems. This analysis minimizes the time of data collection and the resources committed. For example, if you want to measure the accounts payable process, one option is to map the process and then conduct three interviews within a month of each other to measure the parameters in:

- the bills received
- the bills approved; and
- the bills paid.

Another option is to extract the same type of data from the existing information system using digitization. The as-is value stream map should include also comprehensive data on defects, cycle times and inventory. The main stakeholders of the process should always validate the data extracted from the information system.

At this point, it is important to select the team that must map the to-be during another Action Work-Out. It would be beneficial that the team be as much as heterogeneous as possible with:

- Creative people with the task of imagining solutions to the problem posed;
- Professionals who know the process in depth: this should help to stop the wrong actions and recommend those which are potentially correct;
- People with the power and the knowledge to apply the solution found should modify the process now in use.

Possibly the same team should implement, as soon as possible, the decisions made during the Action Work-Out. Persons external to the project team should not redefine the decisions later.

The last part of the set-up phase of the project consists of a meeting involving the team and the stakeholders. The objective of this meeting is the alignment of all parties involved in the as-is process. The sharing of the value stream map, of data, feedback and process objectives, assures the alignment.

The results of the first macro phases of the Lean and Digitize approach are:

- Analysis of voice of the customers (external/internal);
- Selection of the process to improve;
- Definition of the objectives to achieve;
- Setting up of the project team;
- Mapping of the process: value stream map/SIPOC;
- Learning about basic data in the process:
  - volume
  - defects
  - cycle time; and
  - inventory.
- Approval of the value stream map by the actors of the process;
- Detailed definition by the project team of the as-is process.

Definition of the to-be and implementation of the first improvements: the Action Work-Out

In the second phase, the Action Work-Out will define the to-be process (the future state map) (Ulrich et al., 2002). The Action Work-Out does not have a fixed duration in this phase. It usually ranges from two to five days, depending on the size and complexity of the process to be improved and generally begins with the presentation of the project to the stakeholders to describe:

- The problem to solve;
- The objectives to be achieved; and
- Suggestions relative to the possible causes of malfunction or waste of the process under consideration.

A keynote speech by the stakeholders at this presentation could be the following:

We [The stakeholders] appoint you to improve our process. We want the current cycle time of five days to be reduced substantially to XXX. From our point of view, there are the following problems in these phases. You have carte blanche. You can decide what you want, apply the changes when it is necessary and do so as you see fit. We meet in a week for the report [or] We meet tonight for a partial report.

Based on the analysis of the as-is process, and, with the assistance of the Six Sigma, Lean and Digitize tools, the team designs the to-be process.

The current state maps all the sources of waste in the process. The task of the team is to find during the process Action Work-Out!:

- The way to eliminate them;
- Draw the future map of the process;
- Put into practice some decisions to improve the process.

While drawing the future state map, the word Action (in the name Action Work-Out!) requires that all possible changes be clearly defined (and possibly made) during the Action Work-Out. They might for instance influence the layout of an office or a job shop, physically moving work locations, or delete fields of software, or changing the interfaces.

In the Action Work-Out!, the focus is on how one should run the new process. It is necessary to try to put some ideas into practice immediately. While the team draws the future state map, it computes the values of the new cycle times, based on volumes and activity times. This calculation is possible because the team knows all the variables involved.

Continuing with the preceding example:

> *[The project team] we have eliminated the following stages, we decided to change within 60 days this part of the process and we simulated it, reversed these procedures and merged these others. We know the number of operators, we know the time and volume of each phase. Analysing each variable and simulating the entire process, we believe that the new time cycle will be XX minutes. The future state map fully achieves the prefixed objective.*

Normally, during the Action Work-Out, at the end of each day a partial report is prepared to summarize:

- the activities of the day
- the decisions made; and
- the progress in the project.

The team does not necessarily need to prepare PowerPoint presentations. Partial reports can be distributed amongst the various subgroups (if the project is divided into several groups according to skills, knowledge, or just for simplicity). In this way, it is possible to update all the members of the group on the work of other groups.

If the process under consideration is very complex and/or has a strategic value, the team present these partial reports to the stakeholders periodically.

At the end of the Action Work-Out, the team checks that the to-be process aligns with the original objectives. They prepare a final report that lists the actions to be undertaken in the near short, medium and long term, in order to achieve the future state map. The plan of such actions is the kaizen plan. If instead the to-be does not achieve the objectives of the stakeholders, the team needs to plan a new Action Work-Out!.

The results of this new macro phase of the Lean and Digitize approach are:

- Definition of the complexity of the project;
- Planning the duration of the Action Work-Out;
- Presentation of the project to the stakeholders: exposure of the problem, the objectives, and initial suggestions;
- Analysis of the as-is
- The design of the to-be;
- Implementation of the first changes;
- Calculation of the future measures:
    - defects
    - throughput time
    - cycle time
    - inventory.
- Planning and drafting of the kaizen plan;
- Report to the stakeholders.

During the design of the future state map, one may find that there is a need to change a computer application. If this change is minimal, such as a modification of an interface, the team implement it immediately during the Action Work-Out. If there is a need to set different procedures or completely recreate the software, a new Lean and Digitize project can start, with longer durations (90 days or more).

The more complex the problem, the greater the demand for planning for the solution, and the better suited the Six Sigma tools belonging to a classical DMADV project. The Lean and Digitize projects for the implementation of the to-be can last three months, six months, and only more in special cases.

Once the team complete the planned activities through the kaizen plan and verify the correctness of the changes to the process, the final phase of the Lean and Digitize method in GE continues with:

- the training of the operators
- the production launch; and
- the ongoing monitoring of performance.

The project always ends with:

- a lessons learned session; and
- appropriate celebration.

List of References

2008. Third-Party Logistics. OTM-SIG, 50.

Davenport, T.H. 1993. *Process Innovation: Reengineering Work Through Information Technology.* Cambridge: Harvard Business School Press.

Eckes, G. 2000. *The Six Sigma Revolution: How General Electric and Others Turned Process into Profits*, 1st edn. Hoboken: John Wiley & Sons.

Finkenzeller, K. 2010. *RFID Handbook: Fundamentals and Applications in Contactless Smart Cards, Radio Frequency Identification and Near-Field Communication.* Hoboken: John Wiley and Sons.

Nicoletti, B. 2009. *Miglioramento dei Processi di Logistica e Costruzione.* Convegno Annuale della Sezione Informatica dell'ANIMP, Genova, Italy, 23 April.

Nicoletti, B. 2011. Lean Procurement (JIIS). *Journal of Internet and Information Systems*, 2(3), 35–42.

Porter, M.E. 2008. *On Competition.* Cambridge: Harvard Business Review Book.

Ulrich, D., Kerr, S. and Ashkenas, R. 2002. *The GE Work-Out: How to Implement GE's Revolutionary Method for Busting Bureaucracy and Attacking Organizational Problems – Fast!* New York: McGraw-Hill.

Websites

http://www.censis.it/277/280/339/570/573/579/content.asp

http://www.ge.com/ch/it/ourCompany/company/index.html

http://www.ge.com/ar2007/cfs.jsp

10 *Lean and Digitize in Services*

Introduction

Field research (Yilmaz and Chatterjee, 2000) has shown that most processes in services such as transport, billing, payroll, customer order entry, baggage handling, etc., are at less than a 3.5 Sigma quality level. The rate of defects tends to be more than 23,000 parts per million (ppm) or 97.7 per cent efficiency. If the level of Sigma quality processes can improve to something above four Sigma the defect rate would drop to 6210 ppm. This clearly shows a potential performance improvement process of 3.7 times: the yield of the process would reach 99.38 per cent. This would bring significant financial returns for all organizations engaged in continuous improvement programmes such as the Lean and Digitize method. In fact, in most countries the manufacturing sector is less and less relevant. The real economy in these countries involves areas such as finance, consulting, healthcare, retail and logistics, but much less manufacturing, which tends to move overseas to low-cost countries. The Lean and Digitize method can help in this case, reducing the cost of poor quality and obtaining a more consistent process for providing excellent services.

Another important reason for the introduction of the Lean and Digitize method in service organizations is that customer satisfaction is important to reduce variability in processes, rather than just changing the average level of service offered.

Lean and Digitize is a method to improve the profitability of companies and to achieve service excellence through the effective application of statistical tools, teamwork, improvement and process digitization. The popularity of Lean and Digitize in service organizations is growing. Furthermore, many manufacturing organizations are concentrating their Lean and Digitize efforts on service processes internally or in relation to their customers. Areas of particular interest to Lean and Digitize include financel and health, as well as public administration. This chapter presents some of the most common challenges, difficulties, common myths and issues of implementation for the application of the Lean and Digitize method in services.

Services and Manufacturing

In manufacturing organizations, there is a long tradition of using quality methodologies and tools to improve the effectiveness, efficiency and economics of the business. In services, the situation is very different:

* It is often a struggle to develop and implement quality measures;

- In many cases, the processes in the service sectors are not well understood and controlled due to an excessive 'noise'. By this we mean an uncontrollable factor or event (for example, the emotions of the person who delivers the service) during the delivery of a particular service;
- Decisions tend to involve people and the criteria are far less precise. In other words, in services, the contribution of people tends to drive the process, far moreso than in the sector of manufacturing;
- Unlike in manufacturing, in services it is more difficult to define clear and standard processes and the link between process measures and the characteristics of the service offered.

A Lean and Digitize approach is particularly attractive for many services processes due to the need to drive the organization to satisfy customers in a profitable way. In services, it is important to introduce a programme of Lean and Digitize to establish and map the key processes critical to customer satisfaction. According to the literature, services tend to operate at Sigma quality levels between 1.5 and 3.0 (i.e. with a defect rate of between 455,000 and 66,800 defects per million of opportunities). This is not surprising, considering that for decades efforts to improve quality did not include the service sectors.

A number of service organizations have used successfully the Six Sigma and Lean Methodologies (Antony J., 2006). In traditional manufacturing organizations, we are using the experiences of Lean Six Sigma in operations and extending them to service operations (Nicoletti, 2006). A Lean and Digitize approach provides a disciplined method for improving the effectiveness of the service (i.e. the set of desirable attributes of a service), service efficiency (i.e. time and productivity) and the economics of the service (i.e. margins and costs). For example, in a hospital environment, cleanliness is a measure of efficiency of service, but the time waiting for admission to the emergency room is a measure of efficiency of the service (but has impacts on its effectiveness). Service-oriented companies that adopt a Lean and Digitize strategy achieve several benefits (Antony, 2005: 1–12):

- Increased operational agility of the organization;
- Improved teamwork throughout the organizational structure;
- Transformation of the organizational culture approach from being firemen (puts out fires, helps in accidents) to prevention;
- Motivate staff by increasing awareness of the problems by using various tools and techniques. This may also lead to greater job satisfaction for the personnel;
- Reduce the number of activities not adding value in critical processes through their systematic elimination, leading to faster delivery of service;
- Reduce the cost of poor quality (costs associated with late deliveries, customer complaints, resolution of problems associated with errors, etc.);
- Improving the level of the quality of service through the systematic reduction of variability in processes; and
- Improving the effectiveness of management decisions, basing them on data and facts rather than assumptions or gut feelings.

The Spanish group of retailers Zara reviewed their marketing processes and improved both new processes and advanced digitization (Sull 2009).

In 2008 Zara overtook Gap as the largest clothing retailer in the world. This was an example of excellence in managing the supply chain due to its ability to provide new products to its retail outlets quickly. Although the performance of the supply chain is impressive, Zara excels in serving their target customers (young women eager to be trendy) by identifying emerging trends. Zara is very good in identifying these opportunities because it is equipped with systems to:

- Collect market data in real time;
- Integrate statistical reports with periodic utilization of primary market data; and
- Share information broadly throughout the organization.

An interfunctional group in Zara carefully analyses the data on daily sales and stock reports to understand what is selling and what is not. It continually updates its vision of the market. The group examines the twice a week orders received from the chain stores managers. It completes these quantitative analyses with periodic visits to the stores. In this way, they can gather first-hand data that standardized reports may not show immediately. In the summer of 2007, for example, Zara introduced a line of clothes suitable for thin people (slim-fit), including pencil skirts in bright colours. Daily sales statistics revealed that those items were not selling, but the data did not explain why this was happening. Marketing executives of Zara visited the stores to explore the situation in person. They learned that women loved choosing the slim-fitted look, but could not fit into them in their normal size when they tried them on. With this insight, Zara changed the size numbers on the labels, replacing them with smaller sizes, and sales rocketed.

To ensure that the data is widely shared, Zara locates designers, marketers and buyers in in the headquarters of the company at La Coruña. They work in open plan offices where they have frequent discussions, animated meetings and joint analysis of data to:

- Help diagnose the overall market:
- See how their work fits into the organization's strategy; and
- Identify opportunities that might otherwise get lost in organizational silos.

The Results of a Survey in Great Britain

In the following pages, we report the results of a survey on the application of the Lean Six Sigma methodologies in services organizations in Great Britain (Antony et al., 2007: 294–311). The questionnaire used in this study consists of two main sections:

- The first included basic questions such as the type of services provided, the size of the organization, if the organization has a quality management system, the Sigma quality level of the organization, the Six Sigma metrics used, the Six Sigma tools and techniques used, etc.
- The second section aimed to identify CSFs of Six Sigma in service organizations. This section includes 51 variables based on published literature from the main Six Sigma

operators and from academics. The rating scale used was the Likert scale, which provides a better measure of yes/no or true/false. It is useful for ranking the relative importance of responses for respondents, and is quick and easy to complete. In this way, the researchers can quickly spot the critical or most important factors. Researchers were interested to know:

- if the organizations used a formal programme to improve quality
- its usefulness
- the status of implementation and effectiveness of a quality improvement programme etc.

The survey showed that 74 per cent of organizations that responded to the study had some sort of quality system, such as ISO 9001:2008, TS 16949, ISO 14001, etc., and that 26 per cent of respondents were not aware of formal systems of quality in their organizations. The most common initiatives on quality management were the use of Quality Assurance (QA) and Total Quality Management (TQM).

Sixty-four per cent of organizations (16 companies) involved in the survey had used Six Sigma on average for less than three years. Thirty-two per cent of organizations had been involved in a Six Sigma programme for three to five years. One organization claimed to have used a Six Sigma methodology for over five years.

Twenty per cent of respondents were either unsure or unaware of the quality levels in terms of sigma of their core business processes. When known, the average quality of sigma of organizations was between 2.8 and 3.3. The authors of this study believe that this figure may change with increasing sample size. Service organizations tend to overestimate their levels of quality.

The most common Six Sigma parameters used by the organizations included:

- The cost of poor quality (COPQ);
- The defects per million opportunities (DPMO);
- The response time to customer complaints, processing capacity and the number of customer complaints in writing.

Less common metrics used were:

- service times
- reliability of service
- punctuality, such as delivery in time through the process, etc.

The part of the survey developed to identify the CSFs of Six Sigma in the service sector used 13 criteria, already identified as critical by past studies:

- the commitment of senior management and its involvement
- commitment to the level of organization
- cultural change
- link between Six Sigma and business strategy
- integration of Six Sigma with the financial infrastructure
- organizational infrastructure

- education and training
- a programme of incentives
- customer service
- understanding of the DMAIC methodology
- ability to manage projects
- prioritization of projects and their selection
- project monitoring and remediation actions.

In the implementation of a Lean and Digitize project, the CSFs represent the essential ingredients for measuring the success of the initiative. Without them, the initiative has little chance of success. The respondents in the survey in Great Britain (Antony et al., 2007: 294–311) had to classify the CSFs essential for the implementation of a Six Sigma initiative on a scale of 1–5:

1 = less important

2 = not very important

3 = important

4 = very important and

5 = fundamental.

The study showed that the connection between Six Sigma and the business strategy is the most critical success factor. The other most important factors were customer focus and project management skills.

Some of the potential difficulties in implementing a Lean and Digitize project in a service environment include (Antony et al., 2007: 294–311):

- Process problems:
  - In services, organizations rarely describe activities in terms of process. The use of tools such as maps and diagrams of process flow tend to be rare to describe many service processes;
  - The service processes are subject to more uncontrollable factors (psychological factors, sociological factors, personal factors, etc.) than in manufacturing processes;
  - Processes do not tend to be dynamic;
  - The identification of processes that can be measured in terms of defects per million opportunities is not easy;
  - Often in services, the processes' measures consist in discrete data (that is also not continuous). So the process of data collection requires more time because of the need for a large sample size to be valid from a statistical point of view;
  - In service processes, one often has to deal with individual measurements. Therefore, subgroups for a certain period of time (e.g. one week or one month) must be defined;
- Measurement problems:

- The standardized approach DMAIC/DMADV does not always work as it does in manufacturing processes. The measures necessary to monitor service processes are different and therefore metrics must be different;
- The data are not immediately available for analysis and it is more difficult to collect them than it is in manufacturing (for example, because many services are geographically distributed). A basic problem is related to the accuracy and completeness of the data;
- The data source is not always clear: unlike manufacturing organizations, in most service processes customers are also 'providers' of some components of the service. With them, the organization does not always have the power to bargain down. Therefore, organizations must demonstrate service to their customers – 'we are here to serve you' – with the intent to involve them in the process of data collection;
- The measurement of customer satisfaction in a service environment is more difficult because of human interaction and the need to take into account behavioural aspects associated with service delivery. Examples of these behavioural characteristics are a sense of friendship, the desire to help, honesty, etc. These issues tend to have a great influence on service processes and determination on the quality of customer service;
- Much of the data in the service sector are collected manually in face-to-face interactions rather than using automatic data collection as in many manufacturing processes;
- Statistical problems:
  - A transfer function is often not available for many service processes. The application of advanced statistical techniques like design of experiments and the Taguchi method is limited;
  - The data from service processes do not follow the normal Gaussian distribution. This situation can be mitigated through the effective use of data processing techniques (e.g. Box–Cox transformation);
- Issues with people, last but certainly not of lesser importance:
  - Resistance to change in a service is relatively higher than in a production environment due to the strong involvement of the human aspects (human behaviour, friendship, honesty, courtesy, etc.);
  - In the services sector, decisions often require the participation of a human being. As a consequence, the criteria is much less precise;
  - Processes in services, in general, are much more dependent on human and organizational changes which does not occur in manufacturing processes. To change the parameter settings on a specific machine is quite different from changes in personnel training, or adjustments to modified working practices or activities;
  - There is a problem shared by all types of industry. It consists in presenting the reports and recommendations for improvement using the language of business, rather than statistical language. Few managers have a background in statistics. On the other hand, a presentation of the results in a language understood by the staff improves their motivation and their perceptions about the effectiveness of a Lean and Digitize business strategy. From this point of view, the best is to present, for example, the as-is process using a movie or a series of pictures.

Service organizations are increasingly implementing Six Sigma, but they must acquire a different skill or form appropriate to address the issues mentioned above. This envelops a cultural change that is not easily obtained. However, it is a prerequisite for survival in an increasingly dynamic and competitive environment.

Lean and Digitize Services

There are three main problems in services:

- The rigidity of the systems influenced, for example, by the constraints of certain procedures and provisions. It causes increases in the time to go through the processes due to the increased operational complexity. This increase in complexity leads subsequently to an increase in the costs incurred to meet the demands of the customers;
- The process variability is due to the occurrence of anomalies (data entry errors, lost documents, missing or incorrect balance of volume and capacity, etc.). They can lead to delays in delivering services and downtime in operations; and
- The waste of labour corresponds to all those non-value activities added, which involve excessive costs and high processing times. Waste is any operation that impacts on costs but that is not perceived as value added by the customer or by the organization.

It is possible to reclassify the traditional types of waste in Lean Thinking into the types of waste in services, as shown in Table 10.1. Compared to the seven traditional types of waste, there is an additional type of waste which relates to waste in the intellectual resources available in the organization.

The close interdependence between the rigidity of the system, the variability of the processes and the waste of labour, leads to a series of undesired effects in the delivery of services. These involve deterioration in the efficiency of the organization, a decrease in customer satisfaction and a reduced profitability.

There are a series of levers which a Lean and Digitize approach makes available to improve and control the cost structure and minimize the main problems of rigidity, variability and waste.

Table 10.1 The types of waste in the case of service organizations

Waste	Manufacturing	Services
Overproduction	Waste of materials, time, manpower, goods, space, and money	Report not necessary, multiple copies and batch processes involving growth in the number of spreadsheets in Excel
Waiting	Waiting time of operators due to delay of material, failures and set-up	The wait is due to blocked computers during a batch process, to damaged copiers and printers, or waiting for information needed to launch the processes
Transportation	Unnecessary movement of raw materials, half-elaborated and finished products	Unnecessary movement caused by disorganization of the office and by movement of photocopying machines etc.
Processing	Time devoted to unnecessary processes	Any unnecessary step, such as signatures, the double entry of data similar in different offices, or searches due to incorrect storage of data in files
Physical movements	Unnecessary movement of workers during the production of a specific product	Unnecessary movements, such as steps, manual data entry, inappropriate use of photocopies and archives
Rework	Waste of materials, time, and money. Worsens customer satisfaction	Insertions of incorrect data, use of 'closures' to make repairs, incomplete information given to the next process
Inventory	Stocks in transit (work in progress), the material used to hide the problems of balancing of production	Transactions not yet processed
Intellect		Use of experienced personnel in non-value added activities, waste of potential

Levers to Support Change

Lean and Digitize can use four levers:

- lean redesign
- digitization
- centralization and
- outsourcing.

The team redesign the processes following the Lean thinking principles. This results in a simplification of the processes, streamlining of the reporting, standardization of procedures and better demand management.

Digitization should start once the initiative has freed the processes from any possible waste. This allows enhancing the efficiency of the organization and inhibiting the increase in management complexity, variability and inflexibility of the system. Digitization can help services in the design of slim user interfaces and in streamlining operations, for example by introducing tools to analyse the deviations in manual procedures. Such is in the case of Intesa Sanpaolo, the largest Italian bank. A project of Lean and Digitize helped through process redesign and digitization of (Bortolotti 2007–2008):

- A new Web-based integrated procedure for the activation and release of retail banking contracts;
- A new procedure for the disbursement of credit;
- ATMs for payments of services and allowances; and
- International transactions.

A practice widely used is to centralize back-office processes in peripheral offices and administrative centres, once streamlined, not to centralize waste but to maximize productivity by minimizing the transfer of personnel.

It makes sense to analyse the outsourcing of low value-added processes, such as formal control of checks and records in the case of banking services. In this way, it is possible to keep inside the organization only value-added activities, reducing worthless and non-strategic activities.

The application of the levers for improvement in services involves a simultaneous change in behaviour and values. One can get a large increase in performance from the improvement initiative. If it is not supported by a change in values and attitudes of stakeholders, it will eventually return to the old ways of processing and to the old outputs.

For the full success of a Lean and Digitize project, one must:

- Create a strong spirit of emulation both vertically and horizontally in the organizational hierarchy ('I see my managers and my colleagues behave in new ways. I should too');
- Increase the understanding and conviction ('I know what is expected of me. I agree and I find it is important for me'); and
- Develop professional and interpersonal skills.

The Lean Branches

The services tend to be geographically distributed. They often have branches (also called peripheral offices, counters, or something similar). Branches are important to the relationship with the customer. On the other hand, they might not be effective, efficient and economical and should therefore be a primary target for process improvement. There are some very interesting projects on lean branches, for instance in the case of financial institutions (Nicoletti, 2008). The aim is to streamline processes at branches and possibly to migrate their operations on alternative channels.

In the case of financial institutions, the objective of the initiative is moving customers to automated ways of payment and collection. Thus one can free employee capacity in order to use them for more value-added activities, making it possible to move from service to sales: a practice already established in other areas.

The lack of industrialization of banking operations is the origin of some common symptoms:

- The activity of service value-added services are equal in branches to only 15–25 per cent of total operations, often due to a gradual layering of organizational, legal and information technology;
- The time devoted to the sale with the customer 'in front of them' is only a small fraction of the total time available in the branch. This is why the commercial initiative of the resources in the branch is little valued;
- The service times are long and unpredictable with the consequence that the customer experience, and therefore its VOC, is managed or simply left to the goodwill of the personnel of the branch;
- Productivity is highly variable from employee to employee (or branch to branch). This implies that production units are sized for the peak – to ensure an acceptable level of service – with a structural inefficiency in normal times;
- The heterogeneity of operational behaviour creates risks that are difficult to monitor. The poor management of the operations determines usually their overstaffing.

Over the past years, more than 25 banking groups in Europe have experimented, with great success, with the Lean and Digitize method, within broad strategic transformation programmes and in conjunction with the use of more traditional levers such as outsourcing and the centralization of administrative activity (back office) (www.sinedi.com).

The initiative on branches also aims to meet the increasingly urgent requests from customers to have access to services 24 hours a day, seven days a week, wherever they are, through such processes, quickly and easily.

THE LEAN INITIATIVE AT INTESA SANPAOLO BANK (BORTOLOTTI 2007–2008)

Intesa Sanpaolo, the largest Italian bank, has been successful in the migration to alternative channels through the enhancement of continuous services of Internet banking and the introduction of ATM Web (ATMs using Web technology), with the capability to transfer and receive payments, and ATMs with advanced functionality to deposit cash and cheques.

To encourage the migration of customers and the resulting streamlining of workload and procedures at the counters, Intesa Sanpaolo has primarily implemented a promotional policy, enlarging discounts for payments made through Internet banking or the Web ATM, and payments implemented through evolved ATMs. In addition, Intesa Sanpaolo has invested in communications, advertising to customers the benefits in terms of reduced service time and transaction costs on alternative channels.

Figure 10.1 shows how upgrading Internet banking and the introduction of ATMs and

Web ATMs evolved and have freed productive capacity from the branch offices (previously characterized by a high percentage of transactions). It helped to allocate management activities and advisory services with high added value for both clients and employees.

Another benefit of the Lean and Digitize branch is the ability to identify high transactions automatically, which makes it is possible to focus efforts on the most important and profitable customers.

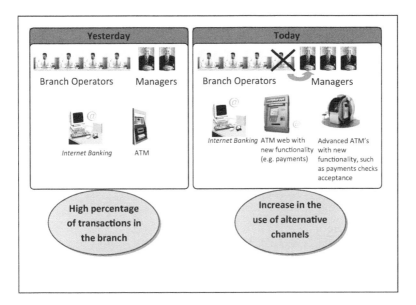

Figure 10.1 The lean branch in Intesa Sanpaolo

The benefits of digitization of branch offices are:

- Release of the production capacity spent on counter activity;
- Allocate capacity released in high value-added activities such as consulting and management;
- 24/7 availability of services;
- Reduction in service time and costs for both the customers and the bank;
- Ability to automatically identify high transactions and transactors;
- Possibility of monitoring results through ad hoc reporting.

Each administrative centre interfaces with the branches through the electronic transmission of documents via a scanner. Automatic workflows manage the movements of the documents.

The project redesigned and optimized both administrative processes and ICT applications, making it was to perform the activities based on the new model of back office processes. The result was productivity higher than in the previous model on all the activities taking place in the branches.

The benefits of the move of processes from branches to mid or back offices were:

- Thanks to the centralization of mid and back office, branch offices were able to devote more time to their main role: advising customers and managing the front line. These activities require their presence on the territory. Therefore they are not subject to further centralization;
- The outsourcing and the elimination of certain low-value-added activities facilitated the work of branch employees;
- The standardization and integration of information systems have simplified procedures;
- Digitization has accelerated the processes and made them more resilient;
- The interface between branch and the administrative centre has allowed the dynamic levelling of the workload;
- The electronic interface has permitted the creation of a system of continuous monitoring of performance (time, costs, quality), through workflow analysis.

In summary, the centralization, outsourcing, standardization and digitization permitted the increase of productivity, and the efficiency and reliability of processes. The results are the

freeing of productive capacity which can be reallocated and reinvested or capitalized as a saving.

List of References

Antony, J. 2005. *Assessing the Status of Six Sigma in the UK Service Organizations.* Proceedings of the Second National Conference on Six Sigma, Wroclaw, Poland.

Antony, J. 2006. Six Sigma for Service Processes. *Business Process Management Journal*, 12(2), 234–248.

Antony, J., Antony, F.J., Kumar, M. et al. 2007. Six Sigma in Service Organizations: Benefits, Challenges and Difficulties, Common Myths, Empirical Observations and Success Factors. *International Journal of Quality & Reliability Management*, 24(3), 294–311.

Bortolotti, T. Academic Year 2007/2008. *An Integrated Lean Six Sigma Model for Process Improvement.* Thesis at the Università di Udine.

Nicoletti, B. 2006. Nuovo Pignone, the Art of Merging Lean Management and Six Sigma. *Computerworld Italia*, 6(December), 1–2.

Nicoletti, B. 2008. *Lean and Digitize: An Opportunity and Best Practices in Banking.* Financial Services Global Leadership Summit, Athens, Greece, 7–9 May.

Sull, D. 2009. *Competing Through Organizational Agility.* Available from https://www.mckinseyquarterly.com/Strategy/Strategic_Thinking/Competing_through_organizational_agility_2488, accessed 5 March 2010.

Yilmaz, M.R. and Chatterjee, S. 2000. Six Sigma Beyond Manufacturing – A Concept for Robust Management. *IEEE Engineering Management Review*, 28(4), 73–80.

Websites

http://www.sinedi.com/italiano/link/pdf/Articolo23.pdf

11 *The Future of Lean and Digitize*

Introduction

In the world of organization, the Lean and Digitize method does not correspond to the last step in the development of methods to support the improvement and process optimization. These methods will evolve further in the future.

Marketing people will decide how to name future methods, after talking of business process re-engineering, business process management, Six Sigma, Lean, Lean Six Sigma, and so on and so forth. It is interesting to analyse which are the lines of development that will make an impact on the methodology of Lean and Digitize.

In describing the development of quality management for Lean and Digitize in the first chapters, we used a Darwinian approach. In this light, it may be interesting to examine the lines of development of the methodology for process management and other aspects. We shall consider how this development will adapt to the major dynamics that seem to shape the future today.

Three aspects are important:

1. the management of processes
2. the administration of physical space
3. digitization.

The development of these three aspects in an evolutionary scenario depends on how the context in which the organization lives might evolve in the future. The world is undergoing a crisis of unusual dimensions associated with the shortage, actual or potential, of resources such as:

- commodities (e.g. copper and, ultimately, hydrocarbons)
- energy
- food
- credit and so on.

Despite this crisis, it seems that certain trends will remain and perhaps accelerate in the future. We refer to:

- volatility
- globalization and
- productivity.

If these are the trends, lines of development of methodologies to support the improvement of organizations will need to adapt to the increasing demands and constraints of these issues:

- The volatility will require more integration, so that weak signals from the outside world, wherever they arrive into the organization, can be quickly transmitted throughout the organization, and agility (Towill and Christopher, 2007: 406–424), so that the organization can change quickly;
- Globalization require increased virtualization, as the cost of energy will not allow excessive movement of resources, including people; and
- Productivity will require even greater automation to support the operations, management and, above all, improvement and optimization of processes and streamlining them to avoid any waste.

In what follows, we examine in detail what these trends will bring in terms of process improvement. We focus in particular on how possible developments in automation will better support a Lean and Digitize project.

The green enterprise or the approach to ecological processes is another aspect that will grow in relevance. Limitation of natural resources and the need to respect the environment will become even more important. The Lean and Digitize method does not take this aspect into account specifically. A lean process almost by definition 'consumes' less than a conventional process and therefore is potentially greener. It is necessary to do more to improve methodology in this direction.

Automation

Against the backdrop of improved productivity, there is very often the assistance of automation. There are, without doubt, 'soft' actions that can improve processes. A rule of thumb states that 50 per cent of improvements in processes is independent of automation, and the other 50 per cent is connected.

If this is true, as can be expected in the future, what will the impacts on the Lean and Digitize method be? One of the technologies developing fast is the use of automation for improved cooperation between people, between institutions or between people and machines, or at least between the machinery and equipment, the so-called Internet of things (IoT) or machine to machine (M2M).

This is an interesting development because organizations have progressed from automation of individual operations to the automation of the workplace, and to the automation of the integration between jobs of work.

The next step, partially already under development, is the automation to support collaboration.

There are wastes even in the processes of collaboration (see the list in Table 11.1 for possible types of waste). The Web can contribute a great deal to the elimination or reduction of these wastes. Think of Web 2.0 (Neal, 2007), which represents the development of the Internet network in the direction of collaboration support. In Web 2.0, the user not only reads information or performs transactions, they contribute to content creation in a website, just like the owners of the site, and do this through blogs, Wikis and so on.

To support collaboration in a globalized world, ICT offers so-called cloud computing. This is a technology but more and more a method that will impact profoundly on the management of organizations.

This chapter will further elaborate these aspects because of their relevance for the future of Lean and Digitize projects.

Table 11.1   Ten possible forms of waste in collaboration

Divergence	Wasted effort due to policy or misalignment of purpose
Misunderstandings	Disconnections in understanding
Little communication	Too much or not enough time spent in communicating
Interpretation	Time spent interpreting communications or components
Research	Time spent in seeking information or reports
Movement	Delivery of components and communications
Additional processing	Creating an excess of information or components
Translation	Time spent adapting objects to new releases
Waiting	Delays due to revisions, approvals or bottlenecks
Misapplications	Incorrect usage of methodologies and technologies

These developments present big challenges in terms of information security and the confidentiality of the organization. Organizations should keep this aspect in mind and take all appropriate precautions for protection.

The increasing pervasiveness of computers, or of its intelligent component the chip, is another aspect that will influence the Lean and Digitize method. The presence of an increasing number of 'smart' components inside for instance household items, represents both an opportunity and a challenge. It provides opportunities in the redesign of processes not available in the past. In effect, this potential will expand even further. To provide an example of how this can support Lean and Digitize initiatives, think of how the presence of chips in machinery allows improvement of service processes with predictive maintenance.

Another development is a digitization based on a new type of architecture: event-driven architecture (EDA) or architecture driven by events. In this approach, the individual components of the system do not mechanically repeat a certain number of operations. They 'react' or even 'predict' them. In more advanced cases, they 'learn' from them how to improve. Based on events, thanks to the initial phase of apprenticeship and forecasting models in the system, this architecture let us choose the best solution for the process.

Web 2.0 and Lean and Digitize

A project is an enterprise limited in scope, time and costs, for instance to develop a product or a process that adds value or brings benefits. These characteristics of projects distinguish them from processes, or operations. They are a permanent or semi-permanent work to produce the same product or service in a repetitive manner. The characteristics of project management are quite different. Therefore, it requires the development of distinct technical skills and the adoption of different management approaches.

The *Oxford Dictionary of English* suggests that organizations in projects are:

> *A collaborative undertaking, which frequently involves research or design. A project is planned to achieve a specific purpose.*

On Wikipedia, the definition of Web 2.0 is:

> *A term describing the trend in the use of the World Wide Web technology and Web design with the objective of enhancing creativity, information sharing and, especially, collaboration among users. The term does not refer to an update of some technical specifications, but to changes in the software development and the end users in the use of the Web.*

At the same time, the execution of a process requires cooperation between the various actors involved (see, for example, the results of a survey on this topic conducted by Oracle in Figure 11.1).

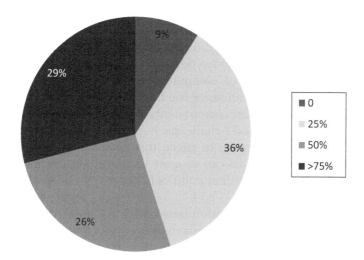

Figure 11.1 Oracle customers whose business processes required collaboration amongst participants (i.zdnet.com)

It is striking that in all definitions the word 'collaboration' appears as an important term. (Web 2.0 has an important set of tools that can support collaboration.) It then becomes clear why it is important to study how Web 2.0 can help contribute to improving the management of projects: this is what we call Project Management 2.0.

Project Management 2.0 is the discipline of organizing resources to determine the full achievement of specific objectives of the project, with the support of Web 2.0.

The primary challenge of project management is to achieve all the objectives and purposes of the project respecting the constraints on purpose, quality, timing and budget. At the second level – but more ambitious – is the challenge to optimize the allocation and integration of resources (money, people, materials, energy, space, supplies, communication, motivation, etc.) required to meet the objectives of the project. Web 2.0 can help members of the project to control all the activities in the project using resources to achieve the objectives and the purposes of the project.

Project management 2.0 should provide support to project teams in the so-called 5 C's:

*   Co-development (working as a team to achieve results);
*   Coordinate (collaborating together, but each member of the group executes their part);
*   Co-decision (by reaching a consensual decision amongst all members of the project team);
*   Committing (engaging people thanks to emotional intelligence in social relationships);
*   Check (verifying the development of the project according to purpose, time, budget and agreed quality).

Web 2.0 should therefore be a great help in making collaboration and innovation more effective through:

*   A wider range of participation (by actively involving more people in the project);
*   Better alignment (ensuring that all project members and stakeholders will receive the same information and thus are on the same wavelength and work in a concerted manner);
*   Increased productivity (by reducing the consumption of project resources and its management, taking into account the cost of meetings and follow-up);
*   Availability of information (ensuring that the correct information is available at the right time to the right team members and stakeholders of the project);
*   Improvement in social dynamics (the motivation of members of the group has not only a rational basis but also depends on the richness of human relationships in the team).

The Table 11.2 indicates some differences between traditional project management and Project Management 2.0.

Table 11.2 The difference between traditional project management and project management 2.0[1]

Traditional project management	Project Management 2.0
Centralized control	Decentralized control
Planning from top to bottom	Planning from the bottom to the top
Authoritarian environment	Collaborative environment
Implied structures	Emergent structures
Limited access and restricted planning	Organized access and without barriers to planning
Local access to information	Global and instantaneous access to information
Limited communications within the project team and stakeholders	Unlimited communications within the project team and stakeholders
Projects separated from the rest of the organization	Holistic approach
Complex instruments	Ease of use of instruments
Rigidity of the instruments	Flexibility of the instruments

Trends

The main reason for moving to Project Management 2.0 is the change in the projects and the context within which it operates:

- Organizations require projects all the faster, because time-to-market is an important competitive advantage;
- In the current crisis, flexibility is essential;
- To reduce costs, there is a trend in projects towards multi-sourcing, based on the use for project development and many different vendors;
- Globalization is driving the development of projects on a global scale, and often with virtual project teams. A virtual team is a set of geographically dispersed project members, in other words, not co-located in the same place. Therefore, the team work without time constraints, spatial or common organizational limits, but with connections based on advanced communication systems. In a virtual project team, resources have complementary skills and are committed to a common purpose, to interdependent performance objectives, and share a work method for which are judged reciprocally. Project members are far more sensible from the point of effectiveness, efficiency and economics of the project;
- The project leader's role is changing: from project manager to a facilitator of collaboration amongst all project members and between the project and its stakeholders.

---

1   An elaboration from Wikipedia

The Tools

In an effort to provide support for better coordination, the development of Web 2.0 allows the introduction of Web-based communities and services, such as social networks, Wikis, blogs, folksonomies and webinars. Web 2.0 offers a rich set of easily integrated components, enabling an organization to reduce costs and increase the capacity of innovation.

In what follows, we examine each of the major Web 2.0 services in detail.

SOCIAL NETWORKS

A social network service is an online community of people who share interests and activities, or are interested in exploring the interests and activities of others who are or want to be in such relationships. Most social network services are Web-based. These provide different ways to allow users to interact and collaborate, such as discussion forums, e-mail and instant messaging services.

The main types of social networks are based on:

- The indices of some categories (such as former classmates);
- Methods to connect with friends (usually with pages of self-description, a description of what people are doing or comments about what people read, have seen, done, etc., including sharing photos, videos, documents, sentiments);
- Recommendations of the work done by other people.

The social network can revolutionize the way a project team can communicate and share information.

Social networks can be very helpful throughout all phases of a project to connect:

- The members of the project to the stakeholders:
- Project members amongst themselves, even if they belong to different organizations or are located in different geographical places.

As an example of the first type, an Italian company, Ducati, used social networks to modify the relationship with their customers. A remarkable number of customers (and potential customers) used Web 2.0 to help to define the characteristics of a new product: a motorcycle.

The second type of network can allow changing the relationships with regard to how information flows from the top of the organization along formal channels to the rest of the project. The hypothesis is that creativity resides in specific individuals or in specific functions. This approach is insufficient. Especially in a project, the information must flow in all directions, with feedback between the different levels. All must work together in the effort of innovating.

To use social networks in projects, organizations should standardize these services to avoid duplication between the members of the project, other stakeholders, or the use of internal networks for interests other than those of the project.

BLOGS

A blog (a summary of the words Web log) is a website, updated by an individual or a group of people with the opportunity to introduce to all comments, descriptions of events, or other material such as presentations or video.

A typical blog combines text, images and links to other blogs, web pages and other resources related to the topic of the blog. The possibility for people who access the blog to leave comments in an interactive manner is an important part of many blogs.

Blogs can collect information or comments, for example in the define and measure macro phase of a project of Lean and Digitize. In a large project like this, blogs can give considerable support in knowing what other project members are doing. With this technology, each member of the team receives information via RSS (see below) of all other members, and other teams responsible for the project. When appropriate, suppliers or other members of the virtual project teams can access these blogs via an intranet or extranet. Other parties can also contribute their contributions in this way. Blogs also allow stakeholders to follow the development of activities without necessarily 'interfering' with inquiries with the members of the project teams.

WIKIS

A Wiki is a collection of Web pages designed to enable anyone with access to contribute or modify content, using a simple mark-up language (Tapscott and Williams, 2006). Wikis provide opportunities for websites for collaboration and contribution to community websites. Wikis are used in organizations to manage the knowledge of the organization or community, and are accessible via an intranet or the Internet. Wikis, created from the voluntary contribution of a remarkable number of people, are the base of the biggest encyclopaedia in the world with over 13 million entries: Wikipedia.

In the management of a project, Wikis can be the repository of specific customer requirements or functional specifications (analyse and process design phase). In the final stages of the project (build, test and deploy), Wikis can be the store for all of the test results. When a problem in a project turns into a topic in a blog, a Wiki could handle it more efficiently until it is resolved and above all documented with the help of all the members involved.

Motorola has introduced blogs, the so-called FAQs (frequently asked questions), used in websites to answer questions regularly asked by visitors to the site), Wiki and forums for internal use. After 10 months, 60,000 of its 68,000 employees used 2,000 Wiki and 2,700 blogs daily.

RSS

RSS (really simple syndication) is a family of Web-feed formats used to publish content, which are frequently updated, like blogs or news headlines, using a standard format. An RSS document contains:

- A summary of the contents of an associated website; or
- The complete text.

RSS feeds allow informing on the activity of a website in an automatic way (push rather than pull. In other words, the information is sent to the user rather than requested by the user.)

One benefit of RSS is the aggregation of content from multiple Web sources in one place. Once the information is sent to the personal computer of the user, it can be read by a software called an RSS reader. This software is Web-based or installed on the personal computer of the user. An RSS publishes the information in a standardized file format once. Many different persons or programs can then access the information. The user subscribes to a power supply providing the supply link in their reader or by introducing an RSS icon in a browser. The RSS reader regularly checks the information that becomes available, enabling the reading of the new content on many similar sites through a single friendly interface. This 'push' from 'one to many' on the Web is useful. The RSS reader alerts the user to the availability of new content. The information can then be downloaded if one finds it interesting.

This model from 'one to many' provides a simple solution for updating all potential users of the updated information during the project.

FOLKSONOMY

Folksonomy (also known as collaborative or social tagging, social classification or social indexing) is a practice and method of work in which collaborators create and manage labels to record and categorize the contents of an electronic archive.

In the case of project management, tagging of folksonomy has the objective of making a collection of information easier to search, discover and navigate over time. A well-developed folksonomy is ideally accessible as a common vocabulary to members and personnel on the project.

With the use of folksonomies on the Internet, users can generally find out who has created a certain tag and see the other tags created by other project members. In this way, users of folksonomy can read all the tags used by another team member. This combination may even make sense for other system users because it gives an advantage to the entire group in indexing the documentation.

Using this tool, project members can tag and share content generated by all members of the project, such as, for example, functional or technical specifics. In other words it tags content in a collaborative way, for example programs or blog portions.

A project is different from traditional situations whereby only the experts in the subject create information. Creative people and consumers of the contents of documents and project results can generate the metadata. In the case of projects, labelling is important in order to standardize the labels that are used by different users (and potential taggers) of documents.

WEBINARS

Using the Web, people can make conference calls. In some cases, it might be also useful to share presentations, images or video via the Web. At certain moments in the life of projects, it may be more appropriate to use the Webinar rather than just conference calls – a Webinar is a new term that describes a specific type of web conferencing. A Webinar can only be one-way, with a single presenter. In this situation, the interaction with other participants in the virtual meeting is very limited (in this case, we use the more appropriate term of webcast). The Webinar can still be much more collaborative, with question and answer sessions, via chat or via voice, to allow full participation of participants. In some cases, the presenter may speak over a telephone line, displaying information on a screen shared with the participants. These individuals can use their own computer to view the content of the presentation and respond with a voice in the conference, if necessary, via an ordinary phone line. More advanced is the use of the computer to make calls using voice over Internet protocol (VoIP) technology.

The Webinar in a project allows the sharing of what the various members of the project are doing and the progress made.

The Tools and Processes

All these tools are important to improve processes. It is therefore interesting to analyse how the process of managing projects could reap the benefits of Web 2.0 using the classification of Lean Six Sigma and decomposing the processes in the macro phases of DMADV. All the tools described are useful throughout the project's life. Some of these are particularly useful in some phases of the project, as summarized in Table 11.3.

Table 11.3   **The most appropriate tools in each macro phase DMADV of the project**

Phase	Tools	
Design	Blog for the development of design requirements	Social networks can help, especially in the case of virtual teams. Webinar for meetings
Measure	Folksonomies for standardization of measures	
Analyse	Wiki for the drafting of functional and technical specifications. RSS to update all components of the project and their changes	
Develop	Wiki to store test results	
Verify	Wiki for verifying the achievement of project results	

A project must be monitored throughout its life. Many of the techniques of Web 2.0 can help in this respect, especially in the planning and operational development of a project. Thanks to the capacity for coordination and communication of Web 2.0, it is possible to solve some of the traditional problems of project programming and controlling automatically.

COMMERCIAL PACKAGES

There are many tools and services available to support Web 2.0, even in project management. So far, their use has been rather limited. The platform of Microsoft Share

Point is interesting enough to support a certain number of functionalities of Web 2.0. Also using Web 2.0 tools like Ajax, the team can customize and make interoperable tools that are quite sophisticated but can also be used by non-specialist users.

Some software companies have developed Web 2.0 software to support project management.

Beyond Web 2.0

Some people are starting to talk about Web 3.0. One can expect that similarly, there will be a Project Management 3.0. Wikipedia defines the term Web 3.0 as a future wave of Internet innovation. However, there is a divergence of views on what direction this development will take. Some developments are possible in the direction of a semantic Web (search tools not only based on keywords but also on the meaning of terms used in research). This will be a very interesting field of development. Similarly, Web 3.0 could use videos and 3D more extensively, thanks to the availability of networks and increasingly powerful tools.

All these aspects are highly relevant in further improving the process of project management.

Cloud Computing and Lean and Digitize

The use of ICT is changing. A new wave is approaching – cloud computing. Cloud computing is the provision of computer resources via the network, ideally through the Internet. It is defined by the National Institute of Standards and Technology (NIST) as 'a model for enabling convenient, on-demand network access to a shared pool of configurable computing resources (e.g., networks, servers, storage, applications, and services) that can be rapidly provisioned and released with minimal management effort or service provider interaction'. NIST has identified five essential characteristics of cloud computing: on-demand service, broad network access, resource pooling, rapid elasticity and measured service.

Such a new opportunity has two impacts on Lean and Digitize. It allows us to use Lean and Digitize to make dramatic improvements in processes. At the same time, it can help in implementing Lean and Digitize itself by offering new ways that Lean and Digitize projects can be managed. It is especially useful when there are multi-locations or virtual projects, either from the point of view of clients, suppliers or team members. In such a situation, the possibility of accessing distributed and distinct computing resources can bring substantial advantages.

Cloud computing is particularly useful to support a Lean and Digitize approach to project management. In this chapter, we consider the opportunities of cloud computing in a couple of specific situations:

- a virtual PMO and
- a helpdesk.

The PMO Case

As an example of the applications of the Lean and Digitize methodology to cloud computing applied to project management it is considered a real application implemented in a large ITC company in Europe, Engineering S.p.A. It has been based on the concept of the resource-based view (RBV) theory. Barbero and Copetti developed a charter for the company's PMO, which they established as a project management centre of excellence known as PMNET (Barbero and Copetti, 2010).

The PMO provides an excellent example of how cloud computing can be used to support project management. The traditional PMO is composed of a certain number of people (in the case of small companies the membrs of the PMO could be just one) who support the project leaders in the way we have presented. With cloud computing this is no longer necessary. The most efficient Lean and Digitize solution is to create a virtual PMO. The best solution is to connect all the project leaders and their senior project team member in a intranet network. Particularly in the case of a multi-company project, it would be possible to connect more than one computer system 'in the cloud', wherever the company was based and independently of where it is based. Once this has been done it is necessary to create a Wiki repository of best practices and make them available to all project leaders. At the same time, it would be possible to create a blog to report new experiences or give project leaders the possibility to put questions and receive answers. The advantage is that the question and answer sessions would be available to all project leaders and could be searched once one project leader has a specific project.

In the case of a programme, this type of solution would be even more powerful. A programme is nothing more than either a large project or a set (or portfolio) of projects. The content (be it specifications, plans or other content) of each project in a programme could be based on different systems or computers. Cloud computing allows their consideration as a unit, supporting both the programme management and the exchange of documents and best practices amongst projects.

The Helpdesk Case

The support units that manage and maintain key elements of the ICT project development infrastructure – such as servers, networks systems and data storage – are liable to performance breakdowns that stem from complex and disordered workflows. Productivity can tumble and the quality of service is low.

The organizations' first response has been in many cases to increase overtime and make spot hires, but this approach led to budget overruns with no real change to the team's workload. A broader transformation is called for. A Lean and Digitize approach can be apply Lean methods to the problems. The key element involves breaking up siloed teams that are dedicated to specific components of the infrastructure and impede a smooth workflow. They can be reconstituted into several distinct teams, each one designed to address a specific level of complexity and type of content. At the same time, the project requires a new dispatcher function to consolidate assignment streams. Thanks to cloud computing there is no need for co-location of these teams and/or a collocation with the project or client teams, which could be dispersed through a large territory.

In a specific case (Andersson, Moe and Wong, 2011), applying this Lean and Digitize approach increased the ICT unit's productivity, speed and quality:

- The number of full-time equivalent positions required fell by 30–60 per cent;
- Average resolution times decreased by 40–60 per cent; and
- The number of incidents per server decreased by 25 per cent.

The intangible improvements included:

- better balancing of workloads
- improved staff morale; and
- increased opportunities for cross-training in technical skills.

Benefits

Cloud computing for project management has several benefits (Asava and Mzee, 2010):

- It supports large complex projects, which in the past were difficult to manage due to limited collaboration, development or network capacities within an organization;
- It enablea the parsing of multiple transactions in a highly distributed environment made up of multiple providers, to be available real-time and aggregated in a suitable way;
- Provides real-time collaboration between globally dispersed teams, clients and suppliers;
- Allows rapid staging, set-up and take-down of a variety of development environments as needed to test/validate an application;
- Allows use of real-time project management software with a wide set of Web-based tools.

These are benefits apply specifically to project management. There are other more general benefits connected with cloud computing. It will:

- Lead to greater resource sharing, greater economies of scale, and greater levels of architectural standardization and process optimization (Gartner 2008a).
- Realize project savings through agility and speed of implementation. It enables projects to cut back on capital spending and optimize operational expenses (Gartner, 2009a).
- Enable users of IT-related services to focus on what the services provide to them rather than how the services are implemented or hosted (Gartner, 2008b).
- Leverage virtually instant agility, flexibility and reach, to dynamically access anything or anybody, and the virtually infinite diversity of available functionalities arising from composite applications and components allowed by cloud computing (Gartner, 2010).
- Provide higher value for creativity and innovation as it enables enterprises to focus on business objectives and, therefore, allocate more resources to solve business

problems. It enables IT availability to broader masses of individuals, thus creating a pool of talent that did not exist before (Gartner, 2009b).

Conclusions

A survey of the *Financial Times* in the USA and Great Britain found that two-thirds of the people involved in the survey had home computing devices more advanced than the ones used in their offices. These people will always ask for more than just traditional project management. They can also use the Web 2.0 type techniques that they use in their personal lives. They have skills and preparation and organizations should care for them, securing the best support possible to increase their productivity and effectiveness at work. This is especially true for the younger generation.

The management of the organization must change. Google is an example of a company piloting new management models (Neal, 2007):

- Hire smart people with whom it is pleasant to work;
- Use flat management structures;
- Allow open communication – no silos;
- Promote the use of e-mail to suggest new ideas;
- Leave 20 per cent of available time in the office to try new products or services for the company;
- Make small projects;
- Push for projects with iterative continuous improvement;
- Try ideas rather than speculate.

There are also (and especially) two important aspects to keep in mind with Web 2.0:

- security and
- the way to introduce these tools into organizations.

Regardless of which tools are used for project management, you need to take into account that key processes must have a secure architecture and that enough training be provided to the users.

Concerning tactics, Gary Hamel (2007) recommends 'Commit to revolutionary goals, but take evolutionary steps towards them.'

List of References

Andersson, H., Moe, G. and Wong, L.A 2011. Data Center Goes Lean. *McKinsey Journal*, March .

Asava, R. and Mzee, H. 2010. Cloud Computing meets Project Management, *PM. World Today* 12(6).

Barbero, M.C. and Copetti, G. 2010. The PMO as a Centre of Excellence [Electronic Resource]: Virtual Community or Physical Unit?, *Proceedings of the PMI Global Congress 2010–EMEA*.

Gartner 2008a. Economies of Scale Are the Key to Cloud Computing Benefits, *Gartner*, June (see also www.gartner.com for more information on the company and their reports).

Gartner 2008b. Cloud Computing: Defining and Describing an Emerging Phenomenon, *Gartner*, June.

Gartner 2009a. Data in the Cloud: Adaptations of Data Management Technologies and Providers, *Gartner*, October.

Gartner 2009b. Economics of the Cloud: Business Value Assessments, *Gartner*, September.

Gartner 2010. Cloud-Computing Service Trends: Business Value Opportunities and Management Challenges, Part 2, *Gartner*, February.

Hamel, G. 2007. *The Future of Management*. Cambridge: Harvard Business School Press.

Johnson, J. 1995. *Chaos Report*. Standish Group. Available from http://www1.standishgroup.com/sample_research/chaos_1994_1.php.

Neal, D. 2007. *Harnessing Web 2.0*. El Segundo: CSC.

Nicoletti, B. 2011, Lean and Digitize Project Management. *Proceedings of the IPMA 24th Congress*, Istanbul.

Oxford Dictionary of English, Kettering: Oxford University Press

Tapscott, D. and Williams, A.D. 2006. *Wikinomics*. New York: Penguin.

Towill, D.R. and Christopher, M. 2007. Don't Lean too Far – Evidence from the First Decade. *International Journal of Agile Systems and Management*, 2(4), 406–424.

Websites

http://en.wikipedia.org/wiki/Web_2.0
http://i.zdnet.com/whitepapers/Oracle_SOA_US_EN_WP_BPMSOA2.0.pdf
http://csrc.nist.gov/groups/SNS/cloud-computing/cloud-def-v15.doc

Index